Dreaming with
the Earth-Mind

Dreaming with the Earth-Mind

Paths to Sacred Activism

KIMBERLY R. MASCARO

Toplight

Jefferson, North Carolina

ISBN (print) 978-1-4766-9655-3
ISBN (ebook) 978-1-4766-5615-1

LIBRARY OF CONGRESS CATALOGING-IN-PUBLICATION DATA

Library of Congress Control Number 2025027563

Front cover image: cross stitch piece titled "Dreams Elements," 2024, in honor of Ancestors and Earth by Kimberly Mascaro.

Printed in the United States of America

Toplight is an imprint of McFarland & Company, Inc., Publishers

Toplight

Box 611, Jefferson, North Carolina 28640
www.toplightbooks.com

To the Ancestors

TABLE OF CONTENTS

DISCLAIMER

This book tells a story. It's a story from my own lived experiences alongside what others have graciously shared with me, on the streets as well as in academic circles, so that I may grow, expand, and develop on many levels. I am grateful for their sharing. What you find in this book are not substitutes for professional counseling, psychotherapy, or medical advice, including psychiatry. If you have any physical or mental health concerns, consult your doctor or other healthcare professional. The author and publisher assume no responsibility or liability for the actions of the reader.

I stand in solidarity with Maui and its Native Peoples no matter where they currently reside. I acknowledge how my residing on the island of Maui, and consuming its limited resources, is a colonial act. In the spirit of reparations, I use my voice (through spoken and written words) as a demonstration of *aloha*.

Acknowledgments

I acknowledge that this book would not have come together if it were not for cherished teachers and elders—the living men and women who have taken me *under their wing* in one form or another so that I may learn, grow, and develop into the person I am today, and the person I am becoming, as I continue to walk a path of collective, collaborative, inner work. Many thanks as well to everyone who shared their wisdom with me, filling these pages through the many interviews and discussions that took place during the past year or so. I am deeply indebted to them all.

I am also so very grateful to my peers (friends and colleagues) and other loved ones who have listened to my stories and stood witness to my lived experiences (especially the most emotionally painful) with deep kindness, empathy, reflective listening, intuitive feedback, and overall emotional intelligence. In total there are too many to list here, as this acknowledgment page would turn into a long chapter in and of itself, and for that alone, I am truly grateful. A bow of gratitude must also be given to those who helped with the editing of the manuscript, along with the entire Toplight team at McFarland & Company, Inc., Publishers.

Because I will always hold a deep appreciation for Maui, given all that this place has taught me, and because this book was birthed on this island, 50 percent of the proceeds I receive from sales of this book will be divided and donated to the organizations listed below for the next five years. If, like me, you too feel inspired to support them, please do.

- **Maui Cultural Lands**: MauiCulturalLands.org
- **Lahaina Community Land Trust**: LahainaCommunityLand Trust.org

- **Kipuka Olowalu**: KipukaOlowalu.org
- **Kimokeo Foundation**: KimokeoFoundation.org
- **Worldwide Indigenous Science Network**: WISN.org

PREFACE

This book, or rather, my storytelling, shares an embodied perspective. It is memoir, biographical, and ethnoautobiographical in that it blends my histories and current experiences with those of traditional practitioners, educators, activists, and members of the community of Maui, a tiny island in the Polynesian Triangle in which I reside as I construct these pages. Through these stories, I hope to lift up and center other voices in their own words, alongside my own.

You will notice the English word *Hawaii* will be used interchangeably with *Hawai'i*, which is how it is written in the Native Hawaiian language, *Ō'lelo Hawai'i*. I offer this work as a gesture of solidarity at a time when, shortly after the devastating fires of August 2023, the United States government continues its militarization efforts directed at Hawaii. Currently, the United States military has plans to occupy even more space on Maui, adding more equipment, such as telescopes, on the sacred Haleakalā, House of the Sun, which is considered an ancestor. Haleakalā National Park is home to endangered species and the Haleakalā volcano, which is dormant. At the same time, land developers are occupying a relatively new plot— 1,000 additional acres in Kihei—for a majority luxury build that, according to those resisting the project, only outsiders/foreigners will be able to afford to occupy.

We directly experience the Earth and everything around us as alive through the ways of dreaming, or the *dream arts*. When we have such an experience of direct revelation, or *gnosis*, how might our perspectives change? How might we make choices that protect and give care to what Source, Pure Consciousness, the Presence, God, *Ke Akua*, the Creator has provided?

This written work is meant to open discussion on current unfolding events, as well as history, and encourage readers to turn inward to remember who we are and take accountability for what we have collectively created. For when we do, I believe we will more deeply consider what can be done for balance, harmonious relations, and sustainability for Earth, all its creatures, and one another.

Furthermore, while I am grateful to anyone who dedicates their time to reading my work, this book's target audience is not locals who identify as *Kānaka Maoli, Kānaka 'Ōiwi,* or *Kama'āina Hapa.* Instead, it is written for others like me: those who are European American, White, born in the United States, educated in the West, in positions of power or leadership, socially or economically privileged, raised in religions whose leaders have excused or dismissed harm inflicted toward others (and the Earth) while simultaneously preaching *love thy neighbor as thyself.* As you continue to read on, understand that raw emotion is present in the forthcoming pages, which I believe must be acknowledged to move forward. Simultaneously, I've been exploring the space of *not knowing.* But, what I do know is that I want to open a space for conversation. I have included the voices of many others, some of whom are my elders. Through my own storytelling, I don't want to inflict further harm. I don't pretend to know the best route or path to take forward, yet I do hope to show through my writing that there is a bigger truth to be explored in order to move forward in wholeness and balance. After all, don't we all, or almost all of us, acknowledge a creative Source? I am a foreigner here. I have participated in the legacy of harm. While possibly triggering for some, to deny the realities of others does not do us any favors in the long run. We must listen to each other, even the perspectives we wish were not so. Also consider this book a call to action.

The more often people authentically connect with something bigger than themselves, whether that be in nature or through a deep inner experience, the less likely they are to withdraw from humanity, be driven toward consumerism, or be distracted from the realities unfolding all around us, outside of an individually focused narrowing worldview. Instead, such experiences of connection and awe provoke a sense of responsibility directed at protecting life in this world—our environment—including a deep care displayed for sentient beings living among us.

Fewer and fewer people across the globe live in traditional ways, and, sadly, through the forgetting of our interconnectedness, our own behaviors are harming us. Only through right relationship do we survive. And as the saying goes, "No one gets out of here alive," yet when our time comes, shouldn't we want to leave a thriving planetary home for those generations that will continue?

Finally, you may notice how some names are capitalized, granting personhood to nonhuman beings. This has been done intentionally to reflect our shared humanity. After all, we rely on one another for survival. Here is what you can expect:

Chapter Summary

The introduction, How I Got Here, provides a backstory. Those pages are a walk-through detailing how I ended up on Maui in the first place and the events that unfolded in my personal life that first year. In addition, just shortly before my one-year anniversary as a resident of Hawaii, a great collective tragedy was unfolding—the worst being the fire that destroyed the community of Lahaina.

Chapter 1, A Brief History of Maui, provides, as the title indicates, a condensed version of some of the major historical moments and impacts of colonization and settler behaviors on the island.

Chapter 2, Indigenous Mind, opens discussion on the terms Indigenous Mind alongside Western Mind. Indigenous knowledge and science alongside contemporary Western orientations are discussed. This chapter features the stories of those with experiences navigating these seemingly opposing worlds.

Chapter 3, Waking Dreams, explores synchronicities, signs, and waking dreams. After defining these terms, meaningful stories and memories from everyday people's lives are included.

Chapter 4, Know Your Medicine, examines experiences of initiation, including dream initiations. Following this, an exploration of European histories, identities, and ritual are discussed.

Chapter 5, Live Your Medicine, describes the art of ceremony. Additionally, ceremonial practices in relation to land as sacred space are included. Sacred activism is also explored, followed by how "seed experiences" can grow into transformative experiences through the dream arts.

Chapter 6, Dreaming with All Relations, expands on nocturnal dreaming. Dreaming with the land, its spirits, visitation dreams, ancestral dreaming, and ecological dreaming are discussed to encourage balance, equity, and healing.

Chapter 7, Journeys into the Dream Arts, begins by reminding dreamers to practice safety as they delve into the dream arts. From there, dream incubation and collective dreaming, as well as shrine and altar-making to demonstrate and encourage a ceremonial life through one's Indigenous Mind are discussed. Concrete practices are shared to promote radically active hope as one way to live.

Chapter 8, the Conclusion, wraps everything together in relation to the major ideas shared throughout this book, from Indigenous Mind and Indigenous Science to personal medicine and the dream arts.

The Epilogue, written in the summer and fall of 2024, provides context for the one-year anniversary of the 2023 Maui fires, which destroyed the town of Lahaina.

INTRODUCTION:
HOW I GOT HERE

My feet walk on a foreign land. I'm in Polynesia, understanding very little about this place. I'm frequently asked, "What brought you to Maui?" Throughout the year, I have turned this question back onto the person inquiring. By doing so, I have learned that many people on Maui (the non–Native individuals at least) sought a place to escape to or a place to start a fresh, new life for themselves. Some expressed how enamored they have been by this island. Some call Maui by another name: Paradise. I don't know why I was surprised. Given the beauty and the extremely isolated geographical location of the Hawaiian Islands, I guess it makes sense. People don't usually land on any of the Hawaiian Islands unless they really want to be here. A typical reply in response to the question "What brought you here?" cites Maui's beauty, natural environment, and slow-paced lifestyle centered around ocean-based activity. Some people relocate to Maui to simply check out. "Everyone dreams of living on Maui," some say. It is a top tourist destination, after all, even if my feelings about the island were more less uniformly enthusiastic and, well, complicated.

My Personal Story of Coming to Maui

"What brought you to Maui?" Sure, it's a seemingly benign question, and yet, for me, this question brings with it layers of discomfort and grief. I've dodged the question many times. While it is true that I've been somewhat nomadic my entire adult life, never having stayed

5

in one place longer than about seven years, I never expected to live here. So, when my partner-at-the-time discussed relocating together to a much warmer place, with my nomadic history and a lifetime of craving warm weather, I naturally thought it a fine idea. We considered possible options such as Florida, San Diego, and the Hawaiian Islands strictly for the heat. Florida was quickly scratched off our list. We realized San Diego, as much as I liked the area, might be a little too cold for us during the winter season. Therefore, Hawaii quickly became the target destination, and even though I had friends scattered across the island chain, I felt some doubt. Long story short, Maui made it to the top of the list. My ex was thrilled. But why wasn't I excited?

The timeline for the relocation plan sped up very quickly—from several years into the future, to a couple of years, and then to the following year. I thought, why the rush? This timeline was moving too quickly for me, but I went along with it to a degree. I rationalized it. After all, I've lived in a half dozen countries and states, so this just seemed all part of my nomadic lifestyle or at least another adventure. Besides, we were planning a life together.

Because he was inspired to transition to Maui as soon as possible, we agreed that I would come out a little later ... six months later, or maybe a year, tops. I just wasn't ready to sell my home (I hadn't owned it for very long) and to so quickly leave close friends and family behind. Temporary long-distance relationships can work more easily for those with virtual jobs. Of this I was certain. I even liked the idea of going back and forth. We looked at the possible months that I could live on Maui and the months I'd likely spend in California during that first year. I documented it the old-fashioned way and held onto that wrinkled piece of paper for months.

Things quickly moved forward in 2022. My partner purchased a dog-friendly condominium so my dog would be welcome. In preparation for his move, we did all the things one does before and immediately after a house enters escrow, such as packing, cleaning, selling items, holding garage sales, and more packing. Afterward, we lived together at my place, temporarily, until his departure date for Maui arrived. Sending him off was bittersweet, but I knew I'd see him soon.

It was around this time, or just a bit before, when a hundred-something-foot pine tree fell on my property. What made this event quite unusual was that having built a multiyear relationship through land stewardship with the dozens and dozens of big trees surrounding my home, I had been talking to one of them, requesting they stand strong and tall. Yet on this day, I looked straight out my living room window, staring at the humongous Pine in front of me, and mumbled something close to, "I hope you don't fall on me. Please stand tall for the year, until I am ready to leave." Then suddenly, crash! Less than a minute later, the ground shook—the double BOOM-BOOM sound was so loud that my neighbors became worried. The sound was heard for many acres past my plot of land, and I shivered with the realization that I had almost died. A seemingly healthy-looking pine tree to my far right came down, literally missing my house where my dog and I stood, along with missing my vehicle, art studio, and propane tank by just a few yards. While I was frightened, nothing was damaged and I wondered how this could be since we were no more than about 15 to 20 feet away from where the tree had landed. It felt like a warning ... a sign or omen.

In disbelief, I called some women I considered wise who quickly affirmed my hunch: "It's a sign." I didn't want to hear this. The price tag on tree removal was high, and additionally I was not ready to go: not financially, not mentally, not emotionally. Furthermore, I couldn't afford to keep hiring "tree guys." Worry, sadness, and despair started to creep in.

Quickly, and out of worry and fear, I made the decision to sell my beloved home, much sooner than I wanted or ever expected I would. Once again, I went into my rational mind, dismissing my deeper feelings and simply going along. My private practice would become a 100 percent virtual one, and my own California-based integrative healthcare team would have to be relocated as well. I was anxious for months. But I've been told that I am a go-getter, a workhorse. So, I made it happen, and happen fast it did. Fortunately, my real estate agent was really on top of things as well. She's sharp, and she prepared me well. Others were supportive too, yet still, I felt down and was exhausted, both emotionally and physically.

Fast forward a couple months, and I was attending an annual conference for the International Association for the Study of Dreams held in Tucson that year at the same time as my home was closing escrow. My heart was experiencing grief, but I told myself it was fate—that the upcoming move to Maui was supposed to happen this way. I tried to let myself go with the flow.

My real estate agent offered me something quite precious as a "thank you, going away, and friendship gift," as she called it. It was a card reading from Nancy Clemens, a spiritual woman and the creator of Dolphin Oracle Cards. Turns out we lived in the same neighborhood! From the reading, we learned that my relocation would lead me into great change and a transformation of some sort—the chosen cards overturned named this explicitly because each card in the Dolphin Oracle deck is labeled with only one to two words on it. This is unlike traditional tarot decks where the imagery can be quite detailed. After the reading, I thought, "Well sure, of course I will experience great change and transformation. I'm moving to Maui, how could I not?" A few months later, I became much clearer in what the cards were telling me.

Soon after relocating to Maui, I was told by a previous neighbor that more trees had fallen. Some had literally struck my former house. Maybe a month later, another neighbor sent me a photo confirming it. Four trees, at minimum, fell onto my former house—the place I loved and once believed would be a long-term home was damaged and in need of repair. Not only did trees crash all around and, literally, right on top of my last home, but my relationship was crashing, too. And there I was, attempting to comprehend the destruction with each passing day on Maui.

Also, in the beginning of 2023 a dream researcher colleague of mine, Ryan Hurd, suggested I meet with someone he respected and adored. I trusted him, so I reached out to her. Soon after, I was enjoying a lovely lunch at Duckine, a restaurant, with Dr. Apela Colorado and her daughter, Chyna. Over lunch, we discussed nocturnal and waking dreams as well as synchronicities. Apela told me about her collaboration with Indigenous populations as an Oneida-Gaul woman; her work at Chartres in France; her late husband, Keola

LeVan Tadashi Sequeira, and his legacy; and her book, *Woman Between Worlds*. I also learned about her organization, the Worldwide Indigenous Science Network (WISN). As we got to know one another further, Apela invited me to her striking and unforgettable home, which was also the WISN headquarters, to talk story and for 'awa ceremonies. She shared with me the history of the home, built by her beloved late husband, Keola. There was nowhere like this in existence on any Hawaiian island any longer. Maui was it!

I'll always remember my very first time at Apela's home. As I crossed the threshold onto the property, passing through a tiny wooden gate, the energy shifted, or maybe it was just my energy. Either way, it was palpable. I felt as if I was entering a sacred space, and with that, I suddenly remembered a powerful dream from several years prior (two months before I received a breast cancer diagnosis): A nocturnal dream I had worked with on and off for years. I titled that dream "The Divine Courthouse."

> *I am viewing a scene from above and also from the back (of the room). I'm either two people simultaneously or witnessing the two people. But were these even people? One body or being is feathered. The other is covered in skin like a reptile—it could be a snake's skin. The feathered body has a wound: either an injury or cut on the left rib area. Some feathers are missing there. The scene is a spiritual or divine courthouse. There are pews like in a church, but this place also has a feeling of being in court for divine negotiation/judgment. Does my rib need aid? I'm wondering. The negotiations taking place involve some thoughts or decisions about others ... about me!—the sense of something taking place related to some aspect of divinity is in the forefront of my mind as the dream ends.*

Apela and I became friends. She continually invited me into her community with open, welcoming arms and love. As the weeks and months passed by, I would be invited to return. I started to feel that perhaps *this* was my purpose on Maui—these people, this organization, as well as this land, and the healing it all could offer. But I only knew part of the story.

I thought about how I could support and serve what was unfolding here, on this little island. Through this process, my dream, which included the common snake-bird motif, also recalled the deity of Quetzalcoatl, the feathered serpent of birth-death-rebirth, except my inner feathered serpent was fractured, split in two, and one part was noticeably wounded. Was a part of me dying so that a healthier part could be born? Is this what brought me to Maui? After all, every aspect of my life changed in such a short period—three years, in fact.

Through my developing friendships I found strength. I was sure to need it. In shock from the betrayal and breakup, and before I could digest all that was unfolding, I was tasked with finding a new place to live with my dog, all the while juggling work and integrative medical treatments … and still trying to adjust to this unfamiliar, foreign land. I hadn't considered that the "change and transformation" Nancy spoke of would have been paired with that much emotional pain and the loss of someone with whom I thought I was building a life.

Thanks to a fast-moving and hardworking real estate agent, I finally secured a place of my own and began the process of moving once again in April 2023. Spring and early summer were equally difficult on many levels, yet I was making friends and beginning to foster meaningful connections through my dance and surf communities. Still, I was far away from "home." Everything was new, and from the emotional pain I was processing, I was still in a dissociative-like fog. It was hard—some days, I felt completely robbed of all joy. Yet even through this very hard time, strangely enough, I felt I was supposed to be on Maui, especially given what it took to get me here. I didn't know why. This simply cannot be a random act, I thought. I kept looking for my greater purpose. Why the heck was I on Maui? This question would stay with me all year.

A few months later as I again pondered what I was even doing on Maui, I sent Apela a text message. I suggested that my purpose was quite possibly linked to her and WISN. In her reply, she joked, "Ya think?" I smiled and nodded in agreement as my conviction grew. I started to accept my fate and open my heart to a new purpose. Soon, things would shift … for the worse.

I scheduled a visit in July to formally interview Apela for an article I wanted to write for my blog, *Conscious Chimera*. Apela's friend,

Teresa MacColl, was also present that day, so I was fortunate enough to have the opportunity to interview her as well. I learned a great deal and was very appreciative of all that they had shared with me. I was so grateful for that day, and naturally, I looked forward to my next visit there. Yet, it was not meant to be. My last time at the WISN headquarters, in what was then Apela's home in the center of the town of Lahaina, was on July 29, 2023, only a week before the deadliest fire in U.S. history reduced the entire town to ashes.

The 2023 Maui Fires and Immediate Aftermath

The entire week of August 7, 2023, was the beginning of a waking nightmare. The strong winds from Hurricane Dora just south of the Hawaiian Islands made for a frustrating beginning to the month of August, but it would soon get worse … a whole lot worse. Fires sparked across the island of Maui, one by one. They quickly spread.

During the evening of Tuesday, August 8, I was busy enjoying local events. First, I met up with a new surfer friend in Kihei to attend the *Waterman* film event together, hosted by Surfrider Foundation. I left that event a little early to make it to my regular Tuesday evening dance class in Kahului. After thoroughly enjoying the hour with my fellow dance-loving friends, we reminisced about the previous Sunday we had all spent together, relaxing, dancing, hot tubbing, and celebrating one of our teacher's birthdays. Feeling content, I walked to my car and began my drive home, back to Kihei.

I had only been cruising down the Pi'ilani Highway for about two minutes when I noticed that my cell phone really wanted my attention—"Hi Sa…," I exclaimed. Before I could finish the greeting, she quickly blurted out her questions about whether I was "freaked out." She was worried for my safety, but I had no idea what she was talking about. She explained that fires had erupted in two Kihei locations (not to mention the rest of the island) as I was calmly cruising south, heading down the highway. By that moment, though, I could start to see an orange-colored murkiness ahead. After that brief exchange, I accelerated to get to my destination a little faster, that being my home in the north of Kihei. As I approached Kihei, I could see the blaze, but I didn't feel too concerned. At the same time, I took notice—I heard my father's voice in my mind, reminding me to always keep the gas tank full, especially during the dry season. We both have had a great deal of direct experience with wildfires, even those huge ones, those called megafires. We survived living alongside several of them in Northern California. In fact, this is the case for my entire family. My own history in Nor Cal as we call it, where I was born and raised, led to my underestimating small fires. I didn't think there was any way that officials would allow hundreds of homes, let alone an entire town on a small island, to burn down. Let alone the economic center! Turns out, I was dead wrong, and grossly naive. But I didn't know it in that moment.

In no time at all, I was paying at the gas pump. Now that my gas tank was full (exhale), I drove up the street across from mine into the residential area to get a closer look. Everyone was on the sidewalks or in the street. Dozens of vehicles had their headlights on and engines running. Okay, people are concerned, I accepted. I took a few photos with my cell phone near the top of Kaiwahine and then turned around. I then drove back down the street heading toward Uwapo Road. Once I parked my vehicle, now that I was home, I came across worried neighbors, also standing outside in the dark. We discussed the situation, then decided to be sure we had everything we needed in our "go-bag." Once I felt mine was sufficiently packed up, the blaring screech on my cell phone ordered: EVACUATE IMMEDIATELY. Time to run!

Alongside my neighbors, I quickly loaded my car with essentials along with my dog. Still, I was skeptical that something like this could ever get so out of control. Getting a lesson from my neighbors, I was educated in a flash on the lack of resources, or rather misappropriated resources, on Maui and was also reminded that helicopters cannot fly in hurricane strength winds. Gulp. Someone said, "There's no CalFire here, Kim." I remained vigilant, as my naivety melted into the background. Following the evacuation orders, I caravanned southward with some of my neighbors. This wasn't the best choice because when we arrived at our agreed-upon meetup point, the smell of smoke was thick. The second Kihei fire, a little farther south, wasn't helping. We couldn't gather any accurate information. It was going to be a long night.

Then, news regarding Lahaina started coming in. Lahaina was completely destroyed. I was in total disbelief, as were most others. How was Lahaina gone? In less than half a day, practically the entire town was wiped off the map. People were missing. Friends became homeless in a flash. Apela was one of them, along with hundreds of others in her community. Many also lost their pets, businesses, and vehicles that day, Tuesday, August 8, 2023. The WISN headquarters, housed in Apela's home, was also destroyed. I personally did not know anyone who lost their life, but the reported numbers of those who died that day increased significantly as the days progressed. Many were elders; some were children. I was in disbelief—how could my government let this happen?

Those first few days immediately after the Lahaina fire were especially critical. While the area was still smoldering, many people were trapped up north on the west side of the island without transportation, road access, water, electricity, shelter—you name it. With grocery stores quickly becoming depleted, water remained unavailable due to damaged infrastructure and melted pipes. Where it was available, it was unsafe to drink. Families with children, even babies, had nothing but the clothes on their backs. Those who survived were in deep pain. I knew I must act fast—I had to help.

Because of my personal history with California fires, I am familiar with disaster protocols. I quickly linked up with other Maui residents, some of whom were new and some of whom were *Kama'āina* ("child of the land"), to begin a multiday process (which eventually turned into a months-long process) of doing the work the government and the NGOs weren't yet doing: purchasing clean water, grab-and-go nonperishables, gasoline, baby formula, diapers, flashlights, batteries, and other essentials. These purchases were possible due to the money generously given to me by friends, family, and colleagues to be directed to early recovery and survival efforts. After purchases were made, the big task of loading these supplies onto boats headed into the region of the disaster—the west side of Maui— just north of the impact zone took place. This routine went on for a long time. Many people expressed how they were angry and frustrated with the relief agencies because they had set up shelters on the opposite side of the West Maui Mountains, in an area (albeit a safe one) that hundreds of people could not reach. The residents were the quickest and most efficient to act in a desperate effort to save their friends and families. People who were so deeply traumatized and in pain stepped up to save their communities from even greater harm. I was struck by the generosity of the people around me. Big wave Jet Ski drivers, who normally rescue surfers, participated in meeting some of the boats and the much larger vessels out in the open sea to transfer the goods onto dry land where displaced families were waiting. Those first 72 hours were especially critical! Four to five days after the fires began, the authorities, some of whom were attending to rescuing people from the ocean, organized and began acting in the arena of food, shelter, and water distribution. Not only were people displaced, but without jobs they had no income to purchase food, or anything, really. Water had to be purchased as well because even if anything would come out of the tap, it was unsafe to drink, or even bathe in. Similarly, the upcountry fire spreading through Kula resulted in the loss of potable water and a great deal of destruction. These were not the only fires that week. Maui faced a true disaster.

Less than two weeks postfire, I flew to California to be with family for a few nights, spending time in birthday celebrations for my mom, brother-in-law, and eldest nephew, all born in August, and holding the memory of my deceased paternal grandmother, whose birthday is also in August. I was very relieved to be in the presence of family, but I also felt guilty and alone. I felt as if I had abandoned post and wondered if anyone around me understood that. Everything going on also triggered me into a deep sadness. I hadn't broken down and cried in front of my parents like that in decades. My time in California would be short, I knew, so I pulled myself together. What did I do? I solicited even more donations in California, acquiring expensive respiratory masks, flashlights, and batteries to bring back to Maui with me. The work of disaster relief became a serious mission. How could it not? Fellow Kihei residents were on a mission to help our west side neighbors as well as those impacted by the fires in upcountry. The initial weeks of intense rapid, frantic action were concluding, but there was, and still is, much work to be done.

Prior to August 2023, I had not been this close to widespread grief in this same way. The entire island, and neighboring islands I was told, felt enveloped in waves of grief and sometimes even a frantic, jittery buzz. This is the kind of loss with no resolution, I thought. It was difficult to imagine how anyone could move forward after such incredible loss.

Even three to four weeks after the fires broke out, small-boat and water-vessel operators were still making deliveries onto the beaches just north of Lahaina. The final supplies I delivered for water transportation were respiratory masks, flashlights, and batteries because these were just some of the items still needed. Maui was in short supply. It was hard to get our hands on more. Later, finally, goods were allowed to be driven north by vehicle without much question. About five weeks after the fire, a neighbor and I visited the area up north on the west side to drop off nonperishable food and additional essentials. Free food pantries had been set up that included essentials (referred to as *Kānaka Costco*); pop-up kitchens offering free hot meals all sprouted in several locations as well. Free therapy services, massage, and entertainment for children could also be found. There were also many highly organized behind-the-scenes efforts—those scheduling shifts for the volunteer mental health providers, for example, and so much more. This was and is one long road. To this day, the people continue to need support from the total devastation of Lahaina even as I write this now.

Months slid by before my own mental fog began to clear. I had been operating in a strange state of mind, sometimes like a zombie. During that time, old wounds resurfaced, both connected to wildfire survival and my recent romantic breakup. I felt great sadness—a safety net was gone. A sense of loss loomed around every corner.

In my downtime, I took solace in reading books. The year 2023 was also the time I spent reading and digesting the book *Women Who*

Run with the Wolves by Clarissa Pinkola Estés. I consider it to be a *long* read, one in which a reader can ponder and take time to savor each chapter. Estés (1995) wrote, "Even raw and messy emotions can be understood as a form of light, crackling and bursting with energy. We can use the light of rage in a positive way, to see into places we cannot usually see" (p. 352). Some days I bathed in an energetic soup of anger but careful not to become addicted to this emotion. I know anger as a sacred ally, so I used that as fuel for creativity. I surprised myself with the spontaneous writings that emerged from within, yet it also felt as if I had been taken over by an outside force. Additionally, Estés (1995) reminded me of the lessons I could learn from that angry energy. By giving it my full attention, I could allow it to teach me, even reshape me in becoming something useful for the community.

From the murky waters of my consciousness during that turbulent season, I wrote a couple pieces copied below, and a third, shorter piece I posted as a blog on my website. They were unlike anything I had ever written before and for the most part spilled out of me as if I was writing for someone else, as if other hands took over my keyboard. I was surprised at what spilled out. It was unlike anything I had ever done. The first one I titled "Impermanence":

> I'm breathing in.... I'm breathing out.... I'm breathing in.
>
> Meditation can teach us many things. One of the many lessons I learned from participating in meditation practice is that emotions, as well as thoughts, come and go. Flowers bloom and wither. Birth is always followed by death. Even stars die.
>
> But who expects their young child's life to be cut so short? The best life-enhancing practices from meditation to yoga to therapy cannot relieve the despair nor the terror of the universal truth due to an injustice.
>
> Nothing, absolutely nothing, is permanent.
>
> Homes and businesses were standing tall, intact. Laughter, smiles, chatter, the pitter-patter of footsteps, the creaking of doors opening, closing. The sound of crashing waves fills the gaps leaving no silence. The aloha—the usual on any given day. A few hours later there was nothing, except for black smoke and soon to follow, flying embers ... thick ash. Shouting, coughing, screaming, wheezing. We can't breathe.

Nothing lasts forever we are told. That's true. But the how and why of endings matter.

How might the impact of the impermanence of life be different from ones that were honored through preparation, ritual, community, and love, as opposed to ones permeated with fear, despair, disorientation, aloneness?

Why were the signs of danger dismissed (for months, even years) knowing so many residents alerted warnings to those officials in power?

Elemental forces of hurricane strength winds and fire joined together while you were mentally asleep or simply uncaring. Children, Elders, died in a horrifying manner. Absolutely nothing, no one, can excuse this reality. When action could have prevented such devastation, will your sympathies ever be enough?

And now, less than a week after the fact, wealthy, privileged, parasites and leeches dial numbers on the daily. How will you protect and honor those who remain ... and the land?

Living children will remember the ones who died. How, if at all, if ever, can justice and respect ever be restored? The next generation has eyes too, and more importantly, lives through their hearts. May impermanence melt away the greed, neglect, and dishonor allowed to manifest on Maui.

The second piece bubbled up after I heard about a group of Maui residents who erected a long display of crosses, in public, for each person who had died in the Lahaina fire. While the gesture is not lost on me, my initial reaction was an angry one because I thought, why would they assume that those who died were all of the Christian faith? When I later drove through the burn zone and passed by the line of large wooden crosses painted in white, I thought, did they ask every impacted family if such a display would be appropriate or representative of that (deceased) individual or family? While many Hawaiians belong to a parish or attend a Christian church, sometimes blending the traditional ways with the foreign religion, how many of the local people (*Kānaka Maoli* or *Kānaka'Ōiwi; Kāma'aina Hapa*) who perished or their grandparents/ancestors experienced religious oppression at the hands of non–Native missionaries and other colonizing forces? After all, up until 1898 *Kānaka Maoli* or *Kānaka 'Ōiwi* were a self-governing, sovereign people until the

United States took the Kingdom of Hawaii. The community of those islands had their own spirituality and religion, their own creation story which was not derived from a Christian agenda. Furthermore, most *Akua* (deities) do not necessarily or primarily even manifest as human (Brown, 2022). That sacred creation chant, the *Kumulipo*, meaning Beginning in Darkness, describes how the world, and life, began according to the *kūpuna*, the ancestors. It is an account of the creation of the world according to Hawaiian tradition. Through this oral tradition, Native Hawaiian peoples understood their familial connection to land and all life, to the gods of sky (*Wākea*), ocean (*Kanaloa*) and earth (Papa/Haumea), and beyond. And, as Indigenous original instructions deliver, how to treat and protect the land and its creatures, as everything is alive and family. I was concerned—I felt like none of this was present or acknowledged when those large white wooden crosses initially went up for display. It was simply a row of crosses, which tells only one story. For some local residents I spoke to (who will remain unnamed), it felt as if a display of dominance stepped forward ... a reminder of who really controls this island.

For better or worse, those feelings and sentiments noted above prompted the piece below:

Tight chest, tense neck, unconsciously holding my breath.
Crosses, over a hundred white crosses, littered along the highway.
Littered reveals my bias. At least I admit I have one.

And the issue I have with the crosses, well, that is my issue: an issue with assumptions and colonial ways. Did you assume your god represents their akua too?

Are you certain the deceased are all Christian? Trees, makau, hearts, ki'i of Kāne and Kanaloa, canoe paddles, lei ... anything from nature—So many options to show allyship. Ignored. Are these crosses for you or them?

Suppressed by Christian colonizers, have we all forgotten how Hawai'i has its own gods? Its own deities? Its own symbols and mele? Are you familiar with any of them? And would it even matter to you?

Everyone is raw. Burning eyes. Blistered hands. Scarred hearts.
This land is now a burial ground. We cry together.

May I suggest continuing your settler ways in private, in your own home, if you must. The public display, so full of assumptions, is disrespectful, distasteful, dismissive.

After the two writings flew out of me, as an expression of anger, I learned how others felt similarly, and I was glad they told me so. While raised in the Roman Catholic tradition, I wasn't taught directly how Jesus Christ was revolutionary. It was much later that I came to understand these aspects of his life, or so it appears from what we know of his life. A lot of what we see in Maui's history—imperialism, militarism, colonization, land and habitat destruction—are in opposition to the spirit of Christ Consciousness, as well as in opposition to the *Kumulipo.*

As stated above, the *Kumulipo* is an account of the creation of the world according to Hawaiian tradition. *Kumulipo* means Beginning in Darkness, describing how the world, and life, began according to the *kūpuna*, the ancestors. Lili'u Loloku Waiania Kamaka'eha, more commonly known as Queen Lili'uokalani (1838–1917), translated this sacred Hawaiian creation chant. She was the first sovereign queen, and the last monarch of Hawai'i, remembered for her love, dedication, and service to the people of Hawai'i and for her resistance to the takeover of the Hawaiian Kingdom by U.S. military and businessmen. The *Kumulipo* can be accessed in a printed version which was translated from the original manuscript that had been preserved by Lili'uokalani's royal family. Queen Lili'uokalani began the translation after the coup, while she was imprisoned in 1895 at Iolani Palace for her alleged counterrevolutionary ways, as she feared she would never be free. By mid–1897 the translations were completed. For an introductory experience, you can locate Shaundor Chillingworth's April 26, 2019, article on the Kamehameha Schools webpage (*https://www.ksbe.edu/article/illustrating-the-kumulipo*), which includes an animated video presentation of the first 28 lines out of the 2,102 lines of the *Kumulipo.*

Upon hearing how others were also upset over the display of crosses, but too afraid to speak out, I decided I would. In doing so, I must also face my own shadow. Since the concept of the shadow will come up throughout this book, let me explain it briefly here. Perhaps you've read the works of Carl G. Jung and have come across his explanation, or one proposed by his students. Simply put, my shadow is the person I don't want to be. The shadow can be individually viewed as hidden, repressed parts of oneself, or collectively as hidden, repressed parts of the collective values of the society in which we participate. In essence, the shadow is that which we do not see or acknowledge. Let's not judge it for now and agree that it is either good or evil. In mythology, the shadow is Trickster energy (Maui has also been referred to as Tricker). We can also look at the term "the shadow" as an imbalance. When we are disconnected from Source we can lose our balance. From an out-of-balance place, whether by dissociation or lack of grounding or awareness, we may experience illness or act out from a polarized stance (i.e., reactivity). When we do not recognize or acknowledge our own shadow, we may overly deflect feedback or even point the finger at others ... anyone but ourselves. As a SoulCollage® facilitator, I turn to founder Seena Frost's explanation of shadow "as vital, primitive energy that is out of balance" (p.73). One way to get a sneak peek at our shadow is to notice what it is we cannot stand in another individual or within another culture or society. That "thing we can't stand" is likely our own shadow—it's an aspect we may be struggling with inside ourselves.

As is the case for so many others, grief, loss, fear and trauma are nothing new in our lives. My identity is bicultural, and through my storytelling one can hear how a fragmented past with intergenerational trauma exists alongside wholeness and gratitude. With the blessings that come with being born into large families on both sides, and the presence of Elders, so too, come the sorrows. I thought nothing of it when I used to tell people how I had attended 30 funerals by the age of 30, not at all realizing the unusual nature of it. When you are fortunate enough to be raised in families with longevity and/or the inclusion of non-blood relatives, thus expanding the family, you also have to say goodbye as they die off one by one. In my family's case, sometimes even three in one year.

My maternal grandmother knew trauma from spousal abuse, her face distorted from heavy-handed violence. My much more resilient mother knows trauma from those memories, and those that later followed her and her only sibling, a little sister, for over a decade in the foster care system. I know trauma from the residual downstream effects on those women's lives, and from contact with those linked to my mother's extended foster family during my childhood and adolescent years. I remember some of the foster kids who came and went. Some I looked up to and was very happy to befriend in my youth, then suddenly they were gone (removed, having gone to a new placement, or having run away). While people experience intergenerational trauma in different ways, for me the worst part was when there were no goodbyes. The pain of those who survived the August 2023 fires yet never had a chance to say goodbye to their loved ones is a pain so great.... It's like we were raised in a world with layers of grief deep in our bones.

Some years later, I found myself serving in the arena of community psychology, accepting job offers with some of the most highly trauma-exposed children in the nation, and later working to help in the healing for families riddled with fragmentation due to the trauma that comes from histories of incarceration, addiction, and interactions with Child Protective Services.

Reflecting on the episodes of my own life, I recognize how we can be guided toward healing. Something deep in my consciousness must have pushed me in the direction of fine art as a major at Sacramento State University just prior to entering those jobs, and I trust that it must have been my loving, wise ancestors that guided and backed me there in that tough line of work. Artmaking allowed me to express myself fully and to quiet down; I credit it for saving my life. Creating art and engaging in those spaces was especially supportive during the decade plus years of working with those traumatized youth—young ones who had experienced and barely survived true horrific acts cast upon them. Later, my nonprofit agency employment involved treating families (primarily women and children) living with addiction. The poverty and violence that is often interwoven with substance abuse all became more than I could take. Fortunately, from my background as a clinician, I was able to recognize that while I carried my own history with me, vicarious traumatization and secondary traumatic stress had also set in. When I looked for help with my full-coverage insurance at the time, there was not any to be found. Eventually, I paid out of pocket to access therapy services to help me recover from the exposure. I was fortunate to have the resources to manage the financial burden.

Privileged with this support, and as resilient as I was, when I finally said NO, I can't continue to do this work (as those working in nonprofit organizations rarely get adequate financial compensation, nor the mind-body-spirit support to sustain themselves in such draining, painful work), I was very soon after diagnosed with chronic fatigue and breast cancer. Left side ... right over the heart.

So, when the August 2023 Maui fires erupted just a handful of months after I was released from that painful relationship, the ugly energy of trauma and those traumatized eyes all around the island were deeply familiar. I hung out at the bottom of the deep well of sadness. The permeating energy generated because of those fires and the massive destruction triggered my nervous system in striking ways. My familiarity with fast action returned as I put all my attention into the immediate relief efforts. As the weeks passed by, I considered the work I had left a few years ago. I struggled to push myself into committing to return to offering trauma therapy to those in need, but I couldn't do it. It was heavier than anything I could hold. I also knew I could not allow cancer to spread and must prioritize parasympathetic nervous system care so that my body could remain in a healing state. It was easy when I offered free guided meditation services to the community, but my mind-body complex wouldn't allow me to return to work as a trauma treatment provider. I felt bad, almost ashamed about this reality, but also knew I was through with self-sacrifice to the point of heading straight toward an early death.

I sat with the contradiction, the cognitive dissonance, as I resided on the island of Maui—occupied land—an embodiment of missionary colonization and militarization. No matter what I gave, or could give, would change that. If I went back to California, my birthplace, the same would be true of my existence there, yet here, so soon after these murderous fires, the reality was ultra fresh. I'd like to think that the insidious removal of Indigenous peoples is a thing of the past, yet looking at Hawai'i, especially Lahaina's not-so-distant history, it becomes apparent that it is happening now. Before I say goodbye to this precious land, I do my best to be *pono*, a term meaning many things, yet here I align with the definitions of being true, sincere, and in balance.

Six to seven months after the fires, post-traumatic stress disorder (PTSD) was setting in for those who literally ran for their lives, some even running straight into the ocean. Some watched as others burned or listened helplessly as others drowned. The deep loss and grief that comes with living as a member of an Indigenous community is now re-triggered across the islands. I continued to be reminded how I was not the only one enraged at the sight of those white crosses. It was like a bold statement some said of "Look, we burned you out and off your land. Now we plant our authority in the ground on the hill overlooking where you were born, where you once made your home. Now it is ours." And as noted above, while I know grief, loss, trauma from my current lived experience in this body I occupy, it is not of this kind, nor anywhere close to this extreme degree. But it does help me empathize and keep me from mentally falling asleep.

Then, not long after those initial anger-fueled written pieces oozed out of my psyche, a final, shorter one came forth. This one held space for the sadness alive in my heart at that time (*consciouschimera.com/blog*):

> I thought I had left trauma work for good; Or at least for the most part after I was diagnosed. My body, my nervous system, my immune system: the impact zone.
>
> Cycles of healing, redefining, reworking, re-examining life, my heart, my mind. Actively turning attention to life's beauty ... and joy. Recalling the cyclical nature of existence itself. And still, maintaining hope.
>
> Now I sit just a few miles south of ground zero. No longer a direct hit to my body, but a scorching of the collective spirit. The sun was not the only force to show no mercy that day.
>
> Today, trauma is the air we breathe. It's not attached to my work, but to my neighbors' eyes. A three-hundred-and-sixty-degree, twenty-four-seven kind of therapy session. One that comes to no end.

Viewing these surprisingly spontaneous writings, recognizing them as a mirror into my soul and a glimpse of my own shadow, I knew I had no other choice than to accept my own dissociation from the unearned privilege and power that has allowed me to live relatively comfortably on Maui. Having enjoyed the benefits of stolen resources, especially of land and water, which set the stage for the devastation of August 2023, how could I help make things right? Some suggested using my voice through writing so that I could help spread the word about what has happened and continues to happen on this land as attorneys, developers, and billionaires partake in the continued land-grabbing unfolding today ... right now.

After these writings poured out of me, when I could finally think more clearly after confronting and processing the rage, disappointment, sadness inside, I felt ready to shift my attention again into what I had begun months ago. I returned to the material gathered from those July 29 interviews with Apela and Teresa, choosing to include them in this book. They are too important for just another blog article, as you will see in the coming pages. In addition, I became inspired to invite others to share wisdom from their own traditions as well, in a shared effort to encourage a return to our spiritual nature so we may care for each other and everything around us as we live out our lives on this sentient planet where everything is alive.

Then, in late fall of 2023, after more emotional processing, I reconnected with Dolphin Oracle Deck creator Nancy Clemens and told her how 2023 unfolded—the good, the bad, and the very ugly. She was not surprised given what came forth in the previous card reading. I shared my unbelievable experiences with the energetic forces of Maui and how, based on some personal experiences that I will keep private for now, I came to see that "Maui karma" as I called it works at lightning speed. Nancy added that the energies of Hawaii, from her lived experience on the Big Island, also quickly work on people in a way that their shadow side becomes apparent and cannot be suppressed back down as it had in the past. One's shadow cannot exist as a skeleton locked into the closet any longer. Instead, shadow reveals itself. This made sense to me given what I witnessed in what had been my home during my first few months on Maui. It also made sense in the year of dreams I had been recalling that reflected the emotional processing of the shock and pain I had experienced along with a slow integration. The same theme shown in 22 dreams, in fact, supporting me to integrate the experiences I lived through and to move forward, came to me over the course of 13 months (by that time). Surrendering to what the foreign land of Maui had to teach me, I made the commitment, recalling how the pine trees ran me off from my previous home with their heart-stopping crash so close to my body, to stay a while longer and learn how to give something of value to this place, from my heart. It just all seemed so strange with how life's events were unfolding (my own, among my Maui friends, and on this land).

By summer of 2024, many *Kānaka Maoli* or *Kānaka ʻŌiwi* and *Kamaʻāina Hapa* of Maui continued to report little in the way of justice. Still, anger remained in the air and, I believe, for good reason. Certain officials still lacked accountability. The price of housing skyrocketed. Evictions were taking place left and right. These reports filled the local news and some relief workers I spoke with reported the same. I saw fire-displaced residents continue to bounce from one temporary housing site to another, their trauma no longer acute, now post-traumatic. Some therapists here, ones I know, had waitlists of more than 150 people. The ashes had settled, but the suffering had just begun.

If you have lived on any of the islands of Hawaiʻi, or are familiar with the history here, you may have a true understanding of *aloha*. You may have seen the reminder on T-shirts that *Aloha* is Law. Truly, Native Hawaiian law is centered on principles of *Aloha ʻāina*, commonly translated to "love the land," however it is also an action verb of stewardship and of defending the land. It is familial. McCubbin, Cristobal and Chin (2021) wrote how as a verb *Aloha ʻāina* calls for "action and is a continual and consistent doing" (p. 259).

As this law is so centered in place and culture, the best place to study it is in Hawaii. Paʻele Kiakona explains *aloha* in how *Kānaka Maoli* or *Kānaka ʻŌiwi* traditionally greeted one another—that is, by bringing heads together, forehead and nose touching, while simultaneously taking a breath in. That's *aloha,* says Pa'ele Kiakona during his interview with Lindsey Davis (ABCNews, 8/17/23). Yet, with all that has transpired, where is the *aloha* when leaders bow down to billionaires and corporate interests? Just look at who owns the largest plots of Hawaiian lands, and what the U.S. military has been allowed to do (the worst may perhaps be the decades of bombing Kaho'olawe). In the spirit of reparations, I write and use my voice because I believe it is *kuleana* (responsibility), as a way of honoring and demonstrating *Aloha 'āina.*

1

A Brief History
of Maui

Ethnographer, folklorist and anthropologist Martha Beckwith, PhD (1871–1959), authored the classic work, *Hawaiian Mythology*. That text contains not only the stories about Maui as a demi-god, but also the many narratives of the Hawaiian people about the Hawaiian gods. The National Park Service website also includes stories of a handful of Hawaii's deities, including Maui (*https://www. nps.gov/hale/learn/historyculture/deities.htm*), who is known as a hero of many things, including but not limited to being a skilled fisherman, the one who brought fire to the people (Beckwith, 1976), and even snared the sun, and thus slowed down the sun (Beckwith, 1976) or the passage of time. I'll leave you with one version of that story below (albeit a version I condensed and abbreviated):

> The sun ran so quickly across the sky that there was no time to do just about anything before the darkness returned. Because of the limited sunshine, Hina (Maui's mother) was unable to fully dry her bark-cloth which was used for clothes and bedding. This was a problem, so Maui took action. From the top of Iao Valley, Maui could see the sun's path. He told Hina about this, along with his plan to make the sun slow down. Hina contributed 15 cords and sent him off with a plan. Maui was tasked with locating his blind grandmother because she feeds the sun. The sun stops to consume the cooked bananas she offers. Knowing this, Maui would steal the bananas just before they were to be prepared by his grandmother so she would search for them and instead find him. At that moment he would identify himself as Hina's son to gain her assistance. This plan worked—Maui's grandmother agreed to help. She provided him with an additional cord, a stone for an adze, and instructed him on how to capture the sun. Maui hid behind

27

the Wiliwili tree as he waited for the sun to arrive. Once he saw the sun's legs, Maui acted quickly, snaring each of them. The sun attempted to retreat, flee, yet Maui quickly secured each cord to the Wiliwili tree as he had been instructed, allowing him to bring the sun back up. To convince the sun that he was serious, Maui struck the sun with his stone adze. The sun promised to go slower from then on, which may have saved its life.

Tēvita O. Ka'ili explores deeper meanings behind the Maui story and offers possible interpretations. Ka'ili wrote the article titled, "The Demigod Maui: Modern Day Lessons from Ancient Tales of Oceania," describing how the sun can be symbolic for chiefs of the highest status and how the slowing down of the sun (no easy task) represents halting oppressive rule, thus allowing greater freedom of the people and granting them time to complete necessary tasks (like the drying of bark-cloth). As noted above, Maui is known for more than just the slowing of time. Regarding Maui being credited for his bringing of fire to the people, Ka'ili (2016) wrote:

> Fire, another Oceanic symbol, signifies knowledge and technology. Maui seized fire from the hording hands of the gods and shared it with the rest of humanity. In this way, Maui democratized knowledge and shared technology freely with the world. It can be seen as an ancient version of open-source. Maui was the champion of the underclass, the dispossessed, and the marginalized.

Maui is known as a Trickster, and such stories are widespread. According to Beckwith (1976), "The demigod Maui is archtrickster throughout Polynesia, but his deeds are rather typical of the *kupua* than of the trickster hero" (p. 430). *Kupua* refers to supernatural powers.

As for Maui's reputation as a clever, shapeshifting hero, Ka'ili explains how Maui's true source of *mana* (supernatural power) is the goddess Hina, variously described as his grandmother, mother, wife, or sister. Maui embodies values of equality and justice, thus transforming society into a more equitable one as one might expect from a grand master trickster of Oceania. As the feminine *mana* flows through him, what is unrealized may become realized, what is impossible becomes possible.

Not long ago, Maui, as a geographical location, was a very different island compared with how it is seen today. Local people speak of the drastic changes that they have seen in their lifetime alone. With the way things are going, Maui, even as it exists today, could soon be long forgotten. From imperialism to colonialism, some claim it to be a cultural genocide—the slow-drip kind. The history of the Hawaiian Islands is lengthy, but below is a brief history.

Historically, the notion of owning land was inconceivable among Hawaiians, including those native to Maui. Resources were shared, not privately owned. Land was used and accessed differently in that many districts existed, with an *ali'i*, or chief, responsible for each one. These *ahupua'a*, or divisions of land, ran from the mountains down to the ocean. All people held a place in society, or rather within the *ahupua'a* in which they lived—some were laborers, some were leaders—all had duties and roles in the community.

Less than 250 years ago, things really shifted. Captain James Cook was the first European to see a Hawaiian island—his arrival at Kaua'i was in January 1778. King Kamehameha the Great desired consolidation of the Hawaiian Islands, which would lead to him governing them (Harden, 2021). In the late 18th century, the kings of each of the Hawaiian Islands would become a thing of the past.

Captain Jean-François de Galaup de La Pérouse was the first foreign body to step foot onto the island of Maui. His 1786 arrival initiated the deaths of Native Peoples. The arrival of missionaries and the resulting spread of disease (Harden, 2021; Berney, 1991) are linked. Kamehameha ceded the Hawaiian Kingdom to Great Britain in 1794. It is still argued today whether this was Kamehameha's true intention.

As the years passed by, the towns we know today—Hana, Makawao, Wailuku, and Lahaina—became ever more populated. Less than 100 years after the arrival of Captain Jean-François de Galaup de La Pérouse, Native Hawaiian deaths skyrocketed again, mostly due to disease brought in by outsiders.

Also, less than 100 years later (1840s and 1850s), pressure from the Western occupiers of Maui led to Kamehameha III being tricked, in a sense, into what resulted in foreign occupation of Hawaiian lands. The Great *Māhele* of 1848 led to the seizing of Native Peoples' land and homes and then being "redistributed outside of their families" (Harden, 2021, p. 100). While some claim that the intentions of Kamehameha III were to protect Maui lands and secure them for Native ownership, the results were in complete opposition to this.

Generations and generations of Native Hawaiian people were familiar with communal ways of living, subsistence, and the *ahupua'a* system. This foreign, Western concept of privately owning land, alongside colonial trickery (recall the language barriers) and occupation by outsiders led to—let's call it what it is—land theft. From there, Hawaiian families had to leave the lands stewarded by their ancestors for generations. Many went to large towns such as Wailuku and Lahaina.

Then came the sugar plantations, and from there, the Masters and Servants Act of 1850 indentured labor system. Samuel T. Alexander and Henry P. Baldwin not only were the first to get involved but also became the largest and most powerful. What were once Maui's natural waterways then became man-made irrigation systems diverting water from the pre-existing watersheds to areas where water was wanted in order to fuel industry. Following the sugar boom, from the 1890s through the 1930s, the pineapple industry grew.

During that era, revolts rose up naturally as a result of the overthrow of the sovereign Kingdom of Hawai'i. That was in 1893. Prince Jonah Kūhiō Kalaniana'ole (born March 26, 1871) joined the revolutionaries to restore the monarchy. The revolution was unsuccessful, and Prince Kūhiō was arrested, charged with treason, and imprisoned for a year. He was pardoned when Queen Lili'uokalani agreed to sign a formal abdication of her throne in exchange for the pardon of her supporters who had led the revolt. The fight between Hawaiians who wanted sovereignty, strengthening of the monarchy, and to remain in control of their own land versus powerful, rich men with access to U.S. government officials, such as Samuel Dole, was on. Queen Lili'uokalani was imprisoned (this was when she began making translations of the *kumulipo*). In the summer of 1898, Hawai'i was annexed without a treaty. Much of this was motivated by powerful individuals who didn't want tariffs placed on sugar. In

1900, Hawai'i was made a territory of the United States, and Dole, the very first governor.

As injustices piled up, so was the strength of those serving the Native community through traditional healing ways. Born in 1889, David Kaonohiokala Bray is one example. Through his family and lineage, he became a *kahuna lapa' au* (medical priest-practitioner) who continuously upheld Hawaiian traditional ways and spirituality (Berney, 1991). Bray gave of himself during the many decades when it was a threat to foreign authorities to do so.

Around this same time, industry's negative impact to the lands of Maui is noted. You can read the report of U.S. forester E.M. Griffith on Hawaiian Forests, presented at Yokohama, Japan, on March 5, 1902, which describes it. Here is a portion of that report:

> The forests on the island of Maui, upon the whole, are in a fairly satisfactory condition although in certain sections they are disappearing very rapidly. Nearly all the sugar plantations and the bulk of the arable land lies between Wailuku and Honomanu and here the forests have been seriously injured by stock grazing.
>
> The sugar planters and farmers in this locality all depend upon irrigation, the water being taken from small streams which for the most part rise on the slopes of Haleakala. For many years, cattle were allowed an unrestricted range in the forests along the headwaters of these streams so that in many sections the forest is either dead or dying.

And a few paragraphs later:

> The government owns some very important forests areas on Maui along the headwaters of the streams and the upper slopes of the mountains which should be segregated and set aside as forest reserves. It will probably be advisable to build fences and necessary to determine which lands are suitable for agriculture and those which should always be kept under timber.
>
> The forests in the Iao valley are very well protected and consequently show no signs of deterioration while the streams are maintained with a fairly even flow. The forests in the remainder of the district of Lahaina show very plainly the effect of grazing and must be much more carefully looked after in order to conserve the all important water supply.

From those eight sentences alone, we can see how government not only views land as a commodity, but also controls it. This report acknowledges that past industry ruined land and water resources to the point that the next industry is concerned. Not once are the local people of Maui mentioned, nor their needs. Instead of looking at destructive short-sighted industrial practices more fully, the primary concerns appear to be related to how to gain the most for future industries.

In 1959, Hawai'i became a state. Also in 1959, David Kaonohio-kala Bray was recognized for over 50 years of service as a *kahuna* by the House of Representatives of the Territory of Hawai'i (Berney, 1991). Bray "is remembered both for his strength of character and his valuable contributions on many levels to the people of Hawai'i and beyond. His legacy continues today" (Berney, 1991, p. 49–50).

In modern times, Prince Kūhiō Day is a holiday formally recognized in the state of Hawai'i. It is celebrated every March 26. It is one of many days in Hawai'i when people remember the injustices that happened then ... and continue to happen.

In addition to the sugar and pineapple industries leaving negative imprints on the land, the cattle industry expanded. All these industries were coupled with importing laborers from several foreign nations. A lot went on here before and throughout the years of World War II. As military presence increased due to the war, those indigenous to Maui were significantly outnumbered. Destruction of Maui continued—another example includes the U.S. military blowing up parts of the reef just off the shore of South Maui so they could make channels for landing craft.

Just a couple of decades after the war, the tourist industry took a front seat (Ka'anapali being the first resort destination in 1961). Kahului, known as "Dream City," was the main trade and service center of Maui. By the decade in which I was born, the 1970s, Kihei, the location from where I am writing this book, became the next target. Locals my age have told me how they remember Kihei and all South Maui as a child: that is, undeveloped, with beautiful beaches and open spaces from Kihei into Makena. Ceremonies were held nearby, just to the south. Sacred space, sacred land, was everywhere.

They tell me how it is nothing at all like it was when they played on the beach with their aunties and grandmothers. Long story short, what had been shared natural resources became owned and occupied by foreigners, in a span of just a handful of generations, forever impacting the land of Maui.

Today we see a notable spike in population growth from residents and visitors, with tourists visiting Maui in the millions per year. There are far more tourists than residents. Additionally, those from the continental United States buy property on Maui—many as a second home or rental property. More and more local people of Maui are leaving. This is also due to the continued acquisition of land by those who were never from here to begin with (Harden, 2021). Corporations, such as Monsanto, and extremely wealthy individuals have bought up large plots of land across the islands, including outside big developers. It appears that none of these people or groups are invested in sustainability. And then ... there's the fires, which destroyed Lahaina because of neglect. You may have heard how dry Lahaina has been (even though it used to be a wetland before outsiders got involved), and how there wasn't enough water in the fire hydrants for Maui's brave firefighters who were fighting the Lahaina fire. You may watch the 2023 reports on Democracy Now! featuring University of Hawaii Law Professor Kapua'ala Sproat (August 18, 2023) or the *60 Minutes* special news reports for further details (CBS).

Lahaina Stolen ... at least that is what the graffiti will tell you. This reflects the history here, and it is also what some *Kānaka Maoli* or *Kānaka 'Ōiwi*, and *Kama'āina Hapa* will tell you if they feel safe enough to speak. Maui resident Pa'ele Kiakona called attention to the realities of generations of Native Hawaiians of Maui who are being priced out, literally pushed out—affordable housing is a major concern as mentioned in his discussion with Linsey Davis (ABCNews 8/17/23). While Lahaina has gotten much of the attention, upcountry resources (both water and land) have also been impacted by these events, both current and in the not-so-distant past, including the very recent 2023 fires (for more on Hawai'i history, see *www. mauicounty.gov/DocumentCenter/View/3231/History, dhhl.hawaii. gov/kuhio*, and *2001-2009.state.gov/r/pa/ho/time/gp/17661.htm*).

Today, the resistance continues. This time, it is regarding the ongoing militarization of Haleakalā, as plans include adding even more equipment, such as large-scale telescopes, at the top of this highly regarded sacred site. University of Hawai'i professor, historian, and filmmaker, Dr. Lilikalā K. Kame'eleihiwa is credited with the following:

> We, the Hawaiian people, who are born from the union of Pap-ahānaumoku and Wakea, Earth mother and sky father, and who have lived in these islands for over 100 generations, will always have the moral right to the lands of Hawaii now and forever, no matter what any court says.

Testimonials, of which the vast majority were in opposition to continued military expansion, were given publicly throughout the summer of 2024. The testimonials reflect the sentiment above. Some have hope, while others are exhausted and let down. They claim how it doesn't matter what is said, even when all local people agree on a decision, because the "government does what it wants." The despair is palpable.

2

INDIGENOUS MIND

To no one type of mind is it given to
discern the totality of truth.—William James

With many thousands of years of history, my profession and academic focus emerged out of the study of the psyche or soul, today known as the field of psychology. While some have argued over exactly where the term was first used and who exactly should get the credit (LaPointe, 1973), we can agree on the root origins of the term itself. The root of the term *psychology* is derived from the Greek *Psyche* as soul or mind, while *logia* equates to study. Going back even further, the term is related to "breath of life." Some believe psychology to be only a few hundred or so years old, dating back to the 1500s when the word was first seen in print (d'Isa & Abramson, 2023), but how is that possible? Humans were making observations and testing out principles of human behavior and capability long before Wilhelm Wundt and the formal discipline of psychology came to be in the 1800s (Jessen et al., 2022). Sigmund Freud, whose background was in the field of medicine, has received so much attention and credit in the field of psychology. He seems to be the person first associated with psychology by the layperson, or everyday people. These assumptions have their limitations. Yet, as we know, so much was understood about human behavior long before those times. In the Western world, concepts related to the mind were discussed before the common era, such as by Anaxagoras (circa 500 BCE), who predates Socrates. Additionally, from an Indigenous lens, psychology goes back thousands upon thousands of years to be included under a large body of Indigenous Knowledge (IK) accumulated from Indigenous ways of knowing as a science in their own right (Jessen, et al., 2022). When brought all together, these knowledge bases can help drive us forward toward a human experience of oneness within our communities and our sentient surroundings.

Collectively, an awareness has been emerging and mirroring back to humanity how deeply we are out-of-balance, or *beyond the tipping point*, as those seeking environmental justice have pointed out to the world. A step in the right direction, toward wholeness, can be seen in the creation of task forces, forums, collectives, and downright direct action. One example is the United Nations Permanent Forum on Indigenous Issues (UNPFII), an advisory body to the Economic and Social Council, which was created in 2000.

For clarity, I will reference ways by which Indigenous peoples are identified, provided by UNPFII. The UNPFII focuses on many issues affecting Indigenous populations from economic and social development, education, culture, and environment to health and human rights. To answer the question of who Indigenous peoples are, the following information is contained on a UNPFII fact sheet (n.d.). There, you will learn that 70 countries are home to more than 370 million Indigenous people whose traditions, ways of life, and circumstances differ from the dominant society of those nations, and whose ancestors were inhabitants before others arrived. Over time, as a result of occupation, settlements, and conquests, these newly arrived groups became dominant. The world's Indigenous peoples include the Lakota (United States), the Mayas (Guatemala), the Aymaras (Bolivia), the Inuit and Aleutians of the circumpolar region, the Saami (northern Europe), the Aborigines and Torres Strait Islanders (Australia), and the Māori (New Zealand). These and other Indigenous peoples "have retained distinct characteristics which are clearly different from those of other segments of the national populations."

Due to the diversity of Indigenous peoples, the following information on the UNPFII fact sheet can serve as a modern guide for understanding the term. It lists:

• Self-identification as Indigenous peoples at the individual level and accepted by the community as their member

36

- Historical continuity with pre-colonial and/or pre-settler societies
- Strong link to territories and surrounding natural resources
- Distinct social, economic or political systems
- Distinct language, culture and beliefs
- Form non-dominant groups of society
- Resolve to maintain and reproduce their ancestral environments and systems as distinctive peoples and communities

The creators of the UNPFII fact sheet acknowledge Indigenous peoples as keepers of "unique languages, knowledge systems and beliefs" and credit them with possessing "invaluable knowledge of practices for the sustainable management of natural resources," citing relationship to and use of traditional lands as essential for groups' survival.

Regarding participation in politics, the UNPFII fact sheet notes commonalities between Indigenous peoples and "other neglected segments of societies," citing as examples "lack of political representation and participation, economic marginalization and poverty, lack of access to social services and discrimination." Indigenous people the world over share similar struggles related to protection of their rights, striving "for recognition of their identities, their ways of life and their right to traditional lands, territories and natural resources."

With such frequent and massive spans of migration across the globe over the last hundred years, fewer and fewer people reside on the lands of their grandparents or even their great-grandparents. The reasons for this are many, however we know that war, land theft, and colonizing forces are often behind those reasons. The term *colonialism* typically refers to military invasion of territories occupied by those with lesser military powers, whereby the result is imposing oppressive conditions and extracting resources from those conquered (Katz, 2017). Assumptions of superiority underly colonization in all its abuse of power leading to further economic and political oppression.

Everyone has Indigenous roots. All people alive today have

pre-colonial roots if we look back far enough. Indigenous people walking the earth today can share thousands of stories from their experiences of wrongdoing by outside invaders and even neighboring groups. These results from captivity, religious oppression, residential schools, violence, and punishment have robbed those historically most closely connected to land and to the spirit of deep inner knowing and connection to source. This, especially, is the case for those indigenous to North America where ways of knowing through dream sharing and interpretation were forbidden as part of missionary colonial dominance (Ward, 2024). At some point, the connection to Indigenous roots was severed for many who have a migration history in their family. For those like me, it may be anywhere from three to five generations ago when an ancestor left Europe or the United Kingdom for the United States and never returned. That migration coupled with efforts made to assimilate resulted in that fracturing. But wait, there's more. Traditional ways of knowing, those ways-of-being-in-the-world emerging from interconnection with spirits of place, ecology and a life of harmonious balance, have been suppressed and strongly discouraged through threat of violence backed by contemporary Western instruction, and the concepts of rationality, dualism, and intellectualism. For example, journalist Jim Robbins (2018) provides a view of Traditional Ecological Knowledge (TEK), suggesting, "TEK is deep knowledge of a place that has been painstakingly discovered by those who have adapted to it over thousands of years." Robbins includes examples of TEK shared by Indigenous community members, such as that related to beluga whales by Inuit Alaskan elders, and salmon in the Näätämö River by Skolt Sámi of Finland, all impacted by the effects of climate change (*https://e360.yale.edu/features/native-knowledge-what-ecologists-are-learning-from-indigenous-people*). From the many reasons listed above, so much has been lost! The Dark Ages throughout Europe did not help either. TEK of herbs, and their use in certain practices, was suppressed by the Church which associated TEK with witchcraft.

Those privileging Western-minded orientations may view traditional ways of being as embedding the Feminine, which has been viewed as inferior (Leonard & Dawson, 2023) in this out-of-balance, overly patriarchal period. These ways include the valuing of dreaming, following signs and synchronicities, ceremony and ritual, and simply quiet time for inward reflection, and other ways by which to connect with our bodies, the land, and to Source.

Within Indigenous time and space exists a vastness that challenges a mechanical worldview. The land, the place you call home, the place you work and vacation, is sentient and conscious; that is, aware of human presence. A dual-directional, human-landscape relationship highlighting caretaking and stewardship takes center stages in Indigenous cosmologies where the spirit of the land shares knowledge with those who know how to listen. Marker, in his 2018 paper on Coast Salish territory in the northwestern United States, writes, "Modernist social systems and knowledge taxonomies have too often followed a colonialist recipe for seeing the landscape as an inanimate surface for extracting, shaping, and constructing the artifacts of progress" (p. 453). What vast differences in viewing the world.

Colonial mentality in environmental and health studies, including research in those areas, has been dismissive of Indigenous ways of knowing since the time of first contact. The dimensions of spirituality existing within Indigenous ecological knowledge, or rather all forms of Indigenous knowledge, have been yet reduced to folklore and mythology (Sheridan & Longboat, 2014, p. 309). Higher intelligence among Indigenous populations moves beyond the confines of cerebral activity (Dumont, 2002). This is an important point that poses a challenge to strictly secular Western-minded individuals.

Indigenous theories of knowledge are not distinct nor separate from relationship with creation/creator and long-term cultural practice in traditional territories over time. According to Sheridan & Longboat (2014), "it is witnessed in the spruce cone load, the behavior of the raven, the smell of the coming rain, and the lunar cycles that compose minds who think with these phenomena" (p. 310).

They provide an example (Sheridan & Longboat, 2014, p. 310):

> The Athapaskan and Tlingit developed a method of studying
> glaciers that related temperature variation to intellectual and
> spiritual adaptation on the part of the glacier. This method, how-
> ever, was eventually dismissed by the ethnocentric conceits of

18th- and 19th-century colonial scientists and naturalists, for whom glaciers could not have memory. Not much has changed since then, as the majority of practicing glaciologists and ecologists today treat glaciers as inanimate objects fit for study and possession.

The Western subject-object distinction, or rather separation, is incompatible with Indigenous systems by which collective, relational ways of existing are primary. Sheridan & Longboat (2014) note additional distinctions between TEK and colonial environmental studies, such as their relationships with water. TEK acknowledges that all life comes from water—it is beyond human existence, our ancestor—and that water is intelligent with a language, gender, and duties. Systematic inquiry among Native Americans over many generations' time has led to such conclusions about natural phenomena (Brown, 1975).

Living from Your Indigenous Mind

Indigenous Mind (IM) is a particular way of viewing, interpreting, and making meaning of the world we live in, often from a non-linear, nonhierarchical lens, without binary distinction between secular and sacred. IM encompasses and includes the planet as a living being that needs love, care, stewardship, and long-term maintenance of sacred spaces. Those living in their Indigenous Minds consider multi-generational lives from ancestors to those yet-to-be born (Dumont, 2002), so there is a way of relating to the land that is very different from those in their secular Western Mind (WM). We have seen in the last several hundred years how, when it comes to land and environment, the secular WM is motivated to extract, control, and manipulate. We see this today all over the world and during the summer and autumn season of 2023 with regards to what transpired in Lahaina on the Hawaiian island of Maui. Local residents openly discussed how elected officials did not prioritize multiple warnings to protect the land alongside the imminent danger in the forefront of daily life on Maui. From that position, Indigenous values have been trampled in favor of colonial mentality birthed from a WM stance. As far Maui goes, as I witnessed in 2023 and 2024, the threat of disaster capitalism loomed. Additionally, and sadly, nature is then, once again, reduced to a commodity.

Consider how IM sits alongside WM:

> The first and most ancient is grounded in traditional territories and maintains the memory of a time before human beings were alive, in the staggering temporal depth and reach of Creation stories. The second is based in the secularity of science and grounded in rationalism, technology, and Cartesian distinctions between humans and nature. This tradition will continue to get the lion's share of recognition as environmental threats, such as global climate change, call for immediate action and because of the hardening of the boundaries between hard and soft science as well as between the physical and the spiritual. (Sheridan & Longboat, 2014, p. 316–17)

Those living in their IM look at the sheer number of natural disasters that took place around the world in the very same week as the extremely devastating Lahaina fire and know that this is not a random roll of the dice. It is a result of climate change, or global warming, human neglect, and the desecration of Indigenous (in this case, Hawaiian) sacred lands and sacred sites. In total, physical health and that of the psyche will suffer greatly. Everything is interconnected. Those operating from their IM strive toward balance, harmony and reciprocation with nature. Had this been the reality, how might things be different today?

As an Aboriginal person, and a member of the Kokatha nation, John Binda Reid explains IM core values from the viewpoint of his early experiences, his upbringing tied to land as a spiritual foundation:

> These core values are not only evidenced between human and human, but also exist between the human and other entities that co-exist within the natural environment in which they live. For example, the reciprocal relationship that has been established between human and the animal species, as well as the reliance of Aboriginal people on different plant species to eat and make medicines from. The people repay the plants, animals and

water sources of their region by not exploiting and taking things in abundance; they only take what they need and leave enough of each species to re-grow, regenerate and repopulate. These systems of reciprocity have existed within the natural environment since the dawn of time; Aboriginal people have observed and have learnt to live within these systems without abusing their relationships with nature. (Reid & Taylor, 2011, p. 5)

IM challenges a Euro-Western worldview of intelligence by which the former is a holistic one to include the totality of the body, mind and spirit. It is heart-centered and relational, rather than primarily brain-centered and cognitive. As Western Science continues to expand and push against its imposed boundaries, there is hope. For example, the HeartMath Institute has confirmed that the human heart directs signals upward to the brain, and that the heart may actually send more signals to the body than the brain—for the heart is in the driver's seat. According to the HeartMath Institute (n.d.), their "Global Coherence™ Initiative is a science-based, co-creative project to unite people in heart-focused love and intention, to facilitate the shift in global consciousness from instability and discord to compassionate care, cooperation and increasing peace." HeartMath caught my attention about a decade or so ago, just before I began a PhD program. I was drawn to their research on heart coherence. Their website explains how "the heart's electromagnetic field is an important carrier of emotional information and how compassionate living from a state of heart coherence can positively affect and lift the vibration of those around us and our planet." As this type of research flourishes, can Indigenous and Western approaches partner for a better world? Imagine what good can come if we learn to hold both positions from a place of wisdom to bring about balance and harmony into the world. Let's look at what Indigenous Science is about.

Indigenous Science Is Science

As a broad, comprehensive system, Kalolo (2022) claims that Indigenous Science cannot be simply explained nor described in one or two words yet points to others who have considered Indigenous Science synonymous with terms such as traditional knowledge. To further understand what we've covered so far and what has been referred to as Indigenous Science, consider the following as stated by Cohen (2023, p. 498):

> Conventional Euro-American scientists and indigenous scientists, or those who research these topics, need to be clear about how they define "science." Western researchers tend to limit science to measurable and replicable evidence with applications to the demands of industry and modern Euro-American society. Western science also does not directly require reciprocity, cultural protocols, or guidance by wisdom-keepers. From the Western academic viewpoint, the efficacy of a plant medicine depends on its chemistry and would not be influenced by how the plant is gathered, by offering prayers, songs, or tobacco, or by invisible *manitou* (spiritual forces).

So how might the two sciences coexist and support one another? Can it be done? In support of considering these questions further, I have included information from the website of the Worldwide Indigenous Science Network (WISN) below. Following that, you'll meet the founder of WISN in an interview I conducted with her in Lahaina in the 2023 summer season just before the fires swept through the town.

Both Western Science and Indigenous Science use "direct observation for forecasting and generating predictions" enabling connections and patterns across cycles of space and time. Specializations include herbalism, weather observation, mental health, and timekeeping with testing to ensure Indigenous Science validity. The main arenas where Western Science and Indigenous Science differ are primarily in the *relationship* with nature. Data generated with Indigenous Science is used to find methods and resources for accommodating nature, as opposed to inserting control of natural forces. Indigenous Science attempts to understand and complete relationships with all living things, as nature is considered intelligent and alive, making nature an active research partner. The purpose is to maintain balance. The Worldwide Indigenous Science

Network (WISN) suggests that "Indigenous Scientists are an integral part of the research process" with "a defined process for ensuring this integrity." In addition, Indigenous Science "collapses time and space," meaning that "fields of inquiry and participation extend into and overlap with past and present" (*wisn.org*). Finally, Indigenous Science is holistic in that it draws on all senses. This is beyond the basic five senses because it also includes psychic and spiritual sensory information. The endpoint of the process is a "balance where creativity occurs." One of my favorite components of an Indigenous Science way of being is that embodiment in the natural world is a given. As a result, that place of balance is considered the norm, not transcendence.

WISN founder Apela Colorado's book, *Woman Between the Worlds: A Call to Your Ancestral and Indigenous Wisdom*, delivers Indigenous wisdom through her direct, lived experiences and long-time, patiently and painstakingly gathered knowledge to promote understanding between the perspectives of the modern world and the Indigenous. After reading her book, I was inspired to learn more. I knew that Apela is of Oneida and Gaul ancestry and that the mission of her organization is to create ethical collaboration between Indigenous and Western ways of knowing. During our time together, I asked her if she would be willing to tell the story of how Indigenous Science came to be.

On July 29, 2023, I sat down with Apela Colorado, PhD, with whom I had spent many months within conversation and ceremony at her home in Lahaina, Maui. One of her past students, Teresa Mac-Coll, MA, was in attendance as well, and both allowed me to interview them on Indigenous Mind (IM), Indigenous Science (IS), and the creation of WISN. The three of us immediately connected by our dreamwork, a powerful way-of-knowing central to IS (Rowe, 2014).

Apela began, "So when I was a young person, growing up between the worlds, it was hard because there were strict racial divisions in the U.S. at that time. It's still harsh, but not like it was then. When I grew up and was in my doctoral program, I started thinking about the disparity between the Indigenous way of knowing, which is the one that can save our lives right now. I reckoned at that time, and still believe, if we linked the Western Science way of knowing with the Indigenous way of knowing. (But not *just* link them, because if you just link them, Western Science, which can be predatory, can devour anything in its path—devour it in the sense that it has to kill it to see how something lives.) So, Indigenous Science works just the opposite of that."

Apela began to wonder how she could halt the predatory effects of Western Science on Indigenous life and people. She said, "It's the scientific truths and discoveries put in the hands of avaricious, unconscious interests that lead to the annihilation of the Earth and Indigenous people who are the people closest to the Earth. I started thinking, *How could I make an interface between the two ways of knowing?* They're both human capabilities, but the way that we exalt over rationality and its analysis shatters life and is leading to our own demise, setting loose enormous cruelty and disparity. Even Mother Earth's creativity is being blocked, from mining, the garbage in the ocean, trash in our air, in our food. This Western scientific and analytic way fuels not only researchers, but also fuels and justifies the behavior of moneymakers, politicians, Wall Street, government, education, everything.... How on earth can we stop the penetration into Indigenous lives and minds? It really matters. Today, Indigenous people are about 5 percent of the global population, and yet 86 percent of the world's remaining biodiversity is on lands that we care for. Who would not be wise to embrace this way of knowing, and even better yet, link it with the good aspects of Western Science so that we can save ourselves and future generations from terrible suffering and cruelty in the future? This was the kind of thinking in my mind as a young person in my doctoral program."

Apela continued, thinking further about that time in her life: "I got stuck in my doctoral program around these very issues. I went to Ivy League schools and was one of the first generation of American Indians to be able to get an advanced degree university education. There were about a dozen to fourteen of us. That generation, and the very few that went before us, encouraged me, and because of changes in policy with the federal U.S. government, a zeitgeist for civil rights for African Americans, and the American Indian Movement ...

because of all those changes in the post–WWII baby boomer generation, it became possible through the American Indian Education Act and the Freedom of Religion Act, and others, for people like me to get an advanced degree. In that advanced degree program, the first question on my mind was, *How can I help my people, how can I help my family, how can I help Mother Earth?* I got stuck writing my doctoral dissertation, and as I said, it was a mild version of the corporate capitalistic greed, but not only that, it was also the dark aspects of human beings. It isn't only institutional desires for wealth that drive things, but it connects with our own shadow selves, with our own personal animus, our own personal desires in the shadow way for control and power, greed and domination. Christians call it the Seven Deadly Sins—we've all got 'em—whether it's Indigenous or non–Indigenous. But the rational mind, and the dissociation and the separation that's come from adhering to analytical thought and its separations, has given just a violent thrust and power to those unexamined aspects of ourselves in life. So, I got stuck because my committee asked me to outline the next six chapters of my dissertation. I couldn't do it. I tried, I tried, I tried. I couldn't do it, and I didn't know why I couldn't do it. I was a single parent with little children counting on me, I had my scholarship that was supporting us, I couldn't afford to lose it, yet I couldn't write. Finally, I went home to Wisconsin and went into a peyote ceremony. In that ceremony, I was given some instruction about what to do when I got back to Boston. I was directed to make an offering to a tree and ask for help. So, I did that, but I was so much in my Western mind at the time, I was very self-conscious."

Apela described the way she followed through. She said, "I found this little, scrawny pine tree by a pond. Pine is sacred to my people. So, I'm looking around, and don't see anyone in the park area, and I kneel down, dig a little hole and make my offering. I'm talking to the tree and asking for help because I am so desperate and so stuck. But part of my mind, a shadow of my Western mind, is saying, *Are you crazy, kneeling and talking to a tree? You need to be home writing and typing, not being here.* But anyway, I did it and a few days later I was at my kitchen table with the papers in front of me. I don't know what I'm going to write, and I thought about my problem with outlining

46

the next six chapters. I thought about how that's just not how we do it, we American Indians, we don't say when we plant our sacred three sisters (corn, beans, and squash), *I'm planting this because I will have 100 baskets of corn at the end.* We plant it with the idea that when we plant these seeds and we care for them and we love them and we communicate with them, they will give back to us." As Apela shared that, I thought about differences not only in agriculture, but also relationship, when it comes to modern versus Indigenous ways regarding plant life—I also thought about my relationship with those pine trees that live on the land of my previous California home. From an Indigenous perspective, the three sisters are known as relatives, and provide just one example of how to "modify the plants to fit the land," as Kimmerer has written (2013, p.138). Apela continued, "You don't know what happens at the end until you get there! Then you can look back and think, *I have 100 barrels or bushels or whatever.* So, I realized we do things differently. I was thinking, *It's almost like ...* then I heard myself say the words out loud: 'It's almost as if we have a science of our own. That's it! We have a science of our own!'"

She smiled and described her process: "So I went and gathered some manila folders, and I said to myself, *Okay, what would a science look like?* You got to have terminology, concepts, etc., so I made a bunch of files then when I was doing that, I looked at them and I realized I didn't have one thing to put in any of them, and I wept. I thought, *I am so lost from who I am and our connections to the Earth.* It was just devastating for me."

Apela released a deep exhale. I breathed right along with her. She continued, "So fast forward to a few years later. I'm in Alberta, Canada, I had finished my doctorate degree, somehow even that insight of how lost I was helped me get through it. My doctoral advisors allowed me to add a chapter at the end of the dissertation where I could finally say what was true for me and the ceremonies I had done to be able to do the research and writing, and how I realized that we have a science of our own, and I wrote about how hard it had been for me. So, I did that, and now I'm up in Alberta, Canada, and I have a job teaching at a university there. But the best part of the job, I was always out and about at Indigenous educational gatherings and ceremonies. I started talking about an Indigenous science, giving presentations, and afterwards I would talk with elders who were there. I remember one education conference in Edmonton talking with these grandmas who wore long braids, the residential school shoes and dresses. I was asking them, 'What do you think about this; I want to talk about our Indigenous way of knowing as Indigenous science.' They just looked down and were quiet for some time. Then one of them, close to me, showed a smile on her face and stated, 'Yes, do it.'

"I also had another experience which convinced me that this was the way to go. I became really interested in the stars and the heavens, in a Western way we might say obsessed, but in a Native way we can say 'the spirit is riding us,' it has us. It was time for me to learn about the stars, the star beings, and the heavens (this is where Western Science can help), so I asked elders about star knowledge, if anything still existed. There were just a few elders that had anything to say because that body of knowledge had been wiped out through the historical process of genocidal and cultural displacement.

"But when I referred to the timing of stellar and planetary cycles, which I learned from Western Science, elders and ceremonialists, these numbers had great ceremonial significance. As I continued my inquiry into stars, and also into any Indigenous archaeology, as there were only two people who had written anything at that time, I would go out at night, even in the bitter cold of Alberta winter, pull my car roof window back, crank the heater on, and stand on a seat with my lower body warm from the heater and upper body exposed, just to be close with the stars. I could see my breath merging with the cosmos, the stars then. I studied petroglyphs because I had to learn my ABCs of Indigenous knowledge, learn how to understand symbols and how star knowledge related to them. That was easily 20 years of inquiry, and worth every bit of it."

Apela then provided details of some of her experiences and with whom she devoted her time. She said, "I was on the northwest coast for a while living and working with Tlingit and Haida Indians. I was adopted by both actually, into the Raven Clan. That was good because the ravens are the oldest people there. Raven's darkness is like the beginning of the world. I met with and was mentored by Chief Donawak—I learned so much from him. He was a traditional chief. He knew the genealogy, all the traditional Raven stories, and when he saw young people who didn't know their genealogy, he made a long house with a totem pole on the front, on the entryway roof, and on the wall, one whole wall, maybe 8 × 10 feet, he wrote complete genealogies of Raven and Eagle clan, a brilliant complex achievement. He impressed upon me the importance of knowing who we are. He also taught me the power of stories because he was a storyteller. He helped me understand some of the meaning of the symbols ... but actually with elders, they kind of don't help you at all. Like any good teacher would do, they put it back on you, like 'What does it mean to you?' They wouldn't say it that way when I asked, they'd just shake their head and tell me a Raven story."

We laughed at this familiar confusion.

Apela described her recollection: "There was one rock in particular that captivated me. It was maybe 4' × 2½' shaped like this oval table (indicating the large one we were sitting around). It had some kind of a water-being carved on it because here's the Pacific Ocean and here's the rocky beach and the big rocks. It turned out that these rocks washed down from the top of the mountain which was connected to the Copper Mountain creation story. When the glaciers retreated, these rocks were carried down from the top of the mountain and they're arranged like that."

I asked, "You can't see them the whole time, right, isn't it dependent on the tides?" Apela confirmed my hunch. "Right, it's covered, and so we are now talking about an Indigenous research archival library. The way it looks is this—there's more than 100 rocks arranged in the tide line, and many are carved. When you arrive there, some of them are submerged depending on the kind of tide, and some of them are exposed. But just because they're exposed doesn't mean you'll see them. Partly through erosion and partly by design, the tide has to come in, pull out, leaving water standing in the faint lines like a printout, and you read, or they tell you, a different story by which rocks are together and can be read."

"That's intense," I exclaimed.

Apela continued, "Yeah, brilliant minds. The way they're carved, nobody knows how they could do that because modern lasers couldn't even do that now ... they are complex designs, curvilinear with uniform grooves. One day while my friends and I were at the site, we spotted a thin, hand-sized disc of greenish granulated stone, obviously one of the tools used for carving. Although the carved image was 15 to 20 thousand years old, lying there next to the boulder, the disc was as if the artist had just dropped it. The geologist of our group couldn't identify the composition except to say its extreme hardness was volcanic. Magical things transcending time happen at sites like this. At this Indigenous petroglyph library, one rock captivated me, it was a design called sea monster—a water spirit—a colossal being representing and protecting the powers of the Pacific Ocean! More typically, in the rest of the Indigenous world, the water spirit is depicted as a snake, but on the northwest coast there are almost no snakes. Here the reptile spirit and protector of the water is 'Wasco,' who has a long lizard-like appearance. In the petroglyph, its jaws, crocodile-like, are open, revealing sharp teeth, its curved tail, scorpion-like, is a stack of graduated circles, each representing a new manifestation of reality."

Apela motioned with her hands as she verbally described the local creature as depicted on the big rock. She explained, "The image incorporates two horizontal Ys so the open ends of each Y face each other. In the middle is a spiral, and underneath it looks like an enormous bird. On the back it's a shark or a whale. Then at the end of the tail, there's a spirit face."

Apela joked, "So in no time at all, like 10 years, I found out (and I recognized it myself) that this is a Thunderbird and on the top a whale or shark, can't really be determined. What it's showing is creation. You could say it's sexuality, lovemaking. In the jaws there's a face—it's about to get munched, implying that we go in there (the jaws) and get our consciousness obliterated. We enter into the water and the spiral takes you, spins you around and you come out transformed. Here's the six segments that constitute the tail of the sea monster, it's manifestation into form, new life. The image outlines the way, showing us the process of Indigenous science or creation science, if you want to put it that way."

I'm left thinking about those initiations in life that take you away from comfort, familiarity, what you know, then push you into the dark depths of pain and despair alone, before releasing hold of you once transformed, like a (s)hero's journey. I chimed in, "And you discovered these rocks when you were in the Pacific Northwest?" Apela nodded, "Yeah, I won't say where because people have been stealing these things because they don't understand the significance or catalytic relationship involved."

She continued to describe the images reflected in the rocks. "At the top there are opposite S shapes. It's opposites coming together. It can be male or female. It doesn't matter—it's dualism coming together."

Apela added, "Why the whale or shark? Because it carries the Akashic records. The Thunderbird is a catalyst of creation. Like lightning, it shakes the earth, it quickens the earth. It's vibration, like thunder, light. Creation in motion. Logically, Thunderbird should be on the top of this image, but it's on the bottom. The front feet of this great water monster or lizard is gripping the Thunderbird. That's because, in Indigenous Science, the mental part has to be in service of the emotional, physical, watery realm of spirit and love."

I jumped in with "And not the other way around." "Yes," Apela said, "it's like a flip, but they are both there."

During this time so many years ago, Apela realized, "Ah, this is the way for our science to work and the way they (Indigenous and Western) can work together." Then, Apela had a new term, Indigenous Science.

At the time, she believed, "I am going to rock the science world with it. I will transform Western Science when they see how perfect this is, this union.... Well, they did not. When I presented at academic conferences, they attacked me, but not all of them. Some good scientists supported me, including David Bohm" (Einstein's protégé, David Pete, David Suzuki, and Elisabet Sahtouris).

As the years passed while Apela added to her Indigenous databank, her organization, with the help of many others, started to form.

She recalled: "These accomplished scientists helped me to form the Worldwide Indigenous Science Network. The name evolved from a conference where I spoke about Indigenous Science. Knowing I lived in Canada, a representative of the Canadian International Development Agency approached me. He really liked what I had to say and asked me what I planned to do next. I told him that what really needed to happen was to get a small group of knowledgeable people together. Our way of transmitting knowledge has been desecrated through genocide and historical forces, along with our sites that hold and transmit knowledge. I reasoned that I needed to have people come together to think and talk about this, and I knew it needed to start with women. This man, Ronald Leger, whom I didn't know, gave me a quick turnaround grant, and about two months later a group of 13 women of diverse cultural and scientific background met in Mexico. In that meeting of 13 women the name Worldwide Indigenous Science Network was birthed."

Apela recalled all of this with excitement. "So that's how the name was born, from 13 women meeting in Mexico. By coincidence it was in this little town which is famous for making these clay trees of life" (referring to the Árbol de la Vida from Metepec).

There's this whole web of relations, Apela acknowledged. "In my book, *Woman Between Worlds*, I try to bring in all my relations, and when I travel, whether I am in Japan, or wherever, I bring them in. Because it's all my relations through sensuality, through couplings, through sexuality if it's a human-to-human form, or it can be like the image we have in there (pointing to another room in her house), the lizard woman goddess—she has a *puka*, or hole, in her belly for that kind of conception, and then one up here (pointing to the head) for this kind of conception. There you go again with the two ways. You can see, being in this house, where seeing and learning from that rock on the northwest coast, and studying the stars, led me to wanting to know more about traditional navigation not only over water but through time. I couldn't find much in my Oneida heritage because we've been living in one place and not migrating anymore. In my research, I came upon the news that Hawaiians were rediscovering the lost art of navigation and rebuilding the oceanic voyaging canoes, and that's what brought me here, to Maui. When I first walked in this house, I learned that the pond next door is where that lizard spirit, that's on that rock in the northwest coast, that story or prediction of the way life unfolds, is right in here on this site, and a woman guardian who lived nearby had been the last cultural or shamanic caretaker. Then we, Keola (Apela's late husband) and I, did more research and found that the Berlin Museum has an original, existing image of it. Eventually we got to the museum and obtained pictures and measurements of the original image. I made offerings, prayed, everything to get permission to recreate her, and that's what you see in our ceremonial room!"

Apela paused, then added, "So you see ... my whole life ... one rock."

Perhaps this is no coincidence, I think, since Oneida connects rock with life, which is Apela's ancestry, and much more recently, she has established relations with a local petroglyph site in Olowalu, on Maui (see Colorado & Hurd, 2023).

I nodded in affirmation.

"So, I'm between a rock and a great place!" laughed Apela. She added, "And I am living on a big rock in the Pacific Ocean." We (Apela, Teresa, and I) all laughed, not knowing what was to come just 10 days later.

Teresa MacColl has an interesting background as well. She worked for the California Department of Fish & Game in the late 1980s. Teresa conducted salmon creel surveys on the Klamath River at the time. Hupa, Yurok, Karuk and other Indigenous groups residing near the Klamath River engaged in subsistence fishing. Teresa told me how she often overheard the racist comments made by anglers who didn't like those who fished differently, and Teresa started to become aware of environmental racism and environmental justice issues.

Teresa later worked as a researcher at UC Davis conducting fisheries studies, only now working with sturgeon. At the start of a project, Teresa had a memorable dream that related directly to her current work-related project. She shared her dream with those she was with and then experienced the dream manifest in just the way she recalled it, later that very same day. She was the first to catch a sturgeon, just as the dream revealed, and the others followed in her footsteps, also as the dream foretold. Teresa, then, followed the dream's lead. She named her sturgeon "Goldie"—the same name her sturgeon identified herself with in the dream. This bold move impacted everyone present. They all started assigning names to their fish, rather than a number, as had been done in the past.

After that time, Teresa became even more connected with the Sturgeon she worked with and began to consider their needs, even intuit their needs. This led to a positive outcome for one sturgeon with a bloated swim chamber (gas in the abdomen) that the campus veterinarian said would die. Teresa had foresight to climb in the tank and rub the sturgeon's belly throughout the day, which led to it releasing the gas and living. This was a turning point for Teresa; the sturgeon spoke to her and told her she needed to do something different.

Teresa told me that she has worked in the science field most of her adult life. There, one is trained to not talk about or have feelings or emotions connected to the animals they work with. Teresa happily reported that she had found a teacher and mentor who she knew loved and cared about fish and ecology in a very deep spiritual, ancestral, and traditional way. "I knew I was on the right path," she exclaimed. This began her training as an Indigenous scientist. Teresa learned how Indigenous Science is a holistic discipline that considers nature to be alive and intelligent.

As part of her training to reclaim her Indigenous mind, Teresa was taught to listen to her dreams and learn the dreaming traditions of her own ancestors. Her cohort (referring to her graduate studies in Indigenous Science) started dreaming together and even dreaming for one another. This is not uncommon among those who work closely with one another and share dreams.

Teresa MacColl introduced herself by name and ancestry: "My tribes are Celtic from Ireland and Scotland, Teutonic, and Anglo-Saxon." She acknowledged the forgetting of Indigenous mind by those Europeans who came to the Americas. Settlers had forgotten their own native tradition in favor of a religion that taught man he must "be fruitful and multiply and fill the earth and subdue it, and have dominion over the fish of the sea and over the birds of the heavens and over every living thing that moves on the earth" (Genesis 1:28 English Standard Version). This view of the natural environment denied there is any spirit in nature.

Teresa explained how she has come across many people of European ancestry who believe their culture is rooted in Christianity and are completely unaware of the tens of thousands of years of pre–Christian heritage and spirituality preceding the last two millennia of Christian experience. Our ancestors were not Christian; not here, not over there, I added—they were connected to what gave them life, and that is nature. Human ancestry is inherently linked with shamanic practice, which again, goes back to its ties with the natural world.

Teresa shared how when St. Patrick came to Ireland in CE 432, he spent nearly 30 years traveling throughout the countryside bringing Christianity to the local people and establishing churches and monastic foundations upon many Druidic sacred sites. While St. Patrick was not the first one to bring Christianity to Ireland, he was responsible "for abolishing pagan rites of the Druids at Tara," she highlighted. Supposedly, first he got rid of the snakes, and then he got rid of the dragons. There were no snakes in Ireland at that time (Mallory, 2016). The Celts used the serpent imagery as a symbol of the universal life energy, a positive symbol of the goddess. So, this legend of St. Patrick ridding the land of snakes and dragons was about the conversion of the pagan priests and the killing of the goddess, the feminine.

Teresa's sharing led to my recalling how serpent or snake and dragon is considered such a positive being in many cultures around the world and how many of those people adorn themselves with related imagery and symbols, often through jewelry worn. I recalled seeing such ancient jewelry while I was traveling through Greece, visiting museums housing such artifacts.

This destruction of the feminine is one of many reasons why we are so out of balance when operating solely from a Western mind. The old way of holding feminine and masculine energy in balance is gone when it comes to how many Westerners live their lives today.

Teresa had more to say about the ancient Celts. Referencing the Scottish Highlands, Teresa explained how you find the *two sights* (*an da shealladh* in Gaelic), also known as the *second sight*. This denotes the capacity to see both the physical waking world, or ordinary reality, and the energetic spiritual world. These worlds are intertwined and connected. Some may refer to the information gathered as a result of such dreaming as prophecy.

Teresa discussed how the connection to the feminine as divine has been lost in the contemporary Western world. She said, "Because of such an imbalance people easily turn a blind eye to the destruction of the planet, as well as our body." *Yes, Western mentality has colonized the female body and notions of femininity for centuries*, I thought. Teresa added, "By connecting with and moving through the deeper issues and energies that are hidden through the colonization of our bodies, our dreams, our ancestors, and the environment, we can regain balance in our own bodies, and become more empowered to reconnect with and heal the larger ecological body, and participate in co-creating positive and sustainable physical, mental, emotional, spiritual, ecological, and ancestral wellbeing."

Reflections and Considerations

Both Apela and Teresa offered me so much to consider. I sat with all they had kindly shared with me for many, many months. I thought a lot about how as Westerners re-establish connection to inherent identity—that's the environment, nature—a reclaiming of what was lost and a re-humanizing can unfold. This hasn't been accepted with much grace in some parts of the world. For instance, look at the reactions targeting Greta Thunberg after her passioned climate speech where she stood up for the youth, the next generation who will have to inherit a suffering planet Earth. Those reactions ranged from calling her brainwashed for believing in climate science, to downright abuse. On another level, some aspects of Indigenous Science have been labeled as evil and illegal to practice, such as in parts of the African continent, even when done for benevolent healing purposes (Mesaki, 2009). In my opinion, we need all types of data gathered and seriously considered so that we come to the least harmful conclusions.

Like Western Science (WS), there exists a method, or tool, for extending a body of knowledge in systems of Indigenous Science (IS). Because the Western Mind (WM) gives much value to linear thinking and processing, people might believe that the Western scientific method is also always a strict linear process. It is not. Both IS and WS have similar underlying systematic methodology. The method rises from the research question one poses. We don't choose it. While I've seen pressure placed on young researchers to conduct quantitative experimental research, by only asking research questions appropriate to that methodology, IS is unapologetic in its inclusion of experiential, embodied, and other data emerging out of one's inner experience through inductive reasoning. Additionally, knowledge gathered from dreams (Rowe, 2014) and other non-replicable sources of data are not tossed out, rather IS respects such data that arise beyond a capacity for measurement among scientific instruments (Cohen, 2023). Furthermore, Cohen (2023) writes, "methodologies that examine interconnections, interdependence, and entire systems rather than a reductionistic focus on isolated events or single chains of cause and effect" are a foundation of IS (p. 498). From what I have learned, IS appears to be aligned with qualitative research methods, and while all research findings can deliver value, it is IS whose core is relationally focused and centered on interdependence. I have not seen this relationship when it comes to Western experimental research.

When we look at IS and WS side by side, it is the way data are acquired, and the drive for doing so, that might show a notable separation—this of course can be debated. From the place of IS, biosphere and ethnosphere, biological and cultural-spiritual, are on equal planes.

IS accepts the value of the scientific method; however, the underlying motivations are different. Consider how IS is driven "by social needs or spiritual imperatives—science for life's sake" rather than "pure science" for science's sake or in an attempt to exercise control, dominance, or financial gain. For example, compare the "Mesopotamian invention of the wheel for transportation and conquest compared to ancient medicine wheels of North America as astronomical or ceremonial calendars and representations of spiritual principles" (Cohen, 2023, p. 499). Another example of ancient social needs or spiritual imperatives might be the drive to construct Newgrange. During this current decade, the tides seem to be changing with young scientists showing concern for the environment with relational respect. For example, preservation over excavation appears to have entered the foreground of scientists' consciousness, at least within the field of archaeology (Colorado & Hurd, 2018). Knowing this, there is hope.

Another example reflects how things might be classified as unique to place and experience. The Evenki are nomadic reindeer herders and hunters of Siberia. They have a "climate science" of their own. Within it exists a variety of classification systems such as those of warm and cold air, of wind, of "clouds and precipitation containing 20 types. The snow typology (25 types) and ice typology (8 types) form a 'physics' of snow and ice" (Lavrillier & Gabyshev, 2021, p. 1911). Lavrillier and Gabyshev (2021) refer to this as part of the Evenki Indigenous Ecological Knowledge System that includes many topographical typologies.

Data gathered from IS are just "as critical to observation networks" ... it "acknowledges and validates that this type of information is just as valuable as Western science data" (Alessa et al., 2016, p. 95). Kalolo (2022) calls for the need for coexistence, all the while calling attention to a number of differences between the two systems. However, even within the differences, there are similarities between the two sciences, such as how manners of diagnostics, prevention, remedy preparation, and treatment are carried out (Kalolo, 2022).

Generating knowledge via the scientific method is a complex task and cannot be reduced to step-by-step, cookie-cutter materialistic measures. Let's look at the steps of the scientific method. First, scientists make observations and ask questions about a phenomenon.

This can be fueled by personal motivation, curiosity, or serendipity (a happy accident), among other experiences. Second, scientists gather data and then make a hypothesis. Third, through testing and data interpretation, outcomes are made about whether to support or oppose the hypothesis. Fourth, this leads to a process of revision or proceeding with releasing the feedback to the scientific community for analysis and replication. Out of this, new ideas are birthed, and scientific theory continues to build.

The steps above, delineating the scientific method, may reflect different language depending on the methodology required to conduct research. As noted, motivations and respect during the process are key. IS centers accountability to all of our relations; that is, human and nonhuman relationships, including plants, animals, and minerals as well as relationships with all elements, natural forces, and every aspect of nature. During such an era, as we face the loss of Indigenous knowledge, this all-inclusive accountability is needed more than ever. All scientists can hone their craft while also placing respect, accountability and relationality at the forefront, but this can become a challenge if the underlying motivation is financially driven, quick productivity.

I see a bright future ahead. The American Psychological Association (APA) has come a long way since it was initially established. At present, the APA has recognized and apologized for its previous years of silence around issues such as systemic racism. The APA currently supports a Liberation Psychology that is inclusive of Indigenous methodologies and the research findings emerging from them. The 2024 APA conference held in Seattle, Washington, included many psychologists showcasing their work centering Indigenous research frameworks and methodologies. Furthermore, shamanic-based research protocols incorporate ceremony and prayer upon contact with sacred sites, as these are considered living (Colorado & Hurd, 2018). Space transforms into place through veneration and intentional art (Gheorghiu, Nash, Bender & Pásztor, 2018). Additionally, it is collaboration within research development that is often for the benefit of all among Indigenous-minded researchers. Considering respectful relationship with the land, there is a balance of give-and-take for the sake of spiritual harmony. As science expands, what might the latest research findings deliver when conducted in context-driven, holistic ways? As we continue to make progress, I remain hopeful.

3

WAKING DREAMS

The universe is too great a mystery for there to be only
one single approach to it.—Quintus Aurelius Symmachus

What is a waking dream? There's no easy answer to this question. The term comes up in poetry, theater, and of course, psychology. When it comes to understanding waking dreams, there are some opposing descriptions within psychological discourse. In the American Psychological Association's psychological dictionary (n.d.), there is a definition for the term "waking dream," which is described as "an episode of dreamlike visual imagery experienced when one is not asleep. The term is sometimes applied to hallucinations, religious visions, and the like" (American Psychological Association, n.d.). It is important to recognize that hallucinations may best be put into a separate category of phenomena. In her book, *Waking Dreams*, Dr. Mary Watkins (1998) wrote, "Waking dreams and hallucinations, however, rely on two distinctly different psychic functions: imagination and perception. Hallucinations purport to deal with external material and perceptual reality, whereas visions are non-corrigible experiences which do not admit of verification or falsification by reference to the perceived world; hallucinations do" (pp. 18–19). Furthermore, "in a hallucination the individual is unable to recognize image as image and external perception as perception" (Watkins, 1998, p. 19). The IM does not draw a hard line in the sand between waking and sleep or dream states, nor does it place various consciousness-based phenomena in boxes. Instead, all of life is an interwoven dream. That includes our abilities to alter it through consciousness.

We can find a more poetic approach in responding to such debates.

61

In *La Vida es Sueño* (Life Is a Dream), 17th-century Spanish drama-tist and poet Pedro Calderón de la Barca wrote,

> What is life? An illusion,
> a shadow, a fiction,
> and the greatest good is small:
> that all life is a dream,
> and dreams are dreams.

In chapter 1, I shared the story of how I met Apela Colorado and her daughter, Chyna. It was strange, yet it confirmed for me that Ryan Hurd was correct and intuitive in his actions that led to that lunch meeting.

During that lunch meeting with Apela and Chyna, while shar-ing stories about our dreams, our ancestry, and our ethnic origins, I abruptly exclaimed how I had always wished to meet Alessandra Bel-loni. I didn't notice in that moment, but Apela and Chyna told me later how they looked at each other right in the eye, as if communi-cating, *Well, are you going to tell her or am I?* Long story short, they told me how they were good friends with Alessandra and that she would be flying in for a visit the very next week. *Wow, this is incredi-ble*, I thought. Truly, I was thrilled! None of these people knew any-thing about how I had wished to meet Alessandra Belloni—a desire I held for many, many years. Alessandra Belloni is a woman from Rome, who currently resides in the eastern part of the United States. She is a woman of many talents with an incredible history and life story. Not only is she a singer, songwriter, dancer, actress, choreog-rapher, and teacher, but she also holds and shares knowledge of the traditional ways of southern Italy. In addition, she authored the book *Healing Journeys of the Black Madonna*. Most recently, Alessandra was featured on the PBS travel series, *Dream of Italy*, hosted and pro-duced by Kathy McCabe. I had been wanting to meet Alessandra mostly because of her teachings of pre–Christian southern Italian folkways, including the healing drumming and trance dances, such as the tarantella.

The way it all played out was quite interesting, yet I found it to be perfect. Apela and Chyna allowed me to pick Alessandra up at

Maui's Kahului airport the day she arrived. Because of the arrival time of her flight, I was able to spend the evening with her before delivering her to the designated hotel in Lahaina. Over dinner, at a restaurant that sadly no longer stands due to the fires that followed only months later, Alessandra told me about a workshop she would be leading in just a few days to come, and that I would be granted a space in that workshop. With great pleasure, I agreed to attend, and from that workshop in early February 2023, I learned to play my first traditional southern Italian rhythms taught by the master herself, Alessandra Belloni.

I was also privileged to see her again shortly before her departure as well where we discussed some of her memories that led her to write *Healing Journeys of the Black Madonna.* Had I not met with Apela and Chyna that week, and at the same time name-dropped Alessandra, I would have missed my chance to meet her.

In my last book, *Dream Medicine,* I shared how meaningful coincidences and profound events seemed to be cast at me at a tender time in my life, waking me up to something bigger, the larger order of life. And now this.... This was the first, but not the last of the synchronicities among these women. Even amidst the chaos in my life at that time, I was starting to become convinced that I was right where I needed to be.

The following year, Alessandra returned to Maui for a brief visit. By that point, I had acquired a little more experience with southern Italian traditional drumming, such as the tarantella. It was uplifting to hear her play and chant once again. I found it inspiring that just a couple weeks later I would be on a plane headed for Ireland with plans to visit sacred sites and bring back with me a *bodhrán,* or traditional Irish frame drum. I've always appreciated and enjoyed all forms of percussion. But it was an impactful health-related dream directing me to the healing properties of drumming and the use of it as a tool for healing through altered states of consciousness that, to this day, has kept me committed.

Cross-Cultural Waking Dream Experiences

In the last chapter, I also introduced Teresa MacColl and referenced her fisheries work with salmon on the Klamath River. Here, her story continues, reflecting some additional ways in which the waking dream might unfold.

In 2004, as a student in Apela Colorado's Indigenous Mind graduate program, Teresa traveled to Scotland for the ancestral journey required of all students. To her surprise, once she arrived in Scotland, she discovered that the four Klamath tribes had also traveled to Scotland. They were there to protest Scottish Power and PacifiCorp. The Klamath dams at the time were owned and operated by Oregon's largest power provider, PacifiCorp, which was a subsidiary of the multinational energy giant Scottish Power. Scottish Power bought PacifiCorp, which operates throughout the western United States, in 1999. In the early 2000s, PacifiCorp proposed a long-term plan for the Klamath River—one that threatened Native Peoples who rely on that river for their way of life.

Writing in the Scottish national newspaper, *The Scotsman* (July 24, 2004), Mike Belchik, a fisheries biologist with the Yurok tribe, concisely addressed why "four American Indian tribes would be compelled" to go to Scotland to demonstrate "for the sake of their fish." "The answer was simple," he wrote. "We seek justice."

> We bring a positive message to the Scottish people, and to Scottish Power. We want the Scots to know that we love our homeland as you love yours. Our homelands are bountiful, and the Klamath River is the vein of life that runs through each of them. When we eat the fish, we give thanks to that fish which is descended from the same fish that fed our grandfathers and grandmothers, our great-grandmothers and great-grandfathers, and so on.

It had been over 10 years since Teresa had worked on the Klamath River, so what were the odds that the Klamath tribes would be in Scotland at the same time as she was on her ancestral journey? For Teresa, this was a waking dream, dream data, and not a coincidence.

In 2005, Scottish Power sold PacifiCorp to Berkshire Hathaway and activists continued the pressure. Soon after, the protests for removal of the dams were successful; a win-win-win for the environment restoration, the fish, and Indigenous people. On March 10, 2023, the Klamath River Renewal Corporation officially broke ground on removal activities for the Klamath River dams, according to Teresa as well as multiple news reports.

On May 8, 2005, Teresa had this dream—a dream she titled "Teaching in Mindanao."

I was outside, near the water, I watched a video I was making. In the video, two women biologists were walking through the water and saying how they were here because it was absolutely gorgeous! A package arrived from "Mindanao." The name seemed important. At the end of my first day of teaching I was writing up our "lessons," and the other teacher arrived.

In February 2008, three years after Teresa's dream, she met Grace Nono on Maui at an Indigenous Mind residency, as part of her educational program. Grace was born and raised in Mindanao.

Teresa said, "I shared my dream with Grace, and she told me she was starting a cultural arts school in Mindanao, which included film and ecology." She said to me, "You dreamed it, it's going to happen," and she invited me to come to Mindanao and teach.

Waking Dreams on Maui

In August 2023, the world became aware of one of the deadliest fires in U.S. history—those on the Hawaiian island of Maui (*https://www.npr.org/2023/08/15/1193710165/maui-wildfires-deadliest-us-history*). With devastating losses of life, Apela and Chyna's survival was a miracle. While their bodies remained intact, everything else, on every level, was threatened. Because Apela and Keola's home, including the WISN office, ceremonial rooms and all of Keola's carvings, was burned to the ground, I asked permission to include additional details of the history of that special one-of-a-kind place, including the dream-like events that, in the end, kept Apela on Maui, instead of remaining a visitor.

Apela explained, "So the house that we lived at was Pakala. Before colonial times, Pakala referred to a small area of Lahaina, a subdivision of land, adjacent to an old pond, probably the most sacred site of all the six islands of Hawaii. Pakala means the enclosure of the sun's rays or of sacred things. Apart from one Portuguese blacksmith named Catalina, the land has always been in the hands of Hawaiian families and, in this case, it was Keola's grandmother's land. Hawaiians have always lived there except for Catalina who was in service to one of the Kamehameha royal family members who was living on the island (*Moku'ula*) at the pond site (the freshwater pond was called *Mokuhinea*) which is where the house is adjacent to."

The island site *Moku'ula* was home to the high chiefs of Pi'ilani since the 16th century and a royal residence for the Kamehameha line in the 19th century (*https://www.lahainanews.com/news/local-news/2018/01/25/new-monument-honors-the-life-of-alice-kaehukai-shaw-kaae/*).

Apela's late husband, Keola, was a *Kahuna Kalai Ki'i* and a *Kahuna Kalai Wa'a* (these are Hawaiian healers and master crafts people). Keola was also one of the founding members of Friends of Moku'ula.

Apela reported how "Keola, who was considered a medicine man of carving, was part of the Hawaiian Renaissance. He helped remember how to make the double-hulled voyaging canoes, and he made the masts for the *Hōkūle'a* (the famous double-hulled canoe), which is famous, but Keola's designs, along with friends of his who worked together, made something like six double-hulled voyaging canoes."

She shared more about his life: "So there was a time in his life, after he got out of the service (Keola served in the U.S. Air Force during the Vietnam War), when he was traumatized by what happened to him there, but he came home. He had seen a lot of the world and decided that even if there weren't many employment opportunities on Maui, there was no place else on Earth he wanted to live ever again, just there. Keola's parents, his adoptive parents actually, gave him a parcel of land that had belonged to his grandma. His grandma spoke fluent Hawaiian and kept him near her. He was sort of her pet, her baby—she would get him to run to get her herbs for her and take him with her when she went visiting other aunties, such as a woman named Alice Kaehukai Shaw Kaae, who was the last person to know certain Hawaiian traditional ways. She was also one who signed the anti-annexation petition of 1897. Keola's grandma would ask Alice for advice on herbs and things since Alice knew traditional Hawaiian ways of healing."

Apela described a little more about his vision for the house he built: "Keola decided that he didn't want to just build an Aura Zome square house like people were building then (in the 1960s and 1970s) or the concrete block houses. Instead, Keola wanted to design something based on the architecture of a traditional Hawaiian grass house, a chief's grass house, but made of modern materials. Because he knew geometry, algebra and trigonometry, he actually could get the angles just right. In Hawaiian art, the angle is everything. It's not embellishment, it's the angle, and the soft curves. So, Keola designed the house when he was working full time as a policeman. He would come home in the afternoon, then start to work with the help of a couple of his friends. Within a few years, they had Pakala built."

Thinking back to when they met, Apela said, "Keola and I met each other in 1991. We lived together in that house and soon became involved in a number of projects. One of the big projects was taking over Kamehameha Iki Park, which is on the ocean. It was with not only the permission, but the enthusiastic support of local government, that we proceeded to start building these 62-foot double-hulled voyaging canoes. When it was about 90 percent complete, there was a board overthrow. It got violent. So, we pulled back from the project. Keola had to deal with the anguish and the pain of being separated from something he had just poured his life into. You see, there is a connection between Hawaiian carvers and the creations they make, especially the canoes, because if you don't have canoes, double-hulled voyaging canoes that is, then you don't have Hawaiians. That's how critical the canoe is in the culture! In fact, even with the creation chant, the Kumulipo, the sections are divided into Wa, or periods of time (the name for canoes is wa'a, by the way), which refers to the companion star to Sirius. Each creation, each new cycle, begins with a canoe. For Keola to be cut off from that caused terrible depression."

Keola recovered. Apela shared the dream: "It was a dream that finally came to him with his grandfather, that brought healing. In the dream, he saw his grandfather writing something (this grandfather was of English descent). In the dream, this grandfather wrote something in English and then he wrote the same thing in perfect Hawaiian. Keola could see the two pages side-by-side. The grandfather said, 'You see what I mean?' And Keola said he did. The dream ended right there. When Keola awoke from this dream he was healed from his depression. That was an issue because Keola was *Hānai*, or adopted, into a Hawaiian-English family. He attended Kamehameha schools, but was half–*Haole*, or half non-native. So, when they did the canoe overthrow, they accused him of not really being Hawaiian to justify taking the canoes away, which caused him great pain. So, that dream somehow did it for him."

Apela described the location of their home and its significance. She said, "The house he built sits on the periphery of the old pond (*Mokuhinea*), which is coupled with the Kaua'ula stream (also referred to as the red stream, which refers to the Menses in the blood) flowed from *Kahalawai*, a.k.a. *Hale Mahina*, down into that 13-acre pond. For reference, *Kahalawai* and *Hale Mahina* are the Hawaiian names for the West Maui Mountains. *Kahalawai* means House of Water, or the Meeting of the Waters, and *Hale Mahina* means House of the Moon, named after the lunar goddess, *Hina*. Additionally, the old pond had a small island in it (*Moku'ula*), about one acre in size. This island (*Moku'ula*) was a significant ceremonial site. The ceremonies that were held there were dedicated to the water spirit of the *Mo'o*, which is the spirit of conception. As I mentioned, the last person that knew those ways was a woman named Alice Shaw, whose full name was Alice Kaehukai Shaw Kaae (her Hawaiian name meaning "sea spray"). She was a friend of Keola's grandma, which meant that Keola grew up around the last caretaker of the pond. Alice died in 1956 and at that time there was no one to take over what she knew and the care of the pond."

A monument dedicated in Alice's memory was installed decades later, in 2018. At the dedication, a small group was present to honor her at the event. Apela and Keola were present. As for the reptile water deities of Hawai'i, the *Mo'o Akua*, they can be found around bodies of fresh water. Water can give life as well as take it away, the power of which *Mo'o Akua* hold. *Mo'o* range in size, from tiny to quite huge, and most are female. A striking, gorgeous woman could actually be a *Mo'o* in disguise, some say, attempting to take on a human lover (Brown, 2022). Early Hawaiian history claims that *Mo'o Akua* held various positions, served a variety of purposes, and made contributions to society.

Apela continued to share memories: "So it happened though, that when I first was getting to know Keola in 1991, he took me next door to meet his sister, and who was there but Noni Shaw, Alice's granddaughter. During our conversation, I told her about an initiation dream I had in a peyote ceremony in 1985 in Navajo land. In the dream, I was under the ocean and this huge *Mo'o*, water spirit, ate me and I just blacked out. Then I came to, inside a bubble because it had breathed me out. I shared that story with Noni. I told her how I had been looking for this place for six years and when I got to Maui, and walked into Keola's house for the first time, I saw pictures of this canoe—its name was *Mo'olele*. When I asked what that meant, Keola explained that *Mo'olele* is the leaping lizard, and the reason he named all of his canoes after the *Mo'o* was because the *Mo'o* is a lizard, and the lizard can go in the water, but it always returns to the land. That's what he wanted all his canoes to do—go into the water, then return. Keola also revealed that the *Mo'o* comes from the pond, right next door. I couldn't believe my ears!"

Even though it was after dark, Apela wanted to see that pond right at that moment. Keola explained how while Apela could walk over to the pond area, the pond did not exist as it had in the past because the plantation filled it in, back in the 1920s.

After describing some of the history of Pakala, Apela's thoughts returned to all they had to deal with during the time of the canoe overthrow. She recalled the devastation: "We worked seven days a week on that project for about three years. We took it from nothing to a $3-million project. The people who took it over made poor choices and did not spend the money wisely. They even sold off the *'iako* (arched crossbeams), and other necessary parts needed for Hawaiian canoe-building."

Keola and Apela turned their attention then to a new development. Apela recalled: "To deal with all that devastation, Keola turned his attention to designing an addition to the house. That addition included an office for me and my work of WISN and a ceremony room. That was probably the best thing we could have done because through that ceremonial room, hundreds and hundreds of people have come through, and WISN still exists some 30 years later, networking healers and shamans all over the world, giving grant money for the protection and the preservation of traditional healers and their knowledge systems."

Built in 1976, the *Mo'olele*, Maui's oldest double-hulled canoe, was destroyed in the August 2023 Lahaina fire. Keola and Apela's house, including Keola's carvings, the WISN office and ceremonial room inside, suffered the same fate. Ku'uwehi Hiraishi (2023) describes and shows photos of the *Mo'olele*, like the one Apela recalled seeing when she first met Keola, in the August 16, 2023, Hawai'i Public Radio article.

Other Views on Waking Dream-Related Phenomena

When we take a step away from the Western-dominated unidirectional, linear-bound views about life, we can see with more open eyes (and a more open mind) how waking dreams, synchronicities and other nonlinear consciousness-related experiences are further data about life and how things work as we exist in this vast multiverse. Finding the words in the English language can be challenging because of its limitations; however, other languages have the words to describe such concepts because they hold great value and are meaningful.

Some of the phenomena discussed thus far can unfold at the

same time, while in other instances, there may be what we could perceive as a significant delay in linear time. The American Psychological Association's (APA) Dictionary of Psychology defines synchronicity from the lens of Carl Jung's analytic psychology as "the simultaneous occurrence of events that appear to have a meaningful connection when there is no explicable causal relationship between these events, as in extraordinary coincidences or purported examples of telepathy. Jung, who first coined the term, suggested that some simultaneous occurrences possess significance through their very coincidence in time." In its simplest description, synchronicity is a meaningful coincidence. On the website of the International Association for Analytical Psychology, Joe Cambray, PhD of Pacifica Graduate Institute, notes how Jung viewed synchronicity as an act of creation in time, thus aligning with the statement above (see *https:// iaap.org/jung-analytical-psychology/short-articles-on-analytical-psychology/synchronicity-an-acausal-connecting-principle/*).

Like so many positions strongly held in mainstream, or Western, psychology and consciousness studies, the views on synchronicity have been challenged and hotly debated. Synchronicity is controversial. This should not be surprising. Western psychology is framed from one cultural context—that is, the Western mindset, where such occurrences might be labeled as superstitious or nonsensical. We must also acknowledge that many of the research findings that sculpted mainstream psychology have come from White, male, middle class, and often well-educated subjects or participants. Both researchers and subject/participants share a similar if not the same worldview. This is, at times, acknowledged and when it is, those purporting a strict mainstream worldview have belittled those who challenge it.

What are we to make of all this? Here are other ways synchronicity has been described. From an evolutionary view, humans tend to make meaning by matching patterns (Kime, 2019). In an evolutionary model, Kime (2019) posited that synchronicity "*is* the feeling of meaning given to a repeated series of events over time which is the inevitable, biological result of repeated experience."

In the past decade alone numerous publications on synchronicity have opened the floodgates for such a phenomenon to make its way into popular culture. Butzer (2021) looks at the highly debated phenomenon of synchronicity from the lens of consciousness studies, first looking at the *why* by naming the two opposing perspectives on the occurrence of synchronicity: first, "cognitive/psychological approaches, which maintain that synchronicity is something that occurs in the mind," and second, the "ontological/metaphysical approaches, which suggest that synchronicity has something to tell us about the ultimate nature of reality" (p. 37). Whether synchronicity emerges from the mind, or whether it speaks to consciousness, often people who experience a strong synchronistic effect in life take pause, and marvel in wonder.

Consider a simple example taken from psychologist and ancestral educator Daniel Foor (2017, p. 48):

> Suppose, for example, that your deceased partner loved lilacs, and on the anniversary of her death you're on the front porch having a drink and feeling sad. At that moment your new neighbor walks over to share with you, out of the blue, that she's thinking of planting a lilac bush and asks if you like lilacs.

An extraordinary coincidence? This seems to go beyond the popular cognitive and evolutionary models. Foor (2017, p. 48) continues:

> You feel a wave of energy pass through your body and sense that something magical is happening, a temporary drawing close of the worlds. You reply that yes, you like lilacs. Even though you have not experienced your partner as a spirit, after the conversation you're left with a sense, against all logic, that she has reached out to comfort you.

In Foor's experience, unpredictable events like these can feel like déjà vu. Have you experienced anything like this before? In addition to the example with the new neighbor and the lilacs, other means through which a synchronistic effect presents itself have been reported such as in writing (street signs, bumper stickers, billboard displays), music (songs on the radio or television), and sightings in nature. For example, let's consider something like the one above: On the day of your wedding anniversary—the first one since your husband's death—you decide to eat at his favorite restaurant because you really miss him. Even though the restaurant is just a half-mile away, you prefer driving this time. You start your car, and the radio turns on immediately, now playing the song you two danced to at your wedding ... your wedding song.

Some have called for empirical research on synchronicity, which is a great challenge, but how important are the findings to those whose synchronistic experiences pierced their soul? Colorado (1995) described her experience of dreaming with one of the most powerful animal spirits in Hawaiian cosmology, *Mano* (shark), which she soon learned was intimately linked with a surprise visitor coming into her and her husband's Maui home. As a kind relationship began to form between them, she discovered the tie between her clan and the visitor's ancestral lineage. In surrendering to something much bigger at play, they took risks and trusted in the mysterious process unfolding. By doing so, they helped each other through great loss resulting in powerful healing (Colorado, 1995). Experiences like these raise big questions. Can mind and matter be considered as one? While many people hold strong beliefs on either side of the debate, the mind-body problem (aka "the hard problem") is nowhere close to being solved. Currently, from a handful of experiments, "the results cannot solve the ontological question of whether consciousness is distinct from the physical. But they do suggest that the roots of the 'hard problem' are partly psychological" (Berent, 2023, p. 564). Still, neuroscientists cannot explain consciousness (Moody & Perry, 2013). If the debate resolves at some point, it may bring Western Science closer to bridging the gaps surrounding these phenomena.

Synchronicity seems to also merge into other areas of consciousness, such as altered states and higher states of consciousness, such as meditation or deep relaxation, visions, and lucid liminal states, occurring when one is technically awake. However, liminal zones can be argued as in-between states. Hypnopompia and hypnagogia come up frequently within the literature on dream and sleep studies. Synchronicities in such altered, or nonordinary, states can get blurry. Sometimes, one might claim to feel a strong presence or encounter an unexplainable force. Other times, a clear sense of one's ancestors is felt. At even other times, one might see or sense a mental image of an object during such a state, then afterwards, when going about the day, that object appears in the physical, ordinary reality. It doesn't end there. Across time and place, people of all backgrounds have reported encounters with the deceased by way of olfactory, auditory, or visual means. For those living more secular-based lives, such experiences can come as a welcome or unwelcome surprise. All these experiences do, however, have a sense or quality to them, leaving believers and nonbelievers alike to feel quite moved, or like a significant or profound occurrence took place in otherwise ordinary life. One's background and culture inform how we describe or explain such phenomena. It's good to keep this in mind as well.

Reading the Signs

The signs are everywhere, around every corner. We can spot them so long as we are present and grounded into our bodies, and open to listening with new ears or seeing with fresh eyes. From there, we can poke holes in consensual and consensus reality.

I met Rebecca (not her real name) many years ago at an event related to our shared profession as psychotherapists. As the time passed, we had gotten to know each other fairly well and so, when a great tragedy struck, I came to learn that her son had passed away. Sometime later, she told me about an experience: "My son, who was a user of street drugs, died on October 2nd a few years ago. Another son informed me of his death, and we discussed the question of an afterlife. That night, I went to bed feeling sad that he had died alone. I woke up the next morning, then went into my office with a cup of coffee. There was a photo of him with his brothers in that room. I sat down and began to read. As I was reading, the battery-operated candles in my office came on unexpectedly. That had never happened before. I knew for certain that it was my son letting me know he was okay."

At the most ordinary of times, in the most ordinary of places, we can have an encounter with a deeper reality, as we stand here at the center of the multidimensional universe (Moss, 2015). Sometimes life offers one or two encounters while for others there are many.

Consider the many experiences shared with me by Cristina regarding her relationship with her deceased mother, Yolanda. Cristina is a Mexican American woman, who shared stories of her experiences that her family has referred to as "signs." I spoke with Cristina who told me a little about her family.

Cristina began to describe her parents' history: "My mom was Mexican American. She was born in Oakland and grew up in San Francisco. My mom's maternal parents were from Mexico. My dad came to the United Sates from Mexico when he was 17 years old. My paternal grandfather died when my dad was five. He was hit in the head by lightning while he was on horseback in a big field. He was the tallest thing around. My dad treats death in a 'matter of fact' manner. To him, it's just something that happens. He was five when he had his first big loss and so he has a more accepting attitude about it. I think he believes in signs and all those things. I notice how he makes a suspecting face when something suspicious happens, but we don't talk about it that much. He grew up on a ranch where animals die all the time. His attitude is that everyone and everything has an expiration date."

Cristina turned her attention to her mother's family. Cristina's mother died from a cancerous brain tumor last year. She said, "My mom's side, on the other hand, regularly mentions things like signs related to the deceased. We'd get together at my grandmother's house and talk about such things. My grandfather passed away when I was eight or nine years old. My mom was so set on getting checked for a brain tumor because her father had a brain tumor. He had had a stroke and passed away within about three years. When we would have family get-togethers at my grandma's house, sometimes the lights would flicker or go out."

Cristina's family understood this to be a sign that her grandfather's spirit was present. Family members were not dismissed simply because they were deceased. The phenomenon was not labeled or explained, it just was. When the lights would suddenly go out, those around might say, "Hi, Papi." They would just address him directly, recognizing that change in the environment was him, or caused by him. Cristina's family members were never afraid to talk about him, which was "really nice," she said.

Hearing this, I imagined that after Cristina's mom passed away, she may have had some expectations, or trusted there would be a continuing of so-called "signs."

Cristina recalled the challenges that came with her mother's diagnosis: "It was hard because the whole time she was sick, we knew she was terminal very quickly. She got diagnosed with the brain tumor on July 1, and then within two weeks she had gone to the ER because she wasn't feeling well. The medical professionals took more scans and by that second week or so, we knew it wasn't good. The medical team discovered it was not just brain cancer, but a very aggressive cancer with a very low success rate of curing it. Even though I knew she was terminal early on, I don't think I had any expectations because I wasn't able to process that she was dying. I knew it, logically. I wasn't in denial. I thought about how to make her comfortable. And about the appointments I must get her to. It was go, go, go, so I don't think I had any expectations as far as getting signs from her.

"Now once she was gone, as far as signs go, I just wanted anything. I wanted to dream about her, or I wanted things to happen. And I wanted it to be so clear—I didn't want there to be any doubt that it was her coming through."

I asked Cristina, "Prior to her physical death, did you have any conversations about that?" Cristina replied, "No, because every time I was with her, it was all logistics and practical matters, instead of spiritual ones. She was tired and I was keeping her company. My aunt and I took shifts—she would go a couple days and then I would go. My aunt sat with my mom in her garden and asked my mom what she was going to come back as in her next life. Why didn't I think to have those discussions?"

Reflecting on her family, Cristina noted, "We're not very religious, as in institutionalized religion, but we are more spiritual, and more in tune with nature. When my mom was sick, my aunt was the only one that had the discussion around 'what are you going to come back to us as?' My mom said she would return as a blue butterfly."

At the time of this interview, it was the one-year anniversary since the death of Cristina's mom. Cristina reflected on her mother's final weeks, and how her mother, after so much medical intervention, had said to her, "I want to go home to God." Regarding her mother's experience, Cristina recalled how much pain she was in—"She was done." Cristina continued, "At the hospice center, my dad and I were wheeling her through the lobby. The lobby has a mural on it of a Hawaiian woman, a profile, with her mouth open. Many colorful butterflies are coming out of it, like a rainbow. I saw that mural just 10 days before her passing. I believe she hung on as long as she did because my dad and I wouldn't leave her side. I don't think she wanted to pass with us there. My dad and I were like security guards at her bedside. She went into hospice on the 16th of October and didn't pass until the 26th, 10 days later."

When Cristina finally agreed to leave her mom's bedside and take a much-needed break, she told her aunt, "Whatever happens while I'm gone, I'm at peace with it." She said this out loud so that her mom could overhear her because Cristina knew her mom wanted to go while she wasn't physically present. While Cristina wanted her mom to stay with her forever, she also honored what her mom needed for herself. She didn't want her mom to have any feelings of guilt. Cristina recalled, "Not even an hour after my dad and I left her side, my aunt called and said, 'Something happened.' She just couldn't name it. I knew my mom had passed then. I told my aunt, 'I'll come right back.' That was also the first time my dad ever left her side."

A few weeks later, Cristina met with one of her clients whom she had not seen since before her mom's death. Cristina provided updates on all that had happened since they had last seen each other. In her house, Cristina showed her client some pictures as they were standing near the door that leads to the garage. She said, "It's a fire door—those really heavy ones—and it doesn't open easily. Yet suddenly, the door opened on its own." Cristina assumed it was her partner, Damarcus, arriving home a bit earlier than planned, but no one was there. Cristina and her client stood there looking at each other. Then, suddenly, the door slammed shut ... again, on its own. Dismissing the unusual experience as wind or something else, Cristina also recognized how open-minded her client was to extraordinary phenomena. Cristina said, "I find it interesting that the biggest, most intense incidents were with that client, and the first ones were when I was talking to her."

She went on to describe the second anomalous event that took place that evening: "We went into the garage, and she was getting ready to leave. That's when we started talking about everything that had gone on, once again. I started to cry and said how I hope I did right by her [in reference to her mom]. I hope I did enough. I didn't know if I did enough, and it was making me cry." Cristina described what took place. After telling the story, she showed me the recording taken by the motion-detecting video monitoring system set up in her garage. The video showed something very strange: a large blow-up workout ball was placed on top of a shelving unit. Because the space was small, the ball was tightly wedged in place. As I'm watching the video, I see the ball being squished down to flatten it out enough so that it could propel itself forward right off the shelf ... yet no one was touching it! How did THAT happen? And what triggered the video monitoring system to come on?

Regarding that event, Cristina exclaimed to her client, "That scared the shit out of me." Cristina's client was scared too. I was shocked and could find no explanation of how this could have occurred—the ball was wedged in, nice and snug. Cristina's client looked at her to say, "See, that's your mom telling you, you did right by her." Cristina tried to dismiss the event in her mind, preferring to believe that it was caused by wind (even though this was in the very back of her garage). Simultaneously, she knew that that ball had never once fallen from that place, as it was so tightly wedged in.

This client to whom Cristina referred met her mom on a couple of occasions. They owned the same make and model of cars and had spoken about them in the past since they each purchased them around the same time. Additionally, both cars have an auto-stop safety feature. Perhaps a connection was established then, in some way, with that commonality between them. So, after those two strange incidents, Cristina's client drove herself home in the same kind of car her mom used to drive. On the way home, Cristina's client reported that her car made an auto-stop before exiting Cristina's neighborhood, yet there was nothing or anyone in the road. While puzzling, she continued home and, on the way, saw a shooting star. Both Cristina and her client considered this to be a communication. Considering all of those things, Cristina exclaimed, "That was an unforgettable day."

Around the one-month death anniversary, Cristina recalled how she noticed more butterflies, either live ones or simply images of butterflies. "I've seen a lot of butterflies in my backyard." Later, she shared her recollections of her discussions with someone she knew from San Francisco, who was of Hawaiian ancestry, about signs of loved ones and the afterlife. While they were near a food truck sitting at one of the tables waiting to dine, Cristina noticed how at least one person at each of the tables had some kind of butterfly tattooed on them. She thought, *What the heck is going on here?*

In recalling an annual neighborhood garage sale, which also became a family tradition, Cristina described how her mom would come out early in the morning to help set up and "how we would have coffee, sit back and chit chat. She loved it because she liked to socialize with all the neighbors and talk to the kids and dogs—it was her thing, she loved it. So, this last January, the annual neighborhood garage sale fell on the day before I was having her memorial here." Because of the timing, Cristina didn't plan to be part of the neighborhood garage sale, but in the end, she decided to put out a couple of things for the big sale anyway. She recalled, "I was by myself early in the morning; I would have normally been with my mom. I was really missing her that day. In the past, she would have sat here with me holding her coffee. We'd hang out. I had put on a T-shirt she had given me with her favorite motto on it: *Un Día a la Vez* (one day at a time). Later in the morning, one of my friends showed up and was hanging out with me off and on, and going in and out of the house. She was helping me with the memorial, too, at that time. She was standing in my doorway when these two ladies appeared. They were looking at my stuff for sale. I heard them speaking Spanish, so I started speaking Spanish. Then, one of them asked how much for the patio umbrella. They were so nice, such sweet ladies and I was like 'you know what, if you want to have it, you can. I'll show you how it works and help load it in the car.' Since the components were so large, she had to make two trips, so we ended up exchanging information. She said, *Me llamo Yolanda* (My name is Yolanda). At that moment, my friend and I stared at her and at each other. I told her in Spanish how that is my mom's name and how she just recently passed away. She said to me, 'We only have one mom,' and she gave me the biggest hug. I tried to hold back my tears and thought, *Oh my god*."

When this woman (Yolanda) returned to load the second piece of the patio umbrella set into her car, she was with someone different this time. The new woman was introduced as her sister, Gloria. Cristina reported, "That's my mom's sister's name."

We have two random ladies with both her mom and mom's sister's name. It was very interesting. Cristina exclaimed, "Yeah, Mom wants to be remembered. For sure. She's like, here I am!"

Cristina also spoke about her personal trainer: "The very next day after my mom's Maui memorial in January, my trainer relocated to Maui from Buffalo, New York. He was compassionate and empathetic to what I was going through. His own mom had passed away the year prior. I had kept up with my workout routine when my mom was sick, just to keep my head clear. He told me, 'I think my mom sent me to you or sent you to me.' He said I was the first evidence of *aloha*."

Cristina recalled how she initially found him: "He posted on an online Maui bulletin board, and I happened to turn on my phone and see his posting right away. I had been researching trainers for myself and I had a strong intuition about him. My mom passed on October 26—that's when he told me, 'I know my mom sent me to you. That's my sister's birthday.'" Cristina continued, "After we had the memorial, my trainer looked at the program booklet, read my mom's obituary which listed her siblings, then told me how his mom's name is Gloria. I love how those two names just keep popping up."

As time passed on, Cristina continued to notice butterflies

everywhere. For instance, she walked past a guy in San Francisco who wore a Yankees baseball hat, but there was a butterfly embroidered on it. It looked like it was part of the hat. So, there are several interesting incidents where things come together like that with people, Cristina revealed.

To honor her mom, Cristina got a tattoo. It shows a gray brain cancer awareness ribbon with blue butterflies. "I was tired that day," she said, "and even more so after getting that tattoo. After leaving the tattoo shop, it was dark out. As I walked along Front Street there was this one streetlamp shining down on one potted plant, lighting up a butterfly image with some numbers—the first two numbers were 54. It was striking because these are my favorite numbers and my mom knew it—the number 54 was an inside thing between us."

Cristina recalled reading an online article about a group of rogue artists putting up an illegal statue in Golden Gate Park during the night on the six-month anniversary of her mom's passing. She told me, "It was a statue of a blue butterfly even though there's no blue butterflies any longer in Northern California. The Xerces butterfly is native to San Francisco, but the Xerces Blue is extinct. My mom used to do walking tours in Golden Gate Park. A big part of me growing up was following her on her walking tours. She was a volunteer for Friends of Rec and Park. So now there's a blue butterfly in Golden Gate Park after six months.... It was a week before my appointment for my tattoo. I already told the tattooist what I wanted done. What's more, the date that the tattoo shop chose for my appointment was May 4th (5/4). My mom was the only one out of eight siblings to have blue eyes. Maybe that has something to do with her statement of returning as a blue butterfly."

Signs and synchronicities can be found in nocturnal dream states as well. Cristina said, "I had wished that she would come to me in dreams because some of my family recall dreaming about her. Fortunately, I did have one memorable dream.

I'm with my family. I can't see them. I just know they are around. We are outside in a park or somewhere like that. Butterflies start landing on me. I exclaim, 'Look, look' and the butterflies just keep coming. I must close my mouth because they are going to go in my mouth if I don't. That's how many there are! It's not weird, or gross, or even scary. Instead, I feel excited, but I know I must keep my mouth closed.

This dream was right before my birthday."

Cristina acknowledged how her mom often threw parties for her and her dad for birthdays and other celebratory events. "We didn't do that for her, so I'm anticipating her second memorial—the big one in California on October 22, 2023. It is the big party I can throw for her now."

We talked about the butterfly tree recently gifted to Cristina and how some of the caterpillars have just transformed into chrysalis. I wonder aloud whether the butterfly will emerge from the chrysalis on the same date as the upcoming memorial. At the time of our conversation, we agree to wait and wonder.

No matter how we label the phenomena within this chapter, such experiences stay with people. They are usually recalled easily, even after significant periods of time. Regardless of one's belief system, the impact of these and related experiences leads to questions about our place in the world, our inter-relatedness and our responsibilities.

This was the case for me, as I stood in a classroom giving a talk on dreams at Yonsei University in Seoul, South Korea. After giving my short talk, each student shared a dream they had collected as a homework-fieldwork assignment. As I listened to the dreams, I was stunned when one young student shared a dream after a death in the family. A blue butterfly entered that dreamscape and was perceived as the deceased loved one. What's more, as a result the dreamer got a blue butterfly tattoo. I was stunned and also paused in admiration as the Great Mystery unfolded.

4.

KNOW YOUR MEDICINE

Some of the oldest labyrinths date back to over a thousand years before the common era (BCE). Several are located in the Mediterranean region, such as southern Greece and the island of Crete. In France, the labyrinth at the Chartres Cathedral may be one of the more famous of the common era. Replicas of ancient and more modern labyrinths can be found across the world in both public and private spaces. Have you ever walked a labyrinth? What was it like?

A labyrinth is not to be confused with a maze. Labyrinths are circular in nature, with one path, unlike mazes filled with dead ends or tricks. It's easy to get lost in a maze, yet labyrinths beckon us to find the way. Their use is quite different. In action, walking a labyrinth is a form of meditation, supporting those in their quest for balance and even spiritual enlightenment. No matter how deep one goes, labyrinths are sacred spaces. Working with circles, spirals and the like induces altered states of consciousness.

Having access to a private labyrinth is a true gift! As a movement meditation tool, usually people walk a labyrinth slowly with great intention, then make a prayer of some sort at the center, before turning around to meditatively walk their way to the exit. But if you have one in your or a friend's yard, for example, an opportunity exists to take it a step further. Try walking the labyrinth as a dream incubation (a practice discussed in more depth in later chapters), then take a nap in the center of the labyrinth. See what dreams come forth! Upon awakening, one can contemplate the dream during the slow, mindful walk out of the labyrinth.

Distant societies frequently encounter each other now, whereas centuries ago they never would have. So often, Westerners who have spent generations in the United States, having lost contact with their own traditional ways and Indigenous medicine, may grasp onto medicine that may not be meant for them. On social media platforms especially, it is common to find people "certifying" or "initiating" outsiders to lead ceremonies that are traditional to groups of people and rooted in a particular area of land. Hence, there is a disconnect. When we deeply understand our own roots and our own history, we can more easily come to understand how these modern-day initiatory rituals and *ceremonies for all*, not only mislead, but could even endanger ourselves and others.

To find our own ancestral medicine ways, we can look back in time from whence we have come. What can we learn about our grandparents and great-grandparents? Many of my own were from Ireland or the Mediterranean region. Luckily, the ancient ways of those areas of the European continent are sometimes easier to rediscover or locate, as far as mythology and folklore goes, than some other areas. Still, the keepers of traditional lore—the poets and seers (*filid*)—engaged in orally passing along ancient tradition are challenging to trace, especially outside of evidence from monasteries written by monks (Mallory, 2016). Some with a long history in the Irish countryside continue to work with the fae folk, fairies, or other entities, as an example of cultural relationships. Demigods are still honored and stories told about their magical powers, such as Cú Chulainn (Mallory, 2016). Greco-Roman cultures, once upon a time, consulted oracles still known to this day, such as Delphi. The ruins of the ancient temples are accessible and some still stand tall today. Another modern-day example includes the traditional ways of healing that continue in the mountainous regions of southern Italy. Beyond these, the megalithic ruins, sacred water wells, and mounds remain in areas throughout what is now Ireland as well as the United Kingdom, and what remains of the temples across the European Mediterranean can be approached, even physically touched, today.

Traditional European medicine ways—our own nearly lost Indigenous Science—included dreamwork, trance, use of labyrinths, and several other ways of knowing that informed an approach to life with a deep relationship to nature and all its inhabitants, including mythological creatures. We don't need to throw the post–Enlightenment baby out with the bathwater. We are safer today to return to these ways. No authorities in the United States will be hanging us, burning us at the stake, or drilling holes in our skulls, known as trepanation (Ghannaee Arani et al., 2012), for madness as was once practiced a few hundred years ago in Europe.

While Westerners are fortunate to have documents, artifacts, megaliths, well-intact tombs, prehistoric cave paintings, and other tangible objects to help us remember who we are, what we have lost from our day-to-day consciousness is our most ancient story of origin, our creation story. This loss has led to negative implications. And while I can share examples below from my father's complex ancestry, Magna Graecia, I believe it is most important to consider how we will choose to relate to it and integrate such a worldview into our lives.

As you'll read below, this is how the creation story may be seen from the point of view of ancient Greece, with Chaos being the primordial goddess of the void, before the more common patriarchal version came about. While the Pelasgian Creation Myth is lengthy, I will share the first two sections from Robert Graves's 1960 book, *The Greek Myths* (p. 27):

In the beginning, Eurynome, the Goddess of All Things, rose naked from Chaos, but found nothing substantial for her feet to rest upon, and therefore divided the sea from the sky, dancing lonely upon its waves. She danced towards the south, and the wind set in motion behind her seemed something new and apart with which to begin a work of creation. Wheeling about, she caught hold of this North Wind, rubbed it between her hands, and behold! the great serpent Ophion. Eurynome danced to warm herself, wildly and more wildly, until Ophion, grown lustful, coiled about those divine limbs and was moved to couple with her. Now, the North Wind, who is also called Boreas, fertilizes; which is why mares often turn their hindquarters to the wind and breed foals without aid of a stallion. So Eurynome was likewise got with child.

Next, she assumed the form of a dove, brooding on the waves and, in due process of time, laid the Universal Egg. At her bidding, Ophion coiled seven times about this egg, until it hatched and split in two. Out tumbled all things that exist, her children: sun, moon, planets, stars, the earth with its mountains and rivers, its trees, herbs, and living creatures.

An interesting point is that the snake-bird motif is at the heart of a vast number of creation stories, according to Dr. Chad Hansen (1995), who delivers a number of them on his website (*http://faculty.collin.edu/chansen/home.html*). Additionally, the void, nothingness, blackness is also at the heart, or rather the very beginning, of many of the world's creation myths, including several additional ancient Greek creation myths.

Here is another ancient story of the Mediterranean regions— this Spider Woman story involves the beautiful young woman, Arachne, who is admired for her skill in weaving, and Athena, the goddess of wisdom, war, and weaving. When everyone asked Arachne if she learned her weaving skills from Athena, she not only denied it but claimed to be a much better weaver than Athena. "Arachne, with the typical arrogance of a young girl, then challenges Athena to a weaving contest in which they must depict a love scene. Arachne mocks the gods in her tapestry, especially Zeus and his polygamy, but her linen is the most beautiful, so she wins" (Belloni, 2019, p. 310). Enraged, Athena destroys Arachne's linen by ripping it up into a thousand pieces, then hits her with a spindle, right on her head! Now, humiliated, Arachne kills herself by hanging from a tree. Athena feels sorry, or rather pity, so she turns Arachne into a spider, restoring her life in this new form. Now Arachne must weave a web forever and ever. So, "Arachne became the Spider Woman who never knew love, still a virgin when she died" (Belloni, 2019, p. 310).

Belloni (2019) explains how, according to this ancient myth, a state of mania spread through Athens in a way that the virgin women began to contemplate suicide. Collectively, these women hanged themselves, "overcome by depression as if they were bitten by Arachne hanging from the tree" (Belloni, 2019, p. 310). This behavior continued until the Sybil (underworld prophetess and oracle of Apollo at Delphi) stepped in by commanding that the women give due honor to the god Dionysus and become initiated into the mysteries ... and well, the story continues from there, but for the purposes of this book, I will stop here. One final point though: Hundreds of years later, when the Catholic Church finally realized it could not stop the celebrations, rites and rituals dedicated to the god Dionysus, the Church replaced Dionysus with Saint Paul. This history relates to the birth of the purification trance dance rituals and music of what is today southern Italy, known as Tarantella (Belloni, 2019). Older women continue to lead this fast-paced musical exorcism of sorts even today (Belloni, 2019). When I have danced next to Alessandra as she plays these fast-paced traditional rhythms, I become exhilarated, not wanting to stop even when physically exhausted.

As people disconnect and split off from nature, including their own natural cycles, the circular nurturing relationship with nature dies with it. The term Normative Dissociation has been used to describe this splitting from one's origins of place, time, history, and cycles of nature, and the implications of such separation (Kremer, 2003; Kremer and Jackson-Paton, 2018). The social norm of Normative Dissociation has at its roots a profound disconnection. It is self-shielding, or splitting off from wholeness, therefore leading to an ever-expanding cultural shadow.

Carl Jung and Jungian psychology gave us the concept of the shadow, which can be personal or collective. Shadow aspects are those behaviors, emotions, events, characteristics and so forth that we, as individuals or societies, deny, repress or simply forget. As I noted earlier, the shadow is the side of people they do not want to acknowledge or be. By turning our back on shadow aspects of self or society, negative consequences thrive, including major power imbalances and even extreme atrocities, such as genocide.

Kremer and Jackson-Paton (2018) assert, "Colonization emerged from a mind out of balance … and is in need of healing" (p. 29). Evidence of colonial thinking can be found on Maui today in many areas. For example, consider the extensive use of natural resources for golf courses and hotel swimming pools, when protests are taking place demanding fair rights to water, or laws that serve individualism over collectivism, or the lack of awareness about ecology and sense of place that has led to the destruction of the Lahaina old pond, the center of the Hawaiian ancestral world until the 1920s.

Kremer and Jackson-Paton (2018) explain decolonization as more than joining with those we, as White, European Americans, have "othered," and encourage turning toward our origins: "Decolonizing is about changing our appropriative and imperial stance toward the world, and is thus not just the recovery of the memory traces of Indigenous presences in all of us, but a creative psycho-spiritual, moral, political and activist endeavor" (p. 25).

When we dismiss or deny our own histories, thus leaving the shadow unacknowledged, there is no way to move forward authentically. When we stand in our wholeness with honesty, we can gently move into the grief that must be processed so that a new way can come to be. Healing needs community.

Another aspect of creation stories of one's ancestors is known as original instructions, which refer to spiritual practices and tenets of sustainability about how to live in balance. Original instructions provide guidance on how to exist harmoniously with ecology through cultural practices—it's our deepest of identities. When we accept our moral obligation to live in balance with the Earth and all creation, we will make progress.

Of those European descendants so far removed, geographically and multi-generationally, from their original lands, how are we to know our original instructions? When I was young, I attended Saint Patrick's School for eight years. It was my Catholic elementary school for first through eighth grade. There, we learned about the story of Adam and Eve. The version I was taught explained how the first woman (Eve) came from the rib of the first man (Adam), and how she basically ruined their wonderful life in a lush, plentiful garden (Garden of Eden). Eden was referenced as a specific place in my Catholic elementary school teachings, but other Christians have said that Eden represents Creation. Eve's behavior was unacceptable. How? By her taking an apple. Eve was not supposed to touch that apple tree, nor interact with a "devilish" snake who was also present. For this, she and Adam were cast out of Eden.

The long-term consequences of Eve's actions resulted in several things, I was told. For example, women would now experience pain during childbirth. Since I have grown up, no longer a child at that school, I have heard the rhetoric spoken about how women's actions are the cause for pain, exile, shame, you name it. I'm grateful how the particular church I attended did not include priests preaching in such extremes; however, friends have told me about their upbringing during times when pastors and priests gave sermons full of misogynistic rhetoric. Such sermons and preaching further divide Eden, or Creation. They are fuel for separation—the exact opposite of harmonious balance.

The story of Adam and Eve might be an attempt to replace our original instructions, but we have the faculties to perceive something much deeper, if only we will listen with different ears and slow down enough to feel. Time in nature supports this, since we can slow our rhythms when away from the busy city life and feel into the creative energies in thin places. Additionally, if we are bound to our apartment or house, or in a city, we can visit archaeology museums or search for ancient images with the help of the internet. Even looking at images of nature brings a relaxation response. At the Calouste Gulbenkian Museum in Portugal, I saw what looked like a large gold coin hovering behind glass in the Arte Greco Romana room. When I approached the glass case to get a closer look, there she was: the goddess Athena sitting on a throne, feeding a serpent coiled around an olive tree. I thought, *Hmm, this seems familiar and yet totally different.*

Jaenke (2020) explains, "Foundational to the shaping of Western consciousness, the loss of primordial oneness is depicted in the creation myth of Western culture, the expulsion of Adam and Eve from the garden of paradise. When ruptures with the caring environment impinge on the impressionable young human, the psychological phenomenon of primal splitting typically results" (p. 20). From there, we perceive ourselves as separate from the other, including all that sustains our lives. Corrective experiences are required to heal the individual, community and environment from the perception of opposition and othering, otherwise we can expect continued negative implications of primal splitting turning into projection and tossed carelessly across the continent.

Jaenke (2020) further describes primal splitting as "an almost ubiquitous cultural phenomenon; it is so commonplace as to appear normative. The penchant for war-making, seeing enemies in the other; the production and release of toxic, anti-life chemicals into the environment; and the splitting of the atom all appear as cultural manifestations of a primal split in the psyche of Western man" (p. 21). Jaenke describes the dualism so deeply entrenched in Western fundamentalism, claiming that fundamentalist religions are expanding. Dualism separates wholeness, creating opposing positions or points of view, such as either/or thinking. Examples of fundamentalist splitting from a religious context could include good or evil, and heaven or hell. Jaenke calls us out in that we are challenged in our ability to differentiate harmonious relations with life force energy from life-opposing forces or energies. Jaenke notes how "the possibility of conducting life from a place liberated from primal splitting is not even on our radar. Amidst this pervasive cultural phenomenon of splitting reality, the dream announces that primal splitting can be neutralized, healed, via a return to oneness. There is a healing balm for toxicity, and it is to be found in the recovery of merger states of consciousness. States of oneness effectively counteract the attack on life, and splitting dynamics, that toxicity represents" (p. 21).

Listening to and connecting with the earth, bare feet on the dirt, can pave the way. We can begin by entering altered states through various means. Consider conscious breath work such as "box breathing," deep prayer, or meditation in labyrinths or on the mat. If you want to go along for the ride, another of the ways we can remember our original instructions, our oldest of creation stories, is to use our natural abilities to dream consciously, in nocturnal states or while awake through trance-like states of consciousness. Through those avenues we have the potential to travel back to our beginnings and remember. And with remembering, we will likely choose the road less traveled, which is one toward inclusion, collectivism, and reduction of harm to each other and all life, including the planet we call home.

Initiation

As *homo sapiens*, we know we emerged from the continent of Africa. From there we spread across the world. It is no wonder why so many of us gravitate to the regions where the earliest of humanity was birthed. For so much of my own life, ancient Egyptian civilization and religion has been of great interest. It felt so important, as it may also have to you, yet to this day, unfortunately, I have not stepped foot on that soil or gazed at the ancient pyramids with my own eyes. Some of the earliest structures in the world were much more than burial tombs. They were doorways—points of spiritual initiation. Bynum (2021) posited, "They were likely the places of initiations into what they perceived as the solar mysteries and the site of resurrection rites for thousands of years" (p. 95).

From Africa, our ancestors of distant past spread out, some making their way across the Mediterranean Sea, for example, settling into various places after millennia of nomadic life. Our ancestors kept busy, interacting with land, dream, and everything around them, even the cosmos. They created the most amazing sites, as we can see from the UNESCO World Heritage list.

In Ireland, dating back to around 3200 BCE, a complex of over 150 monuments exists at Brú na Bóinne, the Palace of the Boyne. They are older than Stonehenge, even predating the Great Pyramid of Giza by 500 years, not to mention the Parthenon (450 BCE) and the Great Wall of China (220 BCE). This rich archaeological landscape, known as Brú na Bóinne, exists in what is today called County Meath, along the River Boyne. The most famous of the ceremonial structures are Newgrange, Knowth, and Dowth. Together, these monuments contain the largest collection of megalithic art in Western Europe, according to Heritage Ireland. But is "art" the most appropriate term?

While the size and scale of Knowth is incredible with its megaliths circling the mound, Newgrange holds one of the very best-preserved chambers of any of the world's neolithic structures. The huge carved rock at the entry point of Newgrange is unforgettable. As an archaeological UNESCO World Heritage site, Newgrange is a special space for more than just that reason, especially during the darkest time of the year. On winter solstice, when the sun shines directly down the shaft there, visitors experience a 17-minute neolithic light show. The incredibly large rock at the entryway shows multiple spirals. That is, creation or birth, transformation or death/rebirth, and celebration or creative forces. Birth-death-rebirth—a never-ending cycle. But it's pitch black inside the Newgrange structure. After walking just a few feet into the chamber along the narrow passageway, you can't see a thing, at least without a flashlight. So, why were those of the ancient past *also* carving spirals in the dark thousands of years ago? Some scholars believe the three large carved spirals (aka triskele or triple spiral) deep inside reflect the Goddess at work (Fox, 2018). I believe these ancestors knew the transformative power of creating spirals in absolute darkness along with the sound that is emitted by scraping rock on rock. Together, the process can induce an altered state of consciousness. Could it be that doing so was a rite of passage or initiation of some sort? Will we ever truly know? Perhaps returning to the location of one's ancestral sites is as well.

The beginning of 2024 was my initiation into Ireland. First, a retired priest from County Cork (what a surprise, another coincidence) was here on Maui to visit Apela and her family. He taught me a few words in Gaelic and some tips for playing the *Bodhrán*, an Irish frame drum, before returning to his home in southern Ireland. My mother has southern Irish DNA, primarily from County Cork. Her foster parents were Irish American as well. I had wished to travel to that part of the world with my mom but in recent years put that hope on a shelf to fade away. Instead, not only did my mom and I spend time together on Ireland's soil, but my sister was present as well, thanks to her employer sending her there for a week of work. Because of the last-minute travel opportunity, only to come forth because of a long-awaited retreat cancellation, I accepted, once again, that Spirit moves us in surprising ways. So, only a short while after meeting the retired Irish priest, we met again on our shared home soil. Taking a train to Cork with my mother was meant to be. So, when I had the opportunity to speak with scholars and tour guides about my views, I discovered I was not alone. They too believed that the ancients knew well how to alter their consciousness with movement and sound. This seemed very important to them. I commented on how I noticed circular and spiral tattoos on them. One tour guide explained how the place "can get to ya," especially given the amount of time spent on that land and the number of times they enter and exit these structures.

And just as I thought I had stood at the foot of antiquity, I was invited to experience a real taste of prehistory. The wait was not long. Funny enough, immediately beforehand, I co-presented on the topic of initiation dreams with Dr. Clare Johnson at the 2024 annual conference of the IASD. The conference was held in the Netherlands at a 12th-century abbey. As soon as the conference wrapped up, I took off for France.

Paleolithic Ancestry

Over the course of the week, I was introduced to those who keep the ancient ways of Occitanie and the Pyrenees alive through traditional ways and the revival of the language, once heavily suppressed. I breathed in the stories and memories shared with me and the group that week with every cell in my being. From scholars and practitioners sharing oral histories of the cave bear and the traditional ceremonies, and journalists reporting on human-wolf shapeshifting, to prayer around ceremonial fire circles at the foot of prehistoric caves of the Perigord and standing below those polychrome paintings, this was the closest I had ever come to a prehistoric European ancestor. I entered the next level of initiation—very different from describing them alongside a PowerPoint slideshow. In total, these experiences left me falling back in time, recalling not only my own transformative experiences, in both dream and wakeful states, but those connected to my European ancestry across time. In my last book, *Dream Medicine*, I quoted Cowen, who authored the book *Fire in the Head: Shamanism and the Celtic Spirit*. Cowen (1993) wrote about Western European caves, stating that "over 200 caves have been discovered ...

elaborately designed with Paleolithic drawing of animals, shamans, handprints, and other esoteric symbols" (p. 123). I never expected to stand inside those caves just a few years later.

I spoke with Dr. Dominique Pauvert, scholar of the religion and spirituality behind European carnival and bear ceremonialism, at great length throughout the summer of 2024. Given my deep curiosity, Dominique and I spent the week discussing his life as a historian and one who participates in traditional practices related to cave bears in southwestern France, the Pyrenees, and the Basque regions of Spain. While the elaborate rituals reflecting the great respect and high status of bears, especially around the time of the bear hunt, in areas of Europe have been reported by anthropologists over the ages, such as Hallowell's 1926 report published by American Anthropologist, *Bear Ceremonialism in the Northern Hemisphere*, this was my first encounter with someone who has been an active participant in ceremonial practices related to bears in these regions.

The original history of carnival in Europe goes back much further than medieval times. It has its origins as a pre–Christian winter festival. Being from the Occitania-Pyrenees-Mediterranean region, Dominique wrote his dissertation on the topic, and later, a book titled *La Religion Carnivalesque*. We met in the Perigord of southwestern France where we spoke about his history and work.

Dominique's journey began in this area, the Dordogne region, because it is where he was born and raised along with his relatives from many generations in the past. "When you are born here, you are born in the prehistory. Everyone knows of the prehistoric time, the flint tools ... it's natural for us." He recalled how he was attracted to shamanic and Indigenous traditional ways, both locally and in the Americas, since he was a boy. He recognized the similarities between foreign practices and those of his ancestors especially in relation to the worship of the Cave Bear, originating in Paleolithic times. Dominique recalled the Native American author, poet, actor, musician, and political activist John Trudell, who reminded European Americans to return to their own ancient, ancestral practices, when inspired by American Indigenous traditional ways.

Dominique also recalled how he attended a festival some years ago while wearing a t-shirt with the image of a version of an Occitan cross. An American tourist noticed and questioned him. He had an Occitan name but because his family immigrated to the United States, his father would not provide him with the information he was seeking, nor teach him the Occitan language. It's a language so few know today. This story was familiar to me in that it is also common for the older generation of Italian immigrant families to tell the younger ones how they don't need to know anything about their ancestral history because, "now we are American." I also recall being told how there was no need to "go back there," since the belief was that there was nothing for us as far as our ancestral lands go. For my grandparents and great-grandparents this was true—they fled during the time of a dictator and escaped poverty. Now though, in just my lifetime, I have witnessed a dialect die. My Piedmontese elders spoke it fluently as I recall listening to it as a child. Yet now, the youngest members of the family, just four generations later, don't know a word.

Dominique continued to maintain his own deep interest in mythology and frequented the bear festivals of the Occitania-Pyrenees-Mediterranean region that grew out of the region's ancient bear cult. He's considered an expert in the bear cult, having been actively involved for over 25 years, and has included his children over the years as they grew. When Dominique attends these events, it is no longer as a mythologist or ethnologist, but as an active participant in the rituals. "These people are my family," he said. Dominique noted the distinctions among the European carnivals that exist today and how the most famous (such as in Venice and Nice, for example) are short-lived and even require payment, excluding community members. This is upsetting for him because the whole point is to be inclusive of all members of society, including "the poorest of the poorest."

"Everybody is accepted during Carnival," he stated.

The Bear festival is a special moment in the long, multi-week winter carnival. Different villages in the region are selected to have a special day focusing on different aspects or groups in the society, such as days for women, for children, and other groups, such as young single people. It's that day when the Bear festival blooms. Dominique stressed how one must be young and fit to participate in this time, as the young men (adolescent age) dressed as bears must run up and down mountains. This requires stamina and strength as they chase the young women—this is a fertility rite of passage in the end. The men would wear fresh sheepskin and tall headpieces, and paint their bodies in the darkest black ashes and oil so their skin appeared to come out of the darkness of the earth, the Underworld. Winter turns to spring. Others dress as the hunter, and the young women dress beautifully to attract the Bear. When the Bear catches a girl, a reenactment of fertility takes place. Dominique highlighted how tourism has negatively impacted these ancient rituals. The tourists get in the way, take photos, and cause other disruptions when their cell phones or cameras get knocked out of hands or bags. Tourists foreign to the regions bring their own perceptions and judgments—there is a mis-mapping of sorts—again not understanding what is unfolding and the significance to the local community.

Dominique explained how there are many details being revealed in these festivals, which may not be noticed by many people, yet have powerful historical meaning, such as how people spin counterclockwise. Some movements are not even conscious, yet he has observed ritual movements and behaviors that many people cannot explain. Dominique explained, "It's a mythical transmission, not a written or oral transmission—there are so many examples of people acting in a mythical way, during mythical moments of the year, yet not recognizing that they are doing so." He continued, "You have a structure: the moment, the situation, the ritual, the place, and so you are in the myth. This meeting, the mythical situation, the mythical story—it's the moment where you meet your ancestors, the animals. You can connect with them, meet with them, live with them. The mythical time is a space—no past, present, or future, not linear." This "space" is the moment when the dead (those outside of society) can return and reenter the city, the "society." Through the mask we enter the Otherworld. The origin of Carnival entails pagan-shamanic practices, and while foreign observers may view the bear festivities as pure spectacle, what is being transmitted and kept alive clearly has great depth.

Dominique provides additional history and context. For those living among the caves and mountains, where the festivals flourish, Bear and horned animals have been revered since Paleolithic times. They are very important because they both symbolize renewal. The bear sleeps in the Otherworld during winter and gives birth during the hibernation of winter ... in December. Dominique highlighted a crucial, yet strange, point: "If you kill a mother bear in November, you will find nothing—the fetus grows after the beginning of hibernation." It's been interpreted in quite a mythical and miraculous way, like the virgin birth. Dominique points out how the pre–Christian story here was used when the church created the Christian story: "Jesus was the Bear."

I'm reminded of similarities from my time in Ireland as well as from studying the work of Peter Knight of England who wrote the 2015 book titled *Stolen Images: Pagan Symbolism and Christianity*. I learned about the vast number of stolen images inserted into Christianity from my conversations with historians, archaeologists, and anthropologists, and from historical documents and museum exhibits. For example, Christian authorities placed churches on top of or right next to ancient sacred springs, but the information Dominique shared was new for me.

The bear reflects the renewal, from the Underworld to this world, including the change of seasons, Dominique explains. He stated, "Bear guides the soul through this yearlong journey, and there is a bear for each season of the year."

Dominique's Aragon ancestors in the Pyrenees spoke Basque in the Middle Ages, the most ancient peoples of Europe. The Basque used to say they were descendants from Bears, like any Pyrenean people. Dominique connected these beliefs with the Christian story. He spoke about Saint Peter, who prior to being canonized was known as Peter the Apostle. Roman emperor Nero ordered his execution. Peter died by crucifixion, many have claimed, although upside down. As the images will show, Saint Peter holds the keys to heaven, deciding who gets in and out. Yet, before Saint Peter, there was a Bear, claims Dominique. The bear is the original Saint Peter. For the Basque, both stand at the gate (to Heaven). Since I also expressed my interest, he added that crosses predate Christianity as well. Crosses with circles around them are quite ancient. Some represent the seasons or rather solstices and equinoxes. Twelve dots surrounding the cross represents the solar calendar. Thirteen would be the moon calendar. I thought, *Yes, sun and moon, masculine and feminine ... it's all about cycles, balance, wholeness.*

Horned beings also symbolize the renewal of life. Their antlers fall off and regrow. In Basque culture and in their carnivals, the bear has horns (horns of different kinds, horns from any horned creature). The entrance of the Bernifal cave, just to the right, you'll find an image of a bear with tiny horns. Only bear or horned animal remains are found in the prehistoric caves of this region. Dominique claims that the true etymology of the name *carnival* is Cernunnos, the ancient Celtic-Gaul horned god. He believes that in the Gaul language *carnivalous* means master of the horn, because he has found the two words to be the most closely related over other interpretations that came later. He explained how during the Middle Ages, the church imposed its will in order to separate the modern day accepted etymology of the word so it would lose its connection to ancient times and therefore its power. What's used today is "a false etymology," he proposes.

While taking in what had been shared with me, the significance of the animals with high status, I found myself recalling some of the creation stories from across the world, and I wondered about something Dominique glossed over. I asked directly, "Do the local people in that region believe that they are direct descendants of the Bear?" Dominique stated, "Yes, yes they do."

The Occitan language, once spoken throughout southern France, was suppressed—children punished and shamed for speaking it. Today there are fewer than a million people who can speak it; thus, the language is endangered because there are few opportunities to speak, teach and transmit it. I was taught a few words in this language by Jean-Paul Auriac during my time in the Perigord region. He is dedicated to keeping the language and the ancient stories alive, having collected the oral histories of his people for many decades. However, Occitan as a social language is virtually nonexistent since it is not spoken in the streets on a day-to-day basis. Dr. Pauvert told me that at the bear festivals in the Pyrenees Mountains, you can hear locals speak in several languages, such as the rare Aragonese, Occitan and Catalan—"We can all understand each other," he said.

I asked a final question. "You told me about the man who noticed your shirt with the Occitan Cross—how do you, Dominique, suggest people like him find his original story?" He stated, "Come back to your land, if you can."

Dominique introduced me to the scholarship of Dr. Roslyn Frank. She has conducted extensive fieldwork that has revealed similar findings to what Dominique shared with me regarding bear ceremonialism and carnival. The bear skulls and bones found in Paleolithic-era caves suggest a strong, pervading bear cult alive and well over the centuries. Altogether, the data suggests a reciprocal relationship among animals, nature and human beings by which they are bound together, and more specifically, that "humans descended from bears" who historically outnumbered human beings (Frank, 2016, p. 344). Frank summarizes a chapter on bear ceremonialism in which she contributed to the 2015 book *Uomini e orsi* (Men and Bears). She wrote how ancient beliefs are shown in the rituals of modern times:

> Carnival time represents the "wild" moment of the end of winter and the beginning of the new season, characterized by the irruption of border figures, animal masks, characters that recall the world of the dead and that carry with them the germ of vital force, the energy that produces the awakening of nature and heralds the growth and fertility of new crops. This wild world presents itself in the form of a contiguity between man and animal: the disguises, the masks, allude to a world in which the characteristics of humans and animals are confused and intertwined. Among these figures, those of the Wild Man, the human being who takes on attributes and aspects of the animal world, and the bear, the animal that comes closest to man and seems to present a deformed image of him, particularly stand out. These are symbolic figures that come from distant times and spaces to tell something that belongs to our common origins. The bear takes on similar attributes and functions in very different contexts, such as the world of the Sámi in Finland or the hunter-gatherers of North America, representing the border between the world of nature and the

human world, between animality and the laborious construction of humanity; a process that has persisted for centuries, perhaps for millennia, and which still cannot be said to be complete.

Frank's earlier works show how what archaeologists have found in caves (bear remains) are also linked to human-celestial relations. She wrote about how the constellations Ursa Major and Ursa Minor (the larger and smaller bear constellations) are historically significant to Europeans and the people who live in the Northern Hemisphere at large. She touches on her fieldwork: "Until recently the cycle of stories and performances associated with the Sky-Bears, particularly Little Bear, had not been identified. Extensive field work over the past 20 years in the Basque region has allowed me to identify three data sets that strongly suggest a cycle of stories and ritual performances dealing with the adventures of an archetypal hero, Little Bear, and his encounters with a series of celestially encoded beings" (Frank, 1995, p. 723). She lists several constellations, including the Lion (Leo), the Hunting Dog (Canis Major), the Hare (Lepus), the Eagle (Aquila), the Dove (Columba), the Three-Headed Serpent (Hydra), the Chained Woman (Andromeda), and the Centaur killing the Beast (Lupus) (Frank, 1995, p. 723–724).

Frank (1995, p. 723–724) elaborates:

> Linked to bear ceremonialism, the cycle of stories composing a type of Bildungsroman, reveals time-factored rituals and sky-texts with a strong shamanistic flavor. Characters in this pan–European cycle of folk tales appear to match many of the other powerful beings that inhabit the European celestial pantheon, e.g., Hercules (Little Bear with his Club) and Ophiuchus (Little Bear when he kills the Serpent-Dragon). The hero's adventures fit into a scenario not unlike the vision quest with its animal helpers characteristic of native American celestial tales in which stories projected onto the stellar screen are acted out ritually, according to time-factored visual elements provided by the apparent movement of the star figures themselves. Undoubtedly, further research will reveal the mechanisms that allowed Little Bear, called "Fourteen" in Basque, to move about the sky, engaging his celestial adversaries and calling upon the aid of his animal helpers.

Being re-exposed to bear imagery in European caves and the ways of Bear in 2024 illuminated memories of dreams past. While Bear appeared in several of my nocturnal dreams over the past decade, even before I lived among them in the California High Sierras and Sierra Foothills (see my previous book, *Dream Medicine*), there is one dream that continued to come to the forefront of my mind. In that dream, I was being hunted by Bear. Fortunately Bear spared my life, even though in the dream, I felt Bear's warm saliva oozing down my neck and head as I lay face-planted on grass. One wrong move and my skull would have been crushed. I awoke stunned and was reminded of Robert Moss—his voice from past workshops I've attended encouraging me to pay attention and remain open. I remember his asking, "What dreams are hunting you?" As I sit here recalling Bear dreams and typing away, I wonder if Bear had been calling, or rather hunting me, patiently waiting for someone new to share its story. Overall, Bear is part of the yearly cycle, change of seasons, fertility, harvest, and wellness (disease prevention). As people of European origin who left their homeland, now residing so far away, in the northern portion of the Americas, the fragmentation is no surprise. It's no surprise that we have forgotten who we are. Could it be that all that we need to do to spark memory is go out on the darkest of nights and look up? By making this a routine, or rather a ritual, we can see Bear disappear and reappear in the night sky just as our ancestors once did. Through such a practice, might we feel a connection to land and sky? Might we remember who we are?

As noted, prehistoric era Paleolithic caves, some with jaw-dropping polychrome paintings and neolithic era megaliths, can be traced across what is today the European Union. These reflect the ancient spiritual beginnings of today's European Americans. Most are near natural water sources, such as rivers, as well as on fertile land, ripe for the civilization's thriving.

As I was on a flight out of Lisbon in July 2024, I viewed a 20-minute documentary called *MEG—Megalithic Route: Temples to Eternity* directed by Tiago Cardoso. This documentary film's description states that "the MEG—Megalith Route runs through 15 municipalities that make up the Viseu Dão Lafões Intermunicipal

Community, covering a length of 500 kilometers, where some of the most extraordinary megalithic monuments in Central Portugal can be found. The route has a total of 26 dolmens, 13 of which are classified monuments." This short documentary film reminded me of when I was in Portugal for the first time, about nine years ago. An Italian friend and I went for a hike and practically bumped into some of these structures. I recall how surprised I was, coming from the U.S., because they were not roped off or guarded as I would expect they'd be. We were free to explore and admire! He and I noticed the significance of the one large flat stone encircled by pillars. We joked how it would be something special to take a nap on that flat stone to see what dreams would come to us.

In Portugal's Viseu Dão-Lafões and Sever de Vogue regions, megaliths from neolithic times are plentiful. Menhirs standing as votive monuments to fertility and celestial phenomena mark the land, and Dolmens that honored the dead. The term Dolmen means stone table. They are prehistoric monuments made of two or more upright stones with a horizontal stone lying across the top. Some Dolmens were quite large and held a treasure trove of artifacts pointing to rituals practiced by important people in those communities, chosen ones, shamans, and the like. This is believed to be the case for a most notable site in the Beira Alta region with human bones dating from 2800 to 2600 BCE, as I learned from the film. Additionally, it appears to have been occupied and continually used for 2,000 years. This special tomb with red-colored paintings depicts animals, humans and other shapes that seem to be showing a combination of two forms. Specifically, and most noteworthy, are the red concentric circles, a human-like figure with stretched skin, and a figure believed to represent a shaman or sorcerer standing above. The paintings all around that central image are primarily deer and canine. Such red paintings are common images in the Beira Alta region, making this a unique location in Portugal. What stands out most to the documentary filmmakers and archaeologists is the motif of stretched skin with a lacy design around the edges. Archaeologists recognize the ancient spiritual past of these places even though the symbols and images engraved on the rock and in the red, black, and white paintings on pillars and in tombs cannot be explained fully by them today. Some suggest that the paintings be read as a narrative. The archaeologists I spoke to view them as a story told by our ancestors.

When visiting such places, keep in mind that they exist, according to the film's scriptwriter, archaeologist Pedro Sobral de Carvalho, as "a tribute to the common ancestor"—the ancestor as entity—so pay respect. Approach with intentionality and awareness. Consider bringing an offering, even a prayer.

Generously, Dominique also reminded me of the scholarship of others like him, such as Dr. Carlo Ginzburg, professor of history and Italian renaissance studies. I had forgotten about his archival research and scholarly works focused on the Benandanti and other European shamanistic cultural phenomena from long ago. One could be initiated at birth by being born with a caul, thus indicating that individual's prescribed future as one who will access altered states of consciousness (primarily through trance and dreams) to help the community by way of curing health-related issues and even ensure a plentiful harvest season (Ginzburg, 2013).

Rediscovering My Italian Identity

In late August 2024, I was able to connect with Alessandra Belloni for a third time. I deeply respect her dedication and talent as a highly skilled musician and practitioner of traditional healing ways of southern Italy. She was born and raised in Italy and came to the United States as an adult. I asked her about why she believes it is important for people to know their ancestral traditions and, particularly, why Italian Americans lost them.

When it comes to European Americans, especially those whose families came from Italy, she told me, "it's important for the people who came here because they have lost touch with their roots. Somehow, the Italian immigrants that came here around the turn of the century knew the music, the dance and the traditions that I present, but as time passed by, they completely lost touch with those ways. Italian Americans did not identify with the true, authentic folk traditions, because, I believe, they were made to feel embarrassed of their roots as they settled into their new life in the United States. At that time, there was a lot of discrimination against Italians. All of it resulted in a crisis of identity."

Alessandra reflected on her experiences when she came to the United States: "It was very hard to start my group and to start educating Italian Americans because they no longer had a direct connection with those folk traditions. Fortunately, it is different now. Younger people have rediscovered the music with the help of the internet. Now, even with all of the complexities, my company has been successful. It wasn't easy."

Alessandra explained, "The Indigenous music and dance, such as tarantella for example, is very wild. It's very sensual. A lot of it has to do with eroticism, as well as the Black Madonna, and the Earth. The Italian Americans in the United States didn't have that connection. After immigrating to the United States, they tried to fit in and be 'American' as much as possible. There was a great deal of pressure to assimilate. You have to become American. You must speak English, and not the dialect."

I shared with Alessandra my own memories of my father recalling moments of discrimination against Italians and Italian Americans in his younger years. I told Alessandra that while I recall my grandmother and other family members speaking their dialect on several occasions, I didn't remember them doing that outside of the home (I presumed for protection from anti-immigrant violence). I also shared my memory regarding the lack of encouragement to learn the language in any serious way or visit the "old country." What was celebrated, however, was the food, and it was amazing. To grow up making gnocchi and ravioli all by hand instilled cultural identity. I also recalled the fiber arts; that's embroidery and cross-stitch. Those were common activities among the females in my family. As for the music, dance, and singing I recall as a child, I can say it was nothing like what I have learned from Alessandra. When I was a child, evenings spent in Italian American clubs featured Italian American polka. While everyone danced and had a great time, this was far from the raw expressions coming out of southern Italy.

Alessandra stated, "I think the value of what I do is to bring those traditions back ... the ones the people left with. I strongly feel that if you are not in touch with your culture, your authentic roots and your origins, then there is a huge identity crisis. People don't really know who they are."

I asked Alessandra how she would encourage people to connect to their ancestral roots. She said, "Go back. Return to your original homeland to go back to those roots."

For Italian Americans who cannot do that, for whatever reason, there are opportunities to work with someone in the United States. Alessandra can teach the traditional chants and music, and I have found her to be accessible. I'm grateful for people like her dedicated to passing on traditional ways.

I have been so fortunate to have been able to walk on the same soil as my ancestors and take in the landscapes they once did. But this is a luxury and a privilege after all—something not available to everyone for a variety of reasons. For those who cannot physically travel due to financial or time constraints, or those of mobility, not all is lost. We can still do what our ancestors did. That is, we can access altered states of consciousness, such as engaging in conscious dream practices as we will explore in the pages ahead. Through those traditional ways, we can soul travel, taking conscious soul flight to distant locations and ask to be shown or given information important to our mission of reconnection.

A rite of passage functions as a reinforcer to a connection with one's spiritual power, thus allowing the initiate to see multiple dimensions at the same time (Kremer, 2007). Such rites mark a significant life change. It acknowledges the end of a time, a chapter in one's life. Similarly, initiations are rites of passage that mark acceptance or entrance into a group or society. The initiate dies spiritually, and through a long, rough journey the initiate is reborn. The former life is erased, destroyed.

Through initiation, we grow up! Our former identity is gone forever. Post-initiation, one moves forward with new gifts. There are many ways to view this process, and the initiation itself can take place over days or even years. In shamanic worldview, initiations signify death and (mystical) resurrection (Eliade, 2004). They may begin in a dream, or in the physical waking state, and progress in a dismemberment process that takes place in an altered state (journey, dream). This is a spiritual experience where one is reborn remembering that we are spiritual beings first and foremost and that our body is a temple for spirit. Although traditionally dismemberment is taken literally, meaning that spirits are seen dismembering the body (down to the divine light) and then reconstructing it, not all traditions view it as a literal, real experience. Some frame the initiatory process as a metaphorical one. This section will reflect several different ways in which to view such transformational processes.

Sometimes, there is a deeper awareness unfolding in the psyche. The heart-spirit connection knows to trust and allow the initiatory process to unfold, however scary it may seem. This part of us, the part in touch with Source, knows that the old way, albeit safe and comfortable for the ego, does not work for our lives any longer. Initiation is the greatest test, for there is no guarantee we will survive it. As mentioned, some initiations are experienced in the physical waking state while most are a combination of dream-journey and waking states (Walsh, 2014). For example, surviving being struck by lightning can happen by day or night, physically awake or in trance, journey, or dream. The same is true for surviving a severe illness with an unexpected recovery. Side note: These consciousness state-based distinctions are a Western construction, rather than an understanding of the shamanic world. In some cultures, such as among Pakistani Muslims, an initiation dream is particularly powerful given its ability to transform the dreamer (Ewing, 1990).

For women, the most powerful of initiations often involve the womb, as it is a place in her body that gives rise to life, creativity, the next generation. There is a birth-death-rebirth cycle at play—a true transformation of the psyche, as myths, ancient narratives, tales guiding the human spirit reflect (Estés, 1995). Through this, women may become teachers, creative types of all sorts, healers, mothers. Joseph Campbell, in conversation with Bill Moyers (1991), notes how females go through initiatory processes biologically—these developmental leaps are nature-based, such as menstruation and childbirth.

Unlike nature's initiations that physically impact female bodies, males are often initiated voluntarily through their community. Some examples include but are not limited to the following: isolation in nature, vision quest, fasting, tattooing, and/or circumcision. For instance, African Zulu tradition incorporates dreaming here. For Zulu males, elaborate rite of passage ceremonies begin with a dream and, in the end, a man comes forth as a fully initiated member of the community (Bulkeley, 2008). In Ojibway tradition, pre-teen and teenage males might fast for up to an entire week as part of their initiation into adulthood. This "prepared them for dreams of spirit guides that gave them personal power" (Krippner, Bogzaran & de Carvalho, 2002, p. 135). Across the world, powerful dreams are a vital part of processes of initiation. This comes up for women around the world during their childbearing years who report what has been called an announcing dream. Announcing dreams are considered a type of pre-birth communication (Mascaro, 2018, 2016, 2013). These communications may emerge in all states of consciousness and give signal that a child is on the way. For more on the announcing dream phenomena, reference the first book by this author, titled *Extraordinary Dreams: Visions, Announcements and Premonitions Across Time and Place*, inspired by this author's earlier doctoral research with pregnant women, which was the first systematic study on the phenomenon.

Beyond nature-based rites of passage, as described above for females, community members in many diverse traditional groups of the world may experience supernatural initiatory processes through visions and dreams as well. This is not limited to cultures or belief systems from the past, for today, many groups throughout the contemporary world hold such worldviews. For instance, Islamic worldview holds the world of dreams to be as real, or even more real, than this physical, material world we currently inhabit. In the supernatural world, sacred beings are real. This worldview is in opposition to a Western one where such experiences and imagery are cast into a system of unconscious projections (Edgar, 2011). In Sufism, the mystical path of Islam, night dream transmission is of great importance, promoting spiritual growth. Among those living through these traditions, dreams are a means to experience direct encounters with sacred beings and the discarnate or deceased, wherein no interpretation is necessary. People's spiritual beliefs and practices are shaped by dreams of deceased loved ones in profound ways throughout what is now China, where shamanism has been active for tens of thousands of years. Across China's vast history, both practical and supernatural dream reports flourish, including reports of shared dreaming, some of which warn of consequences for disobeying the ancestors (Bulkeley, 2008). Initiations and dreaming are intimately tied for those on a Buddhist path with the unfolding of new spiritual beginnings.

Joseph Campbell, who frames initiatory experiences in psychological terms, also reminds us that "leaving one condition and finding the source of life to bring you forth into a richer or mature condition" is the "basic motif of the universal hero's journey"; this psycho-spiritual journey being full of initiatory experiences. I'm reminded of the Korean folktale of Princess Bari. Like the hero's, or in this case heroine's journey, this well-known folktale follows the pattern of separation, initiation, and return.

Such psychospiritual journeys can begin in "The Dreaming," or dreamtime—terms I will use interchangeably throughout this book. Consider the following dream as reported by the dreamer, Robert Hoss, an executive member of the International Association for the Study of Dreams (IASD). This dream came to Hoss during a time when he was in his 20s and on a quest for Truth, albeit an imbalanced one. In the dream, he had been wandering all night, searching for the "Book of Truth" in bookstores and strange lands. Frustrated, he notices an old man off to the left who points to a spiral wooden slide as he looks him dead in the eyes. "Truth Lies Within," states the old man. Robert descends the slide into the earth. While confused at the absence of a book, he sees a "beautiful feminine, almost angelic being in an archway." She has descended a staircase and moves toward him. They embrace, and an "electric exhilaration" is felt while knowing that truth does lie within ... within himself that is. He recognized that the merging of his "masculine intellectual pursuit with this feminine, intuitive, receptive, spiritual, higher self" was the wise lesson (Hoss, 2017, p. 11).

That dream changed Robert's life. His old self died in that he no longer moved through the world in such an imbalanced manner, where he had been ruled by pure logic and intellect. He began a deep and frequent practice of meditation and opened himself to his once dormant intuitive capacities. This metaphorical rebirth gave way to a new existence, a new experience of life, in a variety of ways, including career, lifestyle, and relationships.

For a pictorial representation, look at the Major Arcana of a Rider-Waite-Smith tarot deck. We, as (s)heroes, are born *The Fool*, then move forward along the path (of the Major Arcana) toward *The World*, which signifies a cycle complete. In one lifetime, we may cycle around from the fool to the world many times. Additionally, no one can say for certain whether one or many lifetimes will be needed to complete the inner journey (toward integration and wholeness).

Core Shamanism is a system of shamanic practice developed by Dr. Michael Harner from his anthropological research, field work, and direct experiences spanning decades. Sandra Ingerman is a well-known teacher of Core Shamanism today. Sandra has informed my understanding of the sometimes-confusing process of initiation. She describes initiation as a time when we say goodbye to an old phase of life and hello to a new phase of life. Initiations dissolve what does not serve us anymore. It can be a painful process. Initiations can take place on a collective level, such as COVID-19. Personal initiations such as giving birth, a high school or college graduation, getting a license to operate a vehicle, are some examples of how new responsibilities in one's community emerge as passing through an initiation phase. Hopefully this goes well so we can step into our greatest Light. She encourages us to trust soul, life force, vitality. Our spirit reflects Source. Source lives within us all, in our spirit, she reminds us.

Initiations are reported in dreams and visions, including liminal state experiences from hypnopompia and hypnagogia, and a variety of altered states of consciousness (ASC) such as out-of-body experiences (OBE), soul flight, ecstatic trance and shamanic journeying, in addition to waking state and physical experiences. When one fully commits to walk their spiritual path, initiations arise. However, from a shamanic perspective, the spirit world decides and will send the call. Those elected by the spirits might attempt to decline the invitation, yet a "refusal of the call" (Joseph Campbell's term) "can result in sickness, insanity, or death"—true for shamanic traditions and hero traditions alike (Walsh, 2014, p. 54). Claims and beliefs are tested—it's a time of crisis. Are we ready to take the deep dive? It doesn't matter, because our individual ego does not get to decide.

Initiatory recollections from my own ASC experience began in 2004 with an OBE (when I was learning under gnostic mystics and around the time I began training in hypnosis). While Gnosticism is the mystical branch of Christianity, the term *gnosis* refers to acquiring knowledge through direct experience. In my very first OBE state I walked through the upper level of the two-story townhouse I lived in during that time. As I decided to float down the staircase heading to the ground floor, the residence transformed.... I entered a classroom with children sitting in school desks while examining or studying talismans. As I exited the classroom, unannounced, a huge monster came through the wall. Fully lucid in the OBE state, I remained in place with the knowledge that I was to face this creature. Doing so dissipated its power over me.

The following five nocturnal dreams took place over about a five-year period. As is commonplace among dreamworkers, I will describe the dreams in the present tense. Notice the ancestral and initiatory elements.

Dream One:

Outdoors, in a lot with tall trees, likely Pine, a tornado is just up ahead, too close for comfort. A man just in front has his back to it. I approach the whirlwind with caution and exclaim how it/they are moving/spinning backwards. My father exclaims how the trees can protect us. I hug one tightly. Then, I make it into the large house to our right—it's lit up and seems calm inside. I immediately feed the old woman sitting at the table, providing her with nourishment.

Dream Two:

I'm standing at the edge of a river and notice a large anaconda next to me. I realize how it could be harmful. I slowly walk away from

*the serpent but am followed as I enter into a portable-style build-
ing where I must protect my mother. I shut the door as the serpent
approaches. It easily enters through an opening in the bottom corner of the door. Quickly, I kill the anaconda with my bare hands; it
then appears to transform into a dragon. I climb on and we launch
into the sky in flight. Stars and geometrical shapes illuminate the
sky.*

Dream Three:

*Two female friends, whom I know to live deeply spiritual lives
focused on ceremony, accompany me as I walk down a path. I see
something ahead. There, I stand at the foot of a "fire alta" with dark
green-colored barrier ropes around it. It seems to reflect the importance of this space, thus containing it in some way. At the foot of the
altar, there are serpents that appear to be dead and skulls (human
bones)—it is earthy and feels very sacred. I feed pieces of the serpent bodies to the fire and announce to the dreamscape my commitment to "keep the fire going," as I am held or rather contained
within this space.*

Dream Four:

*I am with a man (who became recently deceased at the time of the
dream, and whom I will leave unnamed due to his fame) in a rural
Spanish-speaking village (sometimes I dream in Spanish and Italian). A magical red ribbon-like serpent appears. It hovers as it
moves toward me and a group of local children I want to protect.
We hide in a little wooden hut. This snake comes in through an
opening and bites me on the ankle or heel. I run to another structure where I know the man is. As I enter, I scribble something down
into a large book placed on a table by the door. Then, I describe to
him what it is like to die, consciously die that is, yet at the same
time I am alive.*

Dream Five:

*I'm in a place that is both indoor and outdoor. I walk through a
doorway to my right. On one side is the physical reality and on the
other side of the doorway is the realm of the dead. I pass through
it, back and forth, several times as I take on the role of psycho-
pomp, or deathwalker, with a family member in the process of tran-
sitioning. When I stand on the side of physical reality, I provide*

instruction regarding this individual's death process, which is informed by the information I absorb when in conversation with this individual's spirit on the other side of the doorway. Of those present for him through the process of death, I am the only one moving back and forth between the two realms, and with important communications.

In the dreams shared above, I interact with the elements, both die and do not die, or assist another in the process, yet it wasn't until a few years after those dreams when I would be faced with the real possibility of my own physical death, in the physical realm, this waking state. Powerfully vivid dreams provided clues, but still, I was left stumped, scratching my head.

This led up to my latest, and most powerful, waking initiation in 2019 when I was diagnosed with breast cancer—quite the *dark night of the soul* (to which St. John of the Cross made reference in his book by the same name). The first and greatest test I was faced with was whether I would do what outside authority figures directed me to do, or whether I would listen to my intuition, the whispers that arose as a result of meditation, in order to find the tools I needed to heal from the disease. The first year, especially, was the most frightening, filled with tricksters, and I saw how half of my community thought I was crazy for not jumping into conventional treatments with immediacy. Through that period, I learned who my true friends were and who actually was my spiritual community. A journey to the lower world led by Robert Moss in one of his workshops showed me that something was wrong—a great injury—a first glimpse of my need for healing. But I needed more information to understand the deeper meaning behind what I was shown, what I experienced.

In addition, my nocturnal dreams showed up as my most powerful guides. I followed them every step of the way even when I did not want nor like their directions, warnings, and guidance. As my consciousness grew throughout this intense process, I was shown in a very vivid, semi-lucid dream a large frame drum. This drum was being held up by the hands of a powerful dreamer I knew, a respected female colleague whom I trusted. Since I asked my dreams to show me what I needed to heal, via a technique called dream incubation (discussed in later chapters), and this was the response, I understood that my (serious) training in Core Shamanism would soon begin—no more dabbling in altered state realities.

The appearance of initiation dreams coming forth during periods of intense personal stress is not uncommon and has been well documented. As an ethnologist, Ewing conducted research in the 1980s that revealed that some people's dreams prompted them to join mystic orders (in this case Pakistani Muslim Sufis), and, in the end, these dreams were responsible for leading to the dreamer's positive personal, spiritual transformation.

I was angry, frustrated, and sad as I awoke from that dream with the frame drum because I was so tired, not wanting to start training in another modality. I recognized the dream directive as a call, so I contacted Sandra Ingerman to locate a teacher meeting her approval. I knew enough not to ignore "the call." So, I surrendered and followed through, admittedly sometimes sulking while doing so. This is how I completed three and a half years of personalized training in core shamanic practice with my teacher, Lena Swanson. All because of a dream. Lena expanded my education of the World Tree (the Axis Mundi) of lower, upper, and middle worlds and mentored me as I moved from theory to praxis. I learned about these places through lots of practice and direct experience/revelation, as required by a shamanic practitioner. Since then, I have experienced many lower world dismemberments. These are part of the healing process.

In his book *Dreamtime & Inner Space: The World of the Shaman*, Holger Kalweit writes (1984, p. 95):

> In many traditions the spirits of the underworld not only take the body of the initiate apart in a most gruesome way—they also put it together again, but in a curious manner which endows the person subjected to such dismemberment with superhuman powers. Such "bone displays" lead to a heightening of the spiritual state, a liberation from the blind causality of everyday life. Bone displays are thus a source of true life and represent a mystical rebirth.

Kalweit (1984) adds that "true transcendence calls for a willingness to suffer a genuine death of ego" (p. 95) and speaks on the dangers involved.

He notes that this is not a "mytho-poetical imagination of death in the form of allegories and archetypes" (p. 96).

Direct healings can take place in dreams as well as imaginal or shamanic journeys and ecstatic trance states. One journey from 2021 provided an experience of being doctored. Through the experience, the tumor mass was removed, the area of my body purified with smoke, and lastly, the open area was filled with small chunks of turquoise. There was more, but that is all I was allowed to see. After the journey concluded, I couldn't deny the experience which was sensory on all levels. To honor this healing, I acquired some beautiful turquoise chips from a friend.

In 2002, author and Andean healer, Marcela Lobos of Chile, experienced a powerful dream in which she was pregnant with a dead baby. I was glued to my seat during her talk on the Shift Network's Shamanic Wisdom Summit. Marcela described how dream-midwives appeared to her in the jungle—these spirits stayed with her for a very long time, helping her release what she no longer needed ... what no longer served her. This was a shamanic initiation that, in total, lasted many years and set Marcela on a path as healer.

From Marcela's personal experience, she was pushed well out of her comfort zone and understands how healing crises can be both physical and psychological (mental-emotional). Death of ego, persona, who we pretend to be in the world by wearing protective masks, and all the unconscious shielding must soften if we are to move forward along the (s)hero's journey, however it likely won't be a linear process. Personal growth can be depicted like the image of a whirlwind or spiral.

Shamanic practice walks one along the path toward inner transformation. Originating in Siberia, the northernmost region of Asia and Russia, shamanism may be thought of as the world's oldest religion, so it is no surprise that these birth-death-resurrection/rebirth psycho-somatic histories have been reported across time and place. From a shamanic lens, recall that these phenomena, such as dismemberment journeys and soul flight/dreaming where one leaves the body, are literal, real, rather than what transpersonal psychology would view as, at times, imaginary or more often, symbolic. Also worth noting for clarification is that while there are many practitioners out there, such as those of magic and healing, for example, there are certain criteria that are met when it comes to true shamans of the world. Shamans access alternate states of consciousness at will, fulfill unmet community needs, and mediate between the worlds of the sacred and the profane (Heinze, 1991, p. 13). Some have said that beyond most healers, you know one is a shaman when she or he can work with spirit in such a way that the result is a change in matter (or the material world). This depth is not symbolic.

From the many mystical traditions, Western alchemy gives way to transformation, as it is about turning base metal, like lead, into gold ... a metaphor for transmuting dense frequencies of impulsivity and animalistic desires, even matter, into higher frequencies of creativity, love, wisdom, and spirit. It's a spiritual alchemy that gives a direct experience of the rebirthing. As a prominent historical Western scientist, Sir Isaac Newton, was deeply involved in tradition of alchemy, recognizing that likely the most crucial factor in the process is the consciousness of the alchemist him/herself (Radin, 2018). While the more complex process of alchemy is beyond the scope of this book, I will briefly describe a foundational component below.

Alchemy proceeds in stages/phases. Each has an associated color. The major or original four are as follows (Hamilton, 2014):

Nigredo (the blackening), which indicates a change is starting to take place, as one's old values dissolve and there is suffering. Notions of a concrete, rational reality shatter in this stage.

Albedo (whitening)—Upon purification, the great inner work toward wholeness begins. The cleaning of the chaotic, muddy, dark previous stages takes place. The hardest part of the work is done.

Citrinitas (yellowing)—There is the peak of Albedo. Now a new way of existing in the world, with profound insight as co-creator with the Divine, opens. We consciously participate in the process of creation. A marriage of spirit and soul.

Rubedo (reddening) is the final of the four phases of

transformation. It incorporates an integration of opposites, self-actualization, and a recognition of the wise source of inner guidance. Here, we come full circle, beginning again where we started but with consciousness of the spirit within in holistic unity.

Within each of these four stages exist seven alchemical operations present within each of the stages. For a deeper dive into alchemy and dreams, I recommend reading *Awakening Through Dreams: The Journey Through the Inner Landscape* by Nigel Hamilton.

In restoring balance and in reviving humanity's ancient culture and religion—both shamanism and mysticism—we must return to "The Dreaming." For in dream, anything and everything is possible. We can heal the world, and each other. A true shamanic alchemical transformation unfolds.

Ritual

Across time, "Ritual is part of every society ... rituals embody and express a people's worldview" (Walsh, 2014, p. 208–209). In writing from the perspective of her ancestors, the Blackfoot peoples, Dr. Betty Bastien (2003) noted, "The ethical and moral behavior identified through customs, language values and roles are often referred to as protocol or ritual. Protocols and rituals encapsulate the responsibilities and behavior that are the means for returning to a state of balance or ensuring good relations" (p. 48). Whether simple or spontaneous, complex or choreographed, "the capacity for ritual is innate, a universally human faculty that is both instinctive and embodied. Although it can be ordinary and secular, ritual particularly offers us a language to express our sense of the sacred" (Brazier, 2018, p. 39). Through a fixed order of actions, gestures, and verbal expression of prescribed words a ritual can impact just about every aspect of existence; that is, crossing the boundaries of sociological and cultural, psychological and spiritual.

An additional aspect includes epigenetics. The Centers for Disease

Control and Prevention and Harvard University's Center on the Developing Child provide thorough explanations on the science of epigenetics. Epigenetics explains how environmental exposures, including exposure from behavior, impact the way our genes express themselves, or in other words, turn themselves on and off. On the one hand, the science of epigenetics teaches us that we have control when it comes to our health and our future—our everyday choices and behaviors matter. On the other hand, epigenetic changes can take place very early on, such as when we existed in our mother's womb. These changes impact development and can be long-lasting, even leading to diseases in a person decades after birth. While diseases can change epigenetics, epigenetic changes can make one more likely to develop diseases (*https://www.cdc.gov/genomics-and-health/about/epigenetic-impacts-on-health.html, https://developingchild.harvard.edu/resources/what-is-epigenetics-and-how-does-it-relate-to-child-development/*).

Engaging in ritualized activity is a behavior that can modulate gene expression. Therefore, participating in meaningful ritualized behaviors in one's environment is one way to impact epigenetic expression. What we do in our lives matters, thus sculpting who we become in mind, body, and spirit.

Anthropologists distinguish between several major categories of ritual, although these can often overlap in practice: magic rituals, which involve an attempt to manipulate natural forces through symbolic, often imitative, actions (e.g., pouring water on the ground to make rain); calendrical rituals, which mark the changing of the seasons and the passing of time; liturgical rituals, which involve the reenactment of a sacred story or myth, as in the Christian eucharist and many other religious rituals (American Psychology Association, n.d.). There are even elaborate Saint Feast Day rituals, especially celebrated in New York, that are widespread among Italian Americans. According to Sciorra (1989), feast days are referred to as "birthdays" and new statues are "baptized" with terrestrial godparents (p. 198).

Consider the altars and shrines found on sidewalks in New York's Italian American neighborhoods, emerging out of the magical religious traditions of Italy. Women are the primary builders and designers of these community-sanctioned sacred spaces (Sciorra, 1989). While most often featuring a lone saint, some of the shrines and altars share space with non–Christian figures, and all these devotional spaces are cared for as well as adorned, sometimes with seashells and large amounts of food (Sciorra, 1989). The adornment and offerings are especially prevalent on the Saint's Feast Day. Sacred figurines may be placed in trees even, in a cave-like structure, or above one's typical visual view. In total, neighborhoods become temples where heaven and earth are linked, communities are tied together, and there is a "softening of the spacial boundaries between indoors and outdoors, private and public" (Sciorra, 1989, p. 197). At times, a deceased family member's image will be included in the sacred space. When it comes to rituals for healing purposes, beliefs about the cause and cure for illnesses are expressed (Walsh, 2014, p. 209) among many societies, including Italian American.

From a secular standpoint, we can even witness rituals in the arena of sports. Baseball players are known for following through with ritualized activities on game day, both on and off the field (Gmelch, 1989). Ritual is everywhere.

Still, traditional, spiritually anchored, ritualized life has been lost for the most part, or at least greatly depleted, among those living in contemporary Western cultures. What is left of major rites of passage, such as giving birth, are placed among sterile, medicalized locations where community support and group ceremony is discouraged for the sake of "cleanliness." Health standards are necessary, so that is not my point here. What I do want to call attention to is that such shifts in society have bred, not germs, but loneliness, lack of meaning, and in some cases, postpartum depression.

The word ritual and related terms such as rite of passage often take place around life transitions, especially the most sacred. There is an initiation of sorts in many of them. Consider the conscious rituals you partake in when a birthday, holiday, or wedding anniversary comes around. Then, of course, the rituals surrounding events where one is changed forever, such as a birth or death, occur. To use death as an example, such a rite of passage involves many others who may perform ritualized acts: "praying over the body, commending the soul to the god(s), and remembering the life of the departed" (Madden, 1999, p. 83), which in today's world may include memorial slide-shows and other personalized acts. We truly live a ritualized life.

Rituals play a role in the daily lives of most people. Sometimes, a ritual is done alone, and other times, it is done with others. Rituals that are unconscious, acted out in a state of dissociation, may best be understood as habits rather than true rituals, which are embodied prayers, sometimes expressed in grander intentional ceremonies. From viewing dated films, I recall one rather unconscious ritual (or rather, an unhealthy habit) with which so many of us are familiar: the cigarette smoked after a sex act. If you are old enough, you'll likely remember seeing this often played out onscreen. Such a mundane ritual was almost expected, as it was part of the culture back then.

Rituals, from a contemporary Western definition, are not necessarily religious or spiritual, yet they can be when one is connected in mind-body-spirit. Church on Sundays, answering the call to prayer, adhering to feng shui, crossing oneself (when passing by a place or location of significance), tracking the cycles of the moon, or bowing to the ocean before swimming in the sea are just a few examples of how spiritualized ritual might enter our lives. The spiritual origins can be animistic, or emerge from monotheistic ceremonial traditions, or otherwise.

I'm reminded of my upbringing in the Italian American Roman Catholic tradition. Daily rituals of prayer, making the sign of the cross at special times and places, and so forth, grew into more detailed, lengthy ritual practices such as the stations of the cross or praying the rosary. One of my earliest memories is of the prayer ritual my sister, mother and I enacted before lying down in our beds in the late evenings, at bedtime:

> Now I lay me down to sleep, I pray the Lord my Soul to keep.
> If I should die before I wake, I pray the Lord my Soul to take.

We chanted that one for many years, as it is a well-known prayer. My sister and I understood its meaning. The prayer is kid-friendly in its simplicity and rhyme. Our culture understood death more than others. We were not afraid to talk about it.

The most consistent solo daily ritual in my life is the logging of my nocturnal dreams and dream-like liminal state visions. Following this I enjoy another ritual which is early morning tea sipped outside alongside chirping birds in the waking state, although I must admit that I seem to remain groggy for some time in a way that feels hypnotic. I do this right before or after greeting and honoring the sun, offering prayers in that cardinal direction. I follow this with a verbal gratitude list. I state five to seven elements of life that I am grateful for, such as my family's support, friends to surf with, the presence of my sweet dog, a place to call home where I feel safe, meaningful work, being born in a place with relatively clean air and water, collaboration with conscious community, and access to healthcare.

Ritual and dream have a relationship in many cultures across time. We have contemporary sleep hygiene rituals for enhancing dreaming (Mascaro, 2021) among today's dream enthusiasts in the United States. Indeed, the modern practice of calling lucid dreams can in itself be seen as a ritual complex involving ancient techniques for shifting consciousness (Hurd, 2022). There are also well-documented accounts of traditional practices where dream and ritual come together. As I am writing this manuscript while residing on the island of Maui, I think about the relationships between the dreams of Native Hawaiian healers (*Kahuna*) and the rituals involved in community member healing (Gutmanis, 2024). The *Kahuna* might dream (*moe 'uhane*) their patient's diagnosis, for example (Gutmanis, 2024, p. 39).

5

LIVE YOUR MEDICINE

Once we become acutely aware of the rituals we engage in throughout each day, we can begin to identify how intentional they actually are, and whether they serve the purpose we intended. When do we engage in isolated ritual behaviors? When are others involved? If we recognize how we care about being called, or initiated, toward something greater than material concerns, will we have the courage to take the next step forward?

Ceremony

When rituals are intentional and become full creative expressions to include working with sacred powers, we have ceremony. Because of the power of Source, rituals open and close ceremonies to contain powerful forces. Sometimes a ceremony may be a public event, or one that brings a community together. Bastien (2003) explains that, in her culture, "ceremonies are for connecting, renewing and maintaining good relations with the alliances to ensure that life returns to a sacred and peaceful way" (p. 48). Indeed, ceremonies help bring balance to the microcosm and macrocosm. In Nepal, elaborate marriage rituals take place in Kathmandu Valley involving ceremonial jewelry (Gabriel, 1999). Gabriel (2007) describes how sometimes up to 200 young Newar girls are adorned in gold jewelry as part of the *ihi* ceremony, which leads up to a symbolic marriage to Vishnu, a Hindu deity who is represented as a wood apple, or bael fruit. Everyone is involved—entire communities participate in a life-cycle ceremony such as this one. Ceremonies appear differently around the world on the surface; however, the underlying spiritual forces are not to be taken lightly.

Lead ceremonialists train for decades or even a lifetime in some cultures so that the community is protected. As members of a Catholic parish, my family participated in frequent rituals and ceremonies. The church or cathedral was the container. The priest would lead a large Mass on holy days to include purification by air/smoke (incense), sound (the chanting/singing of sacred names or scriptures), water (holy water, that is), fire (multiple beeswax candles are lit), and earth (holy communion/body and blood of Christ). These are sacred elements. The priest's job is to work with these elemental powers, through Christ, as the Last Supper is recreated. I recall these, especially from my childhood, since these ceremonies were elaborate, rich, and commanded attention.

The non-profit Worldwide Indigenous Science Network (WISN) brings the following information to light regarding a way by which ceremony may be understood:

> When describing the attributes of ceremony, Western literature explains ceremony in psychological terms: ceremony connects the outer world with the inner world. For indigenous peoples, when the outer and inner worlds connect, we are one with the environment and life, have access to more information and better insights, and new questions may be raised. Ceremony is carried out because it is efficacious and works. (*wisn.org*)

WISN is one such organization that supports Indigenous ceremonies across the globe. Many Indigenous communities have experienced outside oppression directed at their ceremonies through laws, prohibitions and regulations meant to stamp out their existence entirely. Traditional ceremonies deemed a threat to dominant cultural forces, such as the dominant one in which I grew up, have been especially targeted with great force and injustice. Others raised in the Catholic tradition, just as I was, have made claims that Indigenous traditional ceremonies are the work of the Devil. What's more, some ceremonial leaders have been directly targeted and their lives threatened with imprisonment, violence and death. Many of the two to four million Maui visitors per year are not aware that in the 1800s Hula was banned. In the last hundred years or so, people have been threatened with criminal charges and incarceration for practices in North America (Sun Dance) and in Brazil (Capoeira). Yes, this was going on in the 1900s, less than a century ago. Ask a trusted elder. Rune drums were confiscated and outlawed in northern Europe—only recently, after decades of protest, have any been returned to the Indigenous communities whose *Noaidi* (Sámi shaman) members used these drums in ritual practices, viewing them as persons, not material objects.

Anyone can go through the motions of ceremonial activity with objects, chanting, or motions that may not even remotely belong to the said practitioners' own culture. Culturally appropriative behavior can be seen all over the place these days. A superficial dressing up, or even donning the ceremonial garb of other peoples does not enhance a connection with Spirit. Wearing the mask of another culture does not move us forward and can come across as offensive to members of the culture being appropriated. When we dedicate ourselves to reconnecting to our own ancient cultural roots, and move forward from that place, we will likely have a more grounded and more meaningful impact for positive change.

It is a ceremony with impact when the illusions of time and space collapse, and there you are, in the eternal, ever-present *Now*. I'm reminded of when I heard a Catholic priest claim that the whole point of Mass is The Last Supper. During a Mass, The Last Supper is not a re-enactment. Instead, at that moment, Mass participants are living The Last Supper. As the priest shared, "This *is* The Last Supper." As one of the hallmarks of a ceremony, participants enter the omnipresent *Now*, the *All at Once Time*. From that place/space, a shift occurs.

Helena Soholm, PhD, is a transpersonal psychologist and a *Mudang* (Korean Shaman). Helena and I share a deep respect and admiration for a mutual mentor, Stanley Krippner, PhD, who is a professor with expertise in consciousness studies, particularly shamanism, dreams, and hypnosis. Before Helena and I had ever met, Stanley was pivotal during our time as psychology doctoral students and really encouraged our work. He is still influential in our lives today. I was especially drawn to Stan, as many call him, when I came across one of the 2011 publications he co-authored titled *The Indigenous Healing Tradition in Calabria, Italy*, as my father is of Calabrese blood. I learned how what we might call healers or seers living in that territory practice under the dominant authority of the Roman Catholic Church. Church officials allow these people to pray with those afflicted but do not allow them to conduct healing work via traditional folk medicine ways of the region. It is important to note that traditional healing ways of Calabria are a blend of the dozens of cultures and societies that resided on that territory since Calabria has been invaded and colonized dozens and dozens of times over the course of millennia. Still, due to Calabria's isolated position, folk healing traditions have in fact survived and are being practiced today. Also due to the remote location and mountainous geography, Calabria has both resisted forces of Europeanization and industrialization as well as been neglected from modernization, resulting in a labeling of the place and its people as being savage and uncivilized, "perhaps held over from colonialist attitudes" (Krippner et al., 2011, p. 50). In this modern era, a folk Catholicism exists in the rural and mountainous parts of Calabria as "a syncretic mixture of some pre–Christian elements with a dose of Roman Catholicism, still relatively resistant to much of the official church doctrine" (Krippner et al., 2011, p. 51) Folk medicine of Calabria has its own lexicon, including the well-known *malocchio* (evil eye), as well as magical cures to alleviate it. Since "the Calabrian universe is an interconnected whole" being "inhabited by a variety of local spirits as well as by angels, demons, and saints," it seems natural that their use of magic and prayer is done for protection as well as plain and simple common sense (Krippner et al., 2011, p. 52), a gift inherited from their ancestors and sometimes enhanced through a so-called altered or nonordinary state of consciousness. It has also been suggested by some that the land of Calabria itself brings forth the healing element ... the land being the origin of healing. And like so many families whose ancestors have been displaced from wars, poverty, and other hardships, my own is included among them.

Helena understands this connection with the land as well as community. She was born and raised in South Korea, yet it wasn't until she had already resided for several decades in the United States before she would experience *the call* and become initiated as a *Mudang*. In fact, that initiation took place in the same year as her academic initiation as a psychologist. While Helena planned for her entry into the world of professional psychology, her entry into the world of shamanism wasn't planned out in such a way. Helena understands how ancestors and other forces decide who must begin the shamanic path or risk facing the consequences. The call I experienced was in the dream state, after I practiced a dream incubation ritual where I asked to be shown a cure for the cancer that had developed in my body. In the dream, I was shown a frame drum, as noted earlier in the previous chapter, and right then and there I knew there was no going back. Just this knowing caused great stress—all morning I felt angry and cried. I knew the big job that lay ahead of me. I felt too exhausted to embark on such a journey, but I knew there was no other way. Basically, I had to enter an unfamiliar world fully and suddenly where, similar to Helena, I only expected shamanic inquiry to remain scholarly, through academic learning. Like others whose interviews are included in this book, Helena too is an example of a practitioner who operates in the two worlds: that of the Western and that of the Indigenous. Her professional services hold both perspectives equally and she uses her skills and talents to help those seeking healing. This is especially true for those who have unwillingly lost connection to their ancestral lands from foreign adoption.

While I have noted ritual and ceremonial activity linked with certain cultures, it is possible that such activity may all feel unsettling when one has been raised in orphanages, group homes, foster or adoptive families. A fracturing or complete split from one's roots or heritage from being raised through such systems can result in disorientation and profound disconnection. Distraction and dissociation are also a result of such fracturing. Helena explains how modern daily living can lead us away from healing such traumas. She writes that through distraction, "we keep ourselves busy to the detriment of our health (mind and body) so that we can feel good about being productive and therefore having worth." In addition, "work, entertainment, and leisure activities are designed to keep us further away from our authentic selves instead of connecting us to our purpose and to others in a meaningful way." And through dissociation, "we engage in numbing ourselves through food, sex, alcohol, drugs, and technology to disengage from the experience of living in the moment. Mindless activities fill our days leaving us feeling empty and alone" (Soholm, 2020, p. 69).

Take away all the distractions and people notice waves of anxiety, dread, or fear wash over them. From that place (a type of crisis, really), people have an opportunity. They can quickly grasp for more numbing solutions, or face the fears of reality, which would mean putting an end to the distraction, disconnection, and dissociation cycle. This life shift requires honesty and humility. Along that path, albeit sometimes frightening and lonely, deeper meaning and purpose are discovered. Support from psychologists and psychotherapists, people like Helena, can help. As noted, Helena also works with adoptees, and in particular, Korean adoptees who have been raised in Denmark by Danish families. Some may never have the opportunity to know their birth parents. Helena has brought ceremonies to Denmark in service of the Koreans who have remained there yet simultaneously desire re-establishing a spiritual connection to their place of origin. Anyone on a spiritual path can find support right at their feet—that is the land they live on that sustains their very life. The trees provide fresh oxygen, ancestral spirits of place inform the deep listener, and energies that vibrate in any geographical location inhabit every inch of the fabric of life. Healing, transformative work takes courage. I believe it must transpire in order to facilitate collective healing of human consciousness, thus birthing a world where compassion, social justice, kindness, and love are the cardinal points on the inner compass.

When I asked Helena about other potential colleagues of hers who might be willing to discuss my views on this current piece of writing, she mentioned a couple of names. One was Dr. Jurgen Kremer. Trusting her judgment, I kept his name in mind and wrote it down on a scrap of paper sitting on my kitchen table. Soon after,

I went to pay a visit to Apela Colorado again, asking if she had ever heard of him. Apela claimed she had, and even more striking, that he would be flying in the following week to stay with her. I even saw the printed flight itinerary so I would believe what I was hearing. And there you have it, Jurgen Kremer sitting with us on the mat in ceremony the following week!

Anyhow, by this point, things were getting weird. Jurgen's textbook on Ethno-Autobiography, co-authored by River Jackson-Paton, has influenced my own work and writing. How was it that so many synchronicities and coincidences were unfolding with Maui seeming to be at the focal point? Is this, or rather these connections, what brought me to Hawaii, the world's most remote island chain and the most isolated population center and archipelago in the world?

In the book *Braiding Sweetgrass: Indigenous Wisdom, Scientific Knowledge, and the Teachings of Plants*, author Dr. Robin Wall Kimmerer (2013) wrote, "Ceremony focuses attention so that attention becomes intention. If you stand together and profess a thing before your community, it holds you accountable" (p. 249). She continues, "Ceremonies transcend the boundaries of the individual and resonate beyond the human realm. These acts of reverence are powerfully pragmatic. These are ceremonies that magnify life" (p. 249). Kimmerer notices how ceremonies focusing on an individual, such as graduations, weddings, birthdays and funerals, continue powerfully in today's modern culture, but the joy, thanksgiving, and promise of those ceremonies, which are important, are, sadly, no longer extended to celebrating the gifts given to us by nature, including seasons, elements and nonhumans. Have all modern European American people kept the mundane, while ditching the sacred?

Ceremonies bond us with the land we currently inhabit. Kimmerer (2013) points out how "ceremony is a vehicle for belonging—to a family, to a people, and to the land" (p. 37), and that "to have agency in the world, ceremonies should be reciprocal concretions, organic in nature, in which the community creates ceremony, and ceremony creates communities" (p. 250).

What can we do when we are not indigenous to the land we live on? To know it, for starters, we listen deeply. This requires silence.

We introduce ourselves mindfully, we really pay attention, learning how nature communicates. Then listen deeply some more and keep paying attention. After all, way back when, we all spoke the same language. Considering reciprocity and the maintaining of balance, where might we proceed from that point? Recognizing the gifts that the land has bestowed upon us with a grateful heart can inspire giving something back. What creative gifts might you give to nature herself? From prayers and song, to donating to agencies for conservation, or volunteering during land or ocean cleanup projects, options are abundant. Everyone can do that, differently, in their own way, but it must be done.

We have the ability to re-establish the nature-based and Earth-honoring ceremonies of our own ancestors, the way they went about it in "the old country." Find a mentor, whether you can travel back there yourself or not. Through intentional ceremonies centering deep care and love, we can heal the fractures, thus restoring relationships of ecology, environmentalism, humanity, each other. The effects will be seen in the land. After all, nature doesn't lie. She tells it, or rather shows it, like it is.

Sacred Activism

The Hawaiian proverb, *E Hele Me Ka Pu'olo*, encourages one to make every person, place or condition better than you left it. *E Hele Me Ka Pu'olo* also reminds one to always take an offering with you. It's a favorite proverb of mine that reminds me of how to live. We honor *Ke Akua* (The Creator), all creation, nature, by always bringing an offering wherever we go. Offerings can be words, such as prayers, and prayers come in so many forms. Kremer and Jackson-Paton (2018) write that "healing ceremonies, like all stories, have to be shared. Ceremonies are about connection and relationships, with other humans, with place, and with the world of spirits..." (p. 29).

Sacred Activism represents a way of being lived by many groups and communities, as it is connected to their survival. It is a term coined by Andrew Harvey, founder and director of The Institute for

Sacred Activism. But make no mistake, while Harvey coined the term, Sacred Activism has been in practice for eons. It is quite an old idea embodying anti-racist social activism with spiritual practice. Recent examples can be seen through collaborations centered around ecology between Western scientists and those of Indigenous knowledge systems. Relationships to land, diverse species, environmental conditions including health of resources are all linking together for the health and spiritual well-being among all organisms, including humans. The actions to halt the construction of the vast pipelines through Indigenous lands are the most recent example in my mind.

Decolonizing is "a creative, psychospiritual, moral, political, and activist endeavor" by which we turn our gaze upon ourselves (Kremer, 2003, p. 6). I have found that sacred activist behavior contrasts with typical contemporary Westerners who are either solely secular or solely spiritual in their identities, thus creating a separation between environment and their religious or spiritual beliefs. A part of being a sacred activist ally requires cultural sensitivity to the possibility that taking "ownership" of data, research findings or test results may be in conflict to the desires of Indigenous collaborators and even inappropriate if there exists a lack of awareness surrounding beneficiaries. In my opinion, Sacred Activism includes being certain that at the nexus of activist activities, the results delivered are in benefit for, and defined by, those who have historically been severely negatively impacted in the United States, such as Black, Indigenous, People of Color (BIPOC).

From his own history and lived experiences, high school teacher and activist Hawah Kasat (2024) lists the core concepts of Sacred Activism as interconnectedness (one's actions affect the whole), compassion and love (empathic motivators for addressing social issues), and inner transformation (effective activism is rooted in spiritual growth).

In that recent talk (Institute of Noetic Sciences), Kasat shared his core, personal life anchor behind his own social activism. That is that "there are no enemies." He explained that while he used to feel that loving our enemies seemed a form of contradiction, he revealed how his consciousness grew through enhancing and developing into his spiritual practice. This led Kasat to realize that rather than loving our enemies, know that there are no enemies. Creating the "enemy" is another form of othering, he said. This is critical behind Sacred Activism.

When Kasat named Sri Ramana Maharishi, I predicted what he might say next since I wear a t-shirt with the quote he shared. That is, when Sri Raman Maharishi was asked how we should treat others, his response was "there are no others." Until we realize our true interconnectedness, our shared waking dream, this response will seem nonsensical.

Looking back a bit, I can tell you that my own history with activism began in high school. I really, really cared, and I wasn't afraid to show it. I felt so much emotional pain as I witnessed cruelty by the hand of those with money and power. It was also confusing as to how world leaders and even those in my own family didn't seem to be concerned. Fortunately, when my sister came around and announced she would no longer eat meat, I didn't feel so alone, especially at the holidays.

At 18 I began learning Eastern ways. A course in tai chi taught me breathwork, visualization, and moving energy (before I could even really comprehend what that was). This became regular practice, almost daily, in fact. I was entering a spiritually informed world without even knowing it. My martial arts career began there and carried on for the next 25 years. Learning about spiritualities of Asia, atrocities and human rights violations in sweatshops, and the Free Tibet movement, married sacred practice with social justice causes. Spiritual practice and activism were starting to merge, and I didn't see the two as so separate any longer.

Still, by witnessing so many injustices across the globe, anger ran through my blood as my spiritual practices were set aside. I did not know that I was creating poison that I fed to myself—the opposite of good medicine. Honestly, without a core spiritual grounding, I recall how many of us, myself included, started turning toward alcohol as a coping mechanism. It took several cycles of teeter-tottering from more secular-based activism to Sacred Activism. The empathy was there, the motivation and energy were there, but for years, I spiraled into places where there was no connection with my inner Light ... with Source. This worries me because I see the sadness and despair of today's youth as they attempt to fathom how it is that the generations of their parents and grandparents could leave them with a struggling environment.

Elizabeth Lesser is an author and cofounder of the Omega Institute for Holistic Studies in New York. She coined the term "innervism." Innervism is essential, Lesser claims, and describes the kind of activism that requires looking within. She also explains that innervism is inextricably linked to the work of activism in her online talks and interviews.

Through my own history of activism, I noticed how all too often, many activists I knew constantly looked outside of themselves. There was a lot of finger-pointing and blaming, I recall. Those I knew did not want to look inward, nor sit with their shadow. The silence was obviously uncomfortable for them, and it became easier to bypass what was really going on inwardly. I was part of this. It was a period in my life with a lot of anger and it was messy, especially in my adolescent activist years and into my 20s. In so many activist circles at that time, I recall how a lot of drinking was going on. Alcohol numbed us to our own pain, not just the pain of the external world. To quote Lesser in conversation with journalist Maria Shriver: "The most powerful inner work I have done is getting courageous enough to really look at myself...." She suggests that we look at the parts of ourselves that want to grow and change—it is "very liberating." I was able to start doing this when I gained the support of peers, clinical supervisors, and professors once I began a masters in counseling psychology program. I was thankful for the inspiration to embark on the graduate school journey from coworkers at Seneca Center, a nonprofit agency I was employed with from 1999 into 2004. Those years allowed me to draw on previous experiences from years of martial arts training that included meditation practices. That was a source of inner support and strength as I served children with incredible histories of trauma during my time at that agency. As my meditation skills and practice grew, I developed a witness consciousness that allowed me to hold the paradox of showing up in loving service while simultaneously being a witness unattached to outcomes. Together, life was starting to make more sense.

Fortunately, once I entered graduate school, I was well situated back into martial arts circles and deeply engaged in spiritual practices. A great deal of my activism was centered around the needs of children who lived through extreme abuse and neglect, some intentional and some from systemic inequities and violence.

Meditation was a saving grace and during those years of intense practice I came to understand and, with the guidance of others, finally stand firm in the core truth that spirituality and social justice activism cannot exist in isolation, nor separately, unless we are fooling ourselves.

After almost two decades dedicated to working in nonprofit sectors, I had to jump ship. I realized it might be contributing to poor health outcomes for my own body. And as I aged it felt more acceptable to set back physically and instead provide support to social justice causes financially. Of course, I could still show up at demonstrations and cheer on the youth from the sidelines.

Now, I find that I do a much better job of living in balance. I want to encourage those of us who show deep care to our communities near and afar that we can recall how we, too, are also a part of life on Earth and deserving of harmony and justice. We must apply sacred activist principles to our own lives. If we place our focus on too many causes, spreading ourselves too thinly, there will be a price to pay, perhaps sooner than later. Setting boundaries is necessary. Aside from issues that require immediate attention, such as genocides across the globe, we can, for the most part, do as the saying goes: Think Globally, Act Locally. Simultaneously, we can take action to fuel our own bodies in many ways, such as taking a day off entirely, and when the time is right, enrolling in a small, family- or community-run business where meditation is taught.

Only after a couple decades of training and practice in psychology, psychotherapy and spirituality did Sri Raman Maharishi's comment, noted above, make sense. It's challenging for someone like me who was raised in the modern West with a propensity for separation and duality. Our ego can keep us locked into that. Of course, I still get spun out on some days, going toward polarities and grasping onto illusions (as warned against within the writings of Buddhism and Yogic philosophies). When I feel challenged, I remind myself how every new day is an opportunity to stand in wholeness and move in life from a place of oneness. I stand in that commitment now. It is a life-long practice though, a true journey rather than destination. It is good medicine.

Planting Seeds of Experience

Dreaming, too, is good medicine. The following chapters look at ancestral and ecological dreaming, and later, ways to begin or enhance your practice. For the good of all, the dream arts can be gentle while positively impactful.

In the early 1990s, Rhea White, director of information for the American Society for Psychical Research, described "seed experiences," which have the potential for shifting paradigms and personal transformation. White was one of the first to view anomalous experiences as potentially transformative because of their variance from what society considered to be normal. She proposed that exceptional experiences were seed experiences, and that if certain conditions prevailed, the seed would sprout and grow. With cultivation, it could become a fully mature plant. In a similar way, an exceptional experience sometimes almost immediately—but usually over a considerable period of time—possibly aided by additional exceptional experiences, can enable experiencers to realize more of their human potential. At the point where an exceptional experience permanently alters the experiencer's identity and worldview, it becomes an exceptional human experience (Brown & White, 1997, p. 151).

Around that same time, Yvonne Kason, MD, first coined the term Spiritually Transformative Experience (STE) (2000). As an umbrella term for many different types of spiritual or paranormal experiences, an STE is one which has a lasting impact on the individual. As a pioneer in the field, Dr. Kason began to study these phenomena after her own STE. When she survived a plane crash in 1979, the phenomenon she experienced related to that plane crash would change her life forever. Her experience would be classified as a Near-Death Experience (NDE), yet just like the ones listed below, the impact would be long lasting. She would go on to conduct some very meaningful research in the not-so-distant future as she went on a "scholarly quest to understand what on earth (well, not quite earth) had happened to her" (Harrison, 1993, p. 2318).

According to Dr. Kason, STEs have been reported across time and place. They can take place for someone from any culture, regardless of religion or belief system. STE accounts can be located within the writings of all mystical traditions, as reported to have occurred in the lives of prophets, saints, visionaries all over the world. There are an ever-growing number of terms we can hear with regard to STEs depending on whom you read or whom you speak with. Such terms include Exceptional Human, Enlightenment, Transcendental, Extraordinary or Ascension Experiences. Others may refer to STEs by other names found within the literature such as Holy Spirit Quickening or Spiritual Emergencies, in addition to specific terms within the yoga traditions, according to Dr. Kason, who has grouped STEs into six major categories. I will list them just as she has on her website (*https://dryvonnekason.com/spiritually-transformative-experiences*), where you can read about each category in detail. They are Mystical Experiences, Kundalini/Spiritual Energy Awakenings, Near-Death Experiences, Other Death-Related STEs (Including End-of-Life Experiences/Deathbed Visions/Terminal Lucidity; Death-Watch Experiences/Shared Death Experiences; and After-Death Communications), Psychic/Intuitive Experiences of many types; and Inspired Creativity and Genius.

Regardless of the category in which one's experience lies, an STE can result in a person's spiritual growth and personal healing. When considering the term "spiritual," I reflect on Krippner's concept of spiritual, as taken from the Casto Spirituality Scoring System, that encompasses "something of significance believed to be beyond one's full understanding and/or individual existence and that are associated with a sense of reverence" (2016, p. 163).

Healthcare professionals today still have little awareness or training to support those who come to them for help with understanding and integrating their STEs into their daily lives (Woollacott, Kason, & Park, 2021). Yet, I believe the awareness and training opportunities are expanding. It was the last week of August 2024 when I arrived at the annual conference of the International Association for Near Death Studies (IANDS). Dozens of "experiencers" (people who have reported a Near-Death Experience) along with academic researchers, healthcare professionals, reverends and priests or other religious clergy, independent scholars, and more meet to build community and learn about the latest research findings in the field of near-death studies. My colleague, Dr. Bhaskar Banerji, and I had the privilege of presenting for the first time at the IANDS conference. Our co-presentation was titled "Dreams and NDEs as Life-Changing Events." What will live on in my memory for a very long time is all I absorbed that week from listening to the astounding presentations, including how dreaming was highly valued in so many of the conference attendee's lives. In addition, I sensed so much empathy, compassion, and kindness among the people present at the IANDS conference.

At the IANDS conference, I met a couple of researchers from the University of Virginia's School of Medicine, one of which presented on the neuroscience of out-of-body experiences (OBEs). I took a front seat. Marina Weiner, PhD, explained how the Temporoparietal junction (TPJ) is a brain region associated with how humans understand the feelings of others. The TPJ is active as we locate our body in space as well as with our capacity for empathy. Dr. Weiner spoke about how the OBE is a seed experience. With an OBE there is often ego dissolution in an individual, with an increase in prosocial behavior and a capacity for empathy (Weiner et al., 2024). I recalled how my past experiences with extensive and frequent meditation eventually delivered gifts I never could have imagined. When I learned about OBEs, I made it a personal goal to experience one. My discipline paid off. From Dr. Weiner's neuroscience-focused talk, I learned that a set of regions in the brain called the Default Mode Network (DMN) are activated in our day-to-day lives about 50 percent of the time. She explained how the DMN can be thought of as our cognitive and narrative self, helping us to integrate our experiences and know who we are, giving us autobiographical memory. The DMN is involved in daydreaming, remembering and reminiscing, but when one meditates, the DMN quiets down.

One of the other people I met was Jonathan Ellerby, PhD. As an expert in the field of comparative religion, he wrote about the various types of spiritual experiences in his book, *The Seven Gateways of Spiritual Experience*. He found seven types of spiritual experiences: Truth and Beauty, Ordinary Magic, Spirit World, Cosmic Self, Divine Energy, Formless Spirit, and finally, Pure Consciousness. Thinking about these experiences in a hierarchy, for simplicity, moments of awe could be considered an experience of Truth and Beauty, and Ordinary Magic could encapsulate moments of synchronicity. Many people report experiencing the Cosmic Self through meditation, lucid dreams, and OBEs. As we move along, our ego and identity with the self really begin to dissolve. An experience of Formless Self is not common, yet those who report such experiences can tell you how Source is everything—we are all connected. This shift of perspective is even more so in the case of experiences of Pure Consciousness, where there is such a profound merging with Source that there are no boundaries. There is not an experience of a separate distinct self. Instead, we are one with *the all and everything*—silent stillness.

I spoke with Dr. Ellerby after his presentation where he reminded the audience of our shared humanity. He explained how spiritual experiences teach us what it is to be human and the nature of reality. When we understand who we truly are as spiritual beings, we will naturally become advocates for "inclusivity and pluralism" instead of "othering the sentient beings with whom we share this planetary home." Through my own STEs, I have been reminded of this enlightened way of being in the world. I also know how quickly the most profound impacts of such experiences can fade. In my experience, I have come to rely on and trust that with each and every STE, I will be further guided on how to live in the most loving way.

The final keynote presentation, and the one that moved me to tears, was given by "experiencer" Vinney Todd Tolman whose own

Near-Death Experience (NDE) led him to create a nonprofit organization called Living God's Light. During his keynote speech, he explained how he came to learn the gift of being human: Earth school is the hardest to get into and the hardest to graduate from, he said. I was reminded how I have been told that many experiencers contemplate suicide because once we experience our consciousness outside of the physical body, it's rare to desire continuing on with life back inside a body, as most experiencers must go through pain and rehabilitation due to the circumstances of their death. These circumstances range from automobile or other accidents, heart attacks, drownings, accidental overdoses, or whatever it was that led them to face their own death in the first place.

Vinney reminded the audience of our true purpose. He explained how, as humans, we are here (on Earth) to be fully authentic. Life is about more than love, it is about authenticity. He imparted additional wisdom. In response to a question by a member of the audience, Vinney also explained how the polarization we are seeing in these turbulent times is problematic in that we are not here to be "anti" anything. Whatever we are anti, we become. What we hate is like our puppet master.

There was so much richness in Vinney's keynote talk. I was enlivened when he spoke about something I often share with my own clients, which is hypnopompia and hypnagogia, and the power of these liminal states of consciousness. Vinney, however, referred to it as our "Hour of Power." This period refers to the 30 minutes upon waking up and the 30 minutes before we fall asleep every night. During these times, our brain states slow down and we are highly suggestible, similar to how we are suggestible in states of hypnosis. During those two 30-minute blocks of time, we can make autosuggestions for being our highest selves. It's a time to visualize what we want in life and also repeat affirmative statements, or positive affirmations, that align with that vision. As conscious beings, we can experience wonder and manifest so very much!

Finally, I had an opportunity to learn more about a phenomenon that piqued my interest over the years, that is, a shared death experience (SDE). In addition to all he has already contributed, Dr.

Raymond Moody further contributed to the understanding of SDEs. His investigations are brought forth in his 2010 book, *Glimpses of Eternity*. Many people have had an SDE but have not easily found an emotionally safe place to talk about them. This, as you can imagine, is also true for people who experience an NDE. At the IANDS conference, psychotherapist William Peters presented on the SDE, also introducing me to the Shared Crossing Project that he founded. William first defined the term as an experience in which loved ones, caregivers, or bystanders feel they are sharing in a dying person's transition to a benevolent afterlife. He noted the dominant motif of an SDE to be the "journey." Then, William reported on the features found in both the experiences of near-death and shared-death. They include what one might expect, such as transcendent light, encounters with spirit beings, tunnels or gateways, borders or boundaries, and life reviews. But what's more are sublime feelings of connectivity or unity, profound peace, ineffability, and love. After his talk, I asked him about reports of SDEs in the dream state. He confirmed that an SDE can take place when one is asleep; however, the SDE is experienced similarly to a clear lucid dream or OBE. There are no distortions with an SDE—the experience is clear with a particular set of features. For more on this phenomenon, look for the feature length documentary film *Shared Crossing—Life Survives Death*—a first on SDEs! It will be coming out soon.

In total, a vast array of "seed experiences" holds the potential for moving one along their spiritual path. When these "seeds" blossom into an STE, it has the potential to move a loving agenda forward. These experiences allow us to remember our shared spiritual home—they teach us where we come from, and I believe, also teach us to be at our best, not only for our families and communities, but for the greater whole.

Spiritually Transformative Dream Experiences

Where the dream arts and STEs intersect, we can make preparations and have some conscious control. Through using our exceptional faculties for conscious dreaming practices, from dream incubation and sleep-based meditation to experiences of shared dreaming, we can accelerate the development of consciousness. Through that process and its lasting impact—what I will call Spiritually Transformative Dream Experiences (STDEs)—we have an opportunity to heal all sentient beings, including ourselves, from the damage of perpetual unconscious human activity. I believe STDEs to be broader than the experience of a numinous dream because the presence of a divinity or a supernatural quality is not required.

STDEs are in close relationship with transpersonal dreams (Stumbrys, 2018). I agree with Krippner's (2016) proposal that transpersonal dreams are STEs yet wonder if it is true the other way around. That is because the findings from my doctoral study on announcing dreams of pregnant women (Mascaro, 2018, 2016, 2013) and my own most personally profound STDEs related to cancer have been somatic or focused on physical symptoms, bodily conditions, ailments, or illness in various ways, which have sometimes included psychological and even psycho-spiritual issues outside of present awareness. The spiritual transformation develops. Additional experiences in dreamtime, or "The Dreaming," may be needed. With time, integration, and by trusting in the process, STDEs compel dreamers to take action for their health and healing—their highest good— thus transforming lives. In my experience, STDEs can be direct, down-to-earth, practical, straightforward, and as I said, *somatic*, thus centering awareness of the body's own capacities as the healing agent. We can bring together a conscious ability to work with our body in dreamy states of consciousness (from liminal to fully lucid) for healing and recovery. As I always say, "May your dreams be your medicine"—as they have been mine. Through this deepening process we learn that "something" is at play for our highest good alongside where boundaries and limits (or lack of) may exist.

It was just a few years ago when some of my dreams, unfolding around the same time, brought together lucidity, the presence of deceased loved ones, the somatic awareness, health-related information, and energetic self-healing. From this convergence, I felt ever more transformed in that I knew I held within me a capacity to consciously collaborate with my "inner physician" and ancestors for my physical health and healing, and to know when to seek help. I felt an increased capacity to trust both my bodily knowing and my higher consciousness together, while learning their limits. I considered that there might just be deep meaning behind the chronic illness with which I was diagnosed. I began asking the bigger questions. The process was transformative to say the least, but perhaps not necessarily *transpersonal*.

6

DREAMING WITH
ALL RELATIONS

We are all the leaves of one tree. We are all
the waves of one sea.—Thich Nhat Hanh

Tracking, or journaling, our dream recollections is like looking into a mirror. Dreams show many aspects of ourselves, especially the shadow elements of ourselves that can be challenging to own, as far as the ego is concerned. A significant amount of research on dreams and dreaming has demonstrated a continuity between day-to-day thoughts, behaviors, and feelings and what shows up in that person's dreams. In a recent scholarly article titled "You Are What You Dream," Jenkins & Martin (2023) open with the statement: "Behaviors and traits belonging to waking life have been found to manifest in dream content" (p. 434). They also posit that some evidence suggests that the content of one's dreams reflects traits of one's personality (Jenkins & Martin, 2023). To get a clear picture of who we are, relationally speaking, our dreams can tell us a lot and show us the way forward. Furthermore, when we share a dream with someone (which I feel to be a sacred, intimate exchange), we are self-disclosing—we gift the listener with an opportunity to truly see us (Leonard & Dawson, 2023). Outside of contemporary Western science–based dream dialogue, this "someone" can be the spirit world at large to include all beings (human, animal, and other). The dream gifts dreamers with insight, wisdom and knowledge as is the belief among peoples of the Peruvian Amazon (Peluso, 2004) and other areas of the world. We can embody those gifts and speak words of gratitude to Spirit.

Dr. Nicholas Brink describes a shift in perspective when it comes to considering where dreams come from. In the past, he believed dreams to come out of one's unconscious mind; however, through further exploration of the dream world, his direct experiences alongside those of many other advanced dreamers (those well-versed in dream-based practices) have led him to conclude that dreams come from a place beyond the unconscious mind. They emerge from what he calls "the universal mind but what others have called the akashic field, the morphic field, the divine matrix, or the collective unconscious" (Brink, 2022, p. 8).

In the section titled "Ritual" in chapter 4, I introduced the concept of epigenetics. Through epigenetic transmission, we inherit the experiences of our biological familial ancestors. Sometimes aspects of those experiences are revealed in dreams, and even nightmares (Kellermann, 2013). Altogether, this information reflects how our dreaming selves are intertwined with those whom we share this Earth, ancestors of the past, and also something intangible, much larger, such as the Great Mystery.

To dream with our relations goes beyond dreaming with a lover, spouse, or any intimate human relationship in general. We, as humans, are related to everything, such as basic cellular structures, fungi, water, fire and electricity (as in lightning from the sky), for example. If we have fallen for the false belief that human beings are separate, superior and above all other species, then we are in big trouble because without balance there are consequences.

I recall seeing a meme on a social media platform depicting playing cards set up in a way where they were stacked on top of each other forming a pyramid, similar to a "house of cards," like the ones children make. In this "house of cards" formation, the bottom base layer requires the greatest amount of playing cards, while fewer are needed for each ascending layer. Even fewer playing cards are needed toward the top. When complete and fully constructed, the "house of cards" holds the shape of a pyramid. You may have made one just for fun. Of course, with a setup like this, a light breeze could easily dismantle the playing-card pyramid. In that social media meme's imagery, there at the very top was a human figure standing erect, unaware of what made up the foundation on which he stood (and lived). Every level below this delicately constructed "house of cards" pyramid housed other beings such as minerals, fungi, small plants and seeds, large trees, every kind of animal, the natural elements, and anything essential to human survival. The man standing at the top may or may not have been aware of the life "below" him, or how by removing one element below would surely lead to the destruction of the "house of cards." This represents life, except when it comes to sustaining life on our planet, there is no room for play—every layer matters and is essential for survival of all other layers. Those who have lost their Indigenous mind have forgotten something necessary for everyone's survival. That is, everything is interconnected.

In 2022, Eduardo Duran, PhD, taught attendees in one of IASD's Dream Study Groups about how, when it comes to dreams especially, an Indigenous worldview is different from a Western one. He explained that "everything is the dream. Creator and creation is the dream. Dream originates in the void, the emptiness, the nothing. Dream moves from the black world through the realms until it reaches us in the plant world (ego world). Along the way, ego distorts it ... by the time the dream reaches us, it has been distorted." Duran also noted how Westerners often say, "I had a dream," yet this makes no sense in Indigenous cosmology, where we are part of the Creator's dream. Hence, the dream has us. Duran said, "I am just part of the Creator's dream that continues to dream itself endlessly." In the dream that is dreaming us right now, we agreed way back when, in "dreamtime, before the void, to do this ... today." Duran added, "There's a compression space-time that happens in dreams." An example of this is when we experience a prophetic dream, one where we see what will soon unfold in the future. The "black world dreamtime" emerges out of the void, "where Nothing begins to take shape and form"—elements and all we know comes from that place, he said.

Extending this concept, Waters (2022) explains how "for some tribal peoples, there is a conception of the 'void' or 'black-ness,' but those realities are not exactly 'nothing'; instead, they are better thought of as primordial, formless material" (p. 262). Our human

143

egos distort the energy unfolding and so, we see what can happen ... that is, what we have here today.

By working with dreams in a deep way, giving thanks, building relationship with "The Dreaming" or dreamtime (a very alive, conscious realm), this development can lead you to a place of no return, no turning back. Considering that dreams require action, recall all the ways you can say thank you and bring a gift (aka offering) to the dreamtime, and ways by which you can honor each dream given to you through an appropriate act. By doing this consciously, that is, consciously giving something back, you don't set yourself up for something being taken ... for unconsciously offering yourself. We can offer a prayer from the heart center. Duran shared this sentiment: "At the center of the cardinal points is the Axis Mundi. It can be anywhere, like your heart. Your heart is at that center of the cardinal points." A balanced, harmonious relationship requires doing the ritual of consciously making an offering to the dreamtime. If you don't give the offering consciously, one will be taken unconsciously (nightmares, substance abuse, etc.), Duran claimed. You'll pay the debt to make balance and harmony. Always give a conscious offering (tobacco upon the earth, etc.). Why should it be any other way? Duran reminds us, "In order to change something completely, you need to die and be reborn. There's no other way. That's the natural law."

We can die in dream, through a shamanic journey, Duran explained, and even through the process of psychotherapy. And, of course, then there's the other way to die ... leaving the living in grief. And by entering those states of consciousness in an intentional way, we can do work there to restore balance, such as recovering lost parts of ourselves.

In my lucid dream where I asked the dream to show me what I needed to do to heal.... I was shown a reflection of myself meditating and then thrown into the black void. Basically, I needed to go back to the beginning where everything originates in order to restore the balance.

We are nature herself. Nothing more, nothing less. So naturally, when we harm the Earth, we harm ourselves. Equally, when we harm ourselves, we harm the Earth.

When operating from an individualistic, colonial mentality we lose touch with who we are and what we must thank for our everyday survival. It's a kind of soul loss. With that comes a disregard for the land, the abundance of life seen in Earth's creatures, and for our fellow human beings. No matter who we are or where we have come from, Duran and Duran (1985) remind us of an avenue for returning to wholeness and right relations: "Since the unconscious and the manifestations of the unconscious are accessible to both traditional and orthodox Western approaches, it is reasonable to ascertain that dreams can be a vehicle to help in the healing and integration of world cosmologies" (p. 45). Not all is lost as we can simply go inward and return to the integrated fullness that can come with attending to our whole self. We can train ourselves to live consciously, around the clock.

A third of our lives are spent sleeping, yet, for the most part, we have lost touch with our dreaming minds. The part of us that is capable of soul flight has been relegated to a non-existent role as if what we can gain from dreaming is somehow useless. As we lose touch with our dreaming selves, our dream life, we become out of touch with soul. This loss has created problems on such a grand scale.

Because lucid dreaming has become such a popular topic these days, you may already understand the term. But do you know how it came to be in the modern Western world? In 1913, Frederik van Eeden coined the term *lucid dream*. He was a Dutch psychiatrist who was published on the topic. He recorded over 350 of his own lucid dreams and even conducted experiments in them. This is how lucid dreaming became a recognized phenomenon among Western psychologists, psychiatrists, and academics. It was decades later, however, when in 1975, Dr. Keith Herne was able to provide evidence in his laboratory that lucid dreaming was a real state of being.

Consider the long-prevailing attitudes concerning Western lucid dreaming. Being conscious or lucid in a dream is practically sacred to some. Yet, Western mentality saw this extraordinary state as a means for enhancing individual abilities such as making one a better competitor in sports or other skills. Others claimed lucid dreaming to be a perfect state for experiencing instant gratification through dreams with supermodels and gorging on junk food. Now I am not saying that this is true for everyone, but in general, lucid dreaming has been viewed as an exciting avenue for personal development and personal gain among many Western lucid dreaming enthusiasts. It's not all self-centered though. Some inspiring and creative recent research has now proven how, through the use of technology, dreamers can transfer sounds and melodies (music) from the lucid dream state into this physical, waking reality (Raduga et al., 2023), thus delivering a sense of creative beauty to others. Incredible, isn't it?

Over the years, these advances have caught the attention of those seeking to make a profit. Today, big business is motivated to create dream devices for people to become lucid. Why? I believe it is so that employees can be productive and work while sleeping. Lucid dreaming is known to generate insights. But if a corporation is involved and so encouraging of their employees' abilities to lucid dream, I suspect the underlying motivation is for business purposes. By this I mean that making money for the corporate employer is likely what is driving this! It's like the dream arts and capitalism are becoming intertwined.

Lucidity or consciousness in dreaming can act as a spiritual doorway. Now, communities centering collectivism and affirming interconnection with all relations consider dreaming as a state to connect with the animals, land and ancestors of the place that sustains them, that gives them life. Because "lucid dreaming reveals high order cognitive skills during sleep" (Kahan & LaBerge, 1994, p. 257), community members with conscious dreaming abilities may take specific directed action for global healing on many levels. Additionally, they may act as healers for their community, for example, and work with the spirits of the land for maintaining harmony.

Another distinction between Western and Indigenous mentality as far as dreaming goes is related to how life is lived (see Colorado, 1995). Beyond what I noted above, another contrast between the two is how those living through their Indigenous Mind consider how the dream state can be used to make introductions with the land and all spirits involved, especially before physically traveling to a desired destination, as well as ask permission to take from the land.

Dreaming is deeply woven into our social lives, intrinsically. Evolutionary psychological insights suggest that culture is a direct outflow of dreaming. The promotion of sleep and dreaming can be included as part of social activism. Only in the overworked, under-slept population—those in a daily struggle to survive—does sleep become a privilege. Without proper sleep, we cannot dream well. Classism, racism, and other "isms" have negatively impacted this.

One impact from the harsh years of COVID-19 was that some claimed to recall dreams at a frequency and depth unlike ever before. Maybe you were one of the people to make such a report. What is your relationship with your dreams? How do you relate to them? If you have a history of tracking or taking note of your dreams, how do your dreams *grow* you? How have they grown you into who you are today?

Ancestral Dreaming

Ancestral dreaming is a subject that encompasses broad definitions and descriptions. Ancestors could be personal or collective, depending on whom you talk to. Some may consider their ancestors to be part of their bloodline, while others may consider that ancestors go beyond those limits. This is where all sentient beings are included, from animals to elements. My own definition of "ancestor" has been expanding, yet historically, I was focused on my dreams of deceased family members, known as visitation dreams. That was, until dreams of elements and animals got louder. Now I hold all and everything as an ancestor. This requires that I honor them.

I was first taught the art of embroidery as a little girl of about seven years old by my great-grandmother and my grandmother's older cousins from Italy. I practiced embroidery for many years then cast the practice aside for most of my young adulthood. During a guided waking dream-like experience led by Dr. Janet Piedilato (which she also calls imaginal journeying), I remembered and reconnected with this lost art. During the experience, I remained open to receive information I needed at that time and was shown old hands sticking in the way I once had as a child—the way my ancestors had taught me. Since then, I have returned to this practice, and since I enjoy other art forms such as painting and mixed media, I typically add a little cross-stitched X on every new piece as a way to remember and re-anchor myself to my past and my identity—not only to my great-grandmother who taught me, but to the mothers and grandmothers who taught her. This is just one example of building a modern-day bridge of ancestral remembrance through a practice in which all women and girls participated through time and place (from the United States where I was born back to the lands where they came from).

Across time and place, one's ancestors had strong connections with the land on which they spent their entire lives. It was the place that sustained them in numerous ways. This included all forms of life. Today, in Western societies at least, its people "suffer from a form of fragmentation due to a lack of contact with their own ancestry" (Bogzaran & Deslauriers, 2012, p. 137). Still, we know due to biological similarities that our ancestors did in fact dream; however, "how they understood dreams as possibly different than the reality of waking experience is a matter of speculation" (Bynum, 2021, p. 92). For contemporary Westerners who still recall their dreams, they might discover how following a dream that guided them to a specific place or encouraged engagement in a particular activity can reweave that once lost connection and re-anchor them to their ancestors.

Kimmerer (2013) stated, "Indigenous is a birthright word," and asked about how immigrants and their descendants can enter into "deep reciprocity that renews the world" since the long "soul-deep fusion with the land" is absent (p. 213). I believe we can dream our way back home, for starters. Everyone has an Indigenous ancestor, and they dreamed. It may be difficult to imagine having a deep connection with "the all and everything" because, as modern people, we can sometimes feel overloaded, even bombarded, with ringtones, screens, billboard advertisements, vehicles, electricity, alarm clocks, and so much more. The noise just doesn't stop, regardless of how easy living day-to-day has become. What seems so great, and convenient, comes with a cost. With our commodity mindset, we have paid for these distractions and conveniences with lack of quality, restorative sleep and the fruits of deeply knowing our full selves. Our European ancestors knew who they were and what they had been up to during the 24-hour cycle—that is, while their physical bodies both slumbered and moved about. Evidence exists that reflects how they were connected to spirit, other nonhumans, and the land in all states— dreaming and waking. They experienced the full picture that allowed them to make decisions with multiple data points, not just with one or two sensory organs.

Dreams can also connect past events with how the future will be influenced. There are many examples where dreams have been the environment for answers to come forth regarding locating the body of missing persons, for example among the Sámi. Obtaining this information and sharing it with worried or grieving family members can impact their future, especially when it comes to closure and making peace with tragedy and loss (Kramvig, 2015).

As humans, we come from water. As a primal element, water carries memory. When we dream with ancestors, we are not *just* talking about visitation dreams with deceased loved ones (a topic I touch on throughout this book), or using dream spaces to gain information, no matter how critical. We are talking about that *plus* dream visits with all our relations, that is, everything from which we are descendants.

With my sun sign in Pisces, I joke about my connection with water, even though I was born just a day over the cusp. Still, as a human descendant of water, I trust that element to show up in dreams to guide the way when I need it. Sometimes, water in my nocturnal dreams acts as a looking glass with treasures just under the surface. Other times it rises up in a huge tidal wave formation reflecting the spiritual essence behind it. In other ocean dreams, I skillfully surf the waves and survive being in her power while surrendering to the ocean—she is the boss. Other times, I drink life-giving water offering eternal youth. And at other times, water shows me how dirty it is as it runs through pipes and clogs important household structures. Dreaming with water reveals much of what I need to know when it comes to how I must proceed at any given time, always for balance, which is to my benefit. I trust water and respect that element deeply (as I do all others). If you like, return to the dreams in the previous chapter. Notice the elemental forces represented there.

Kramvig (2015) explains, "Dreaming can be seen as the part in between. In Sámi the concept of *adjagas* relates to this moment of being and not being awake at the same time. It is a tender moment and still full of potential" (p. 190). Connection with nature, the land (Sápmi territory in this case), spirits, and ancestors are common in such a space, in such Indigenous knowledge systems. Dreaming is an Indigenous spiritual practice. How have elements shown up in your dreams or visions, as teachers, such as water, fire, or air, for example?

When I posed this question to a colleague, who goes by Diya, she spoke about her relationship with the water element, but in particular, the waters of creation. Diya is a PhD candidate whose dissertation is based on ancestral dream knowledge.

In our conversation, we spoke about many aspects of water-nature, such as water being the source of all creation and how water holds memory, as well as water being an amplifier of energy. Diya connects with water in many ways, including through dance and storytelling. She explained how connecting with ancestral water sources enhances both personal growth and environmental protection. By connecting with nature, we foster a deeper relationship with ourselves ... after all, we are nature.

When I asked Diya about what she could tell me regarding waters of creation, she reported the following: "So, I can tell you about the seven mothers of creation, my understanding and my connection to them. Across cultures you would hear about the Seven Sisters: the Greeks, the Aboriginal Australian stories, even within the Pacific Island stories. That's mostly connected to the Pleiades. But for me, it was revealed and taught through dreams, part of those dreams was through memories (i.e., remembering what was it like to first come into being). I remember emerging from the primordial waters. It was in that moment of emergence, when I felt the separation between myself as a separate being, yet still connected, and supported on the water. In one of these dreams, I was in San Luis Obispo, California, but far from the coast. I was right in the city, in the flow, and in the dream, I could hear the ocean waves crashing and I knew, I even remember saying to myself, the beach is far away, so what's going on here."

Diya described the dreamscape: "The entire space is dark, some twinkling lights, I thought, 'Oh, that must be the stars,' and then feeling myself on the surface of the water. I had the realization that I was just brought into being and feeling that emergence. I could feel female forms that were formless supporting my emergence from the water. So, my understanding of water as the source of creation for all existence comes from those dreaming experiences like this one."

Diya recalled a series of dreams over a span of 20 years of the waters showing itself. She said, "If you wish to understand water, you have to understand movement. In order to move water, you have to understand movement. In order to move water, you are being brought back to the beginning which is up in the cosmos. The very thing that creates the element that we know as water will reveal itself: I am a consciousness that brings these elements together. So, for me the waters represent beginning and then there's another aspect with memory, or rather, water as a vessel for memory. We see that very prominently in pregnancy, especially within the womb. The womb is the container. Within that container, you have the amniotic sac, where the memory stored in the mother's body goes to work. Then what happens when we're born ... we emerge. Birth equals emergence. It also equals the transmission of memory, and the transmission of knowledge." I jumped in: "Yeah, and I see this image of being fully created in the waters of the womb come in literally, emerging out of water from the literal place."

Diya continued: "Water is also amplifier. It's a really good amplifier for all types of energy. There have been a couple of dreams where past sacred dancers would be teaching some of us students in the dreams, but their feet are in water. As they're doing the dance, the memory of the dance is not only being transmitted to us, but its effectiveness is amplified by the water that they're standing in.

Through this action the effect of the dance will affect the environment. That is also the teaching within the dream—we are transmitting this memory to you through the medium water but also when you do the dance and your feet are in water, you are amplifying that energy."

Diya added, "For example, it would be a marvelous accomplishment if I can master how to stand on the wet sand at a beach without sinking...." Laughing, she continued: "How do you master the skill of not sinking? I don't know. But maybe if I have a bamboo platform that would be stable in the sand so that each time the water comes and I'm doing the dance, it's taking that energy back out. It reverberates outwards in a cyclical motion."

I clarified, "So you take the movements, or dance (what's shown to you) through the dream and then do it with feet in water in a literal way, in the physical waking reality, as a way to give it back to transmit it, to communicate it, outward."

Diya agreed: "Yes. That's the part that ties back into the request from the Mother of the Waters for my dissertation. How do I do that? How do I find the space at the shore where I can actually practice that? Where can I find and train students to actually do that, to show the ocean that, yes, we are really connecting to you? This is how we're giving our thanks to you. We are pulling from our awareness of connection to the cosmos because that is also how you were brought into being. You wouldn't be here without all of the elements that came together. That's something I'm still hoping manifests itself in some way before my dissertation is over, but to be able to communicate that to people.... Wouldn't that be a wonderful goal to work towards? You know, for a little girl to want to become a sacred dancer for the water. For any of this to unfold, I have to make sure I'm connected to my body, I'm respecting my body, and also understand that in giving prayers to the water, the water understands that I respect it, and have this connection to it. But I also want it to carry this message that it's a relational reciprocity working together to ensure that all is well, all will be well, that we're working together to make sure that that balance is maintained."

"It's quite the opposite of an extractive relationship where we are just taking water, or rather using water for our benefit, and really not even having much awareness that we are from water or even made up of water," I added. "What you are speaking about is the opposite of taking, or an extractive one-way transactional relationship. Actually, it's not even a relationship when you do it like that."

Diya reflected: "What I love about the Pacific Islands is that they remind me of the origin stories of creation, such as from the Iao Valley where you have this expanse of water, and then the mound emerges from creation. It's also like a lotus flower on the water, as the first born. Or how when a lotus flower resting on the water does open, a deity emerges from that opening. One of the stories that was shared in the ancestral dreams shared this message, 'you will find me in the waters of creation, and the fruit I brought forth was the sun.' If we look at it from a cosmic perspective, the sea of stars, the stellar nursery, the gases that come together, churn together, from that what's born is light. It's the same within the watery creation stories where you have the first emergence of land or illumination for the rest of creation to happen. So, with the Pacific Islands and the tectonic plates beneath it, you've got the earth, you've got the fire, magma. With all of that churning happening beneath the water, you have the potential for the 'new' to emerge.... There's this concept in Buddhist thought called *dependent origination* which basically explains there are causes and events that came together for something to be or come into being. You see that with underwater volcanoes. New land is being created and emerging; however, there are events and elements that come together for that to happen. I just think being in a location on the planet where creation constantly comes to pass is a really good real-world example with nature that parallels a lot of the creation stories. So why can't people take inspiration from that as well? In some of these creation stories the emergence of the first lands, the causes and conditions of that is where things were pristine and in balance. So how do you get back to balance? You've got to get back to the elements of creation at the beginning of time. And if you're in a space where it's constantly happening, how do you inspire yourself to be parallel to that, to work with that?"

Considering everything that was shared, Diya further reflected on her understanding of her relationship to water: "With water, it's always from a creation perspective. That helps me to constantly remember to go inward first, because there's water within myself. In thinking about how the waters create, it is always from within the waters—they're at the top. So going back into myself, or communicating with water from within myself, that is where creativity happens, where guidance can happen. It's on the inside, because that's how creation happens, from the inside out. There are also stories where there's an external influence that helps to jumpstart the internal and that's not to say that's wrong. It's just another act of creation, but for me, my relationship to water connects back to those past life memories of emerging from the water. So, it's a container of emergence, of support, of creation."

I considered how "when we have that experience of our relationship with the water, I imagine people would be more moved to protect it, to see it as a relative, which of course will have a natural consequence of protecting land and everything related to it. I'm also thinking about external and internal factors. As humans we really need to seriously consider the kind of positive changes we must make for the survival of our species, this place we call home, which is very watery. One way is to look within, to dream, and connect with those forces inside ourselves. We can have a relationship that inspires connection and doing the right thing."

Diya provided a way to begin the process of re-establishing connection. She instructed:

"Get a sheet of paper, a pencil and a clear glass. Pour some water in the glass. Now really look at the water. Consider what it is you are staring at. Can you see that as an ancestor?

Define water. Define ancestor. Look at the etymology of those words—the concept of them. Ask yourself, what are your ancestral lineages? Look at the modern way of how we relate to water, and then look at the old ways of how they (your ancestors) connected to water. Consider these side by side, how are they different? How are they similar?"

I exclaimed, "This practice can bring us to seeing water as much more than a commodity!"

Diya expanded on her thinking: "Exactly. Now when I said connected, it's important to ask, how are you connected, in the old ways of connecting, that is. We come to realize that we once had a deeper relationship to water. So really explore that. Remember, all life starts to grow in the womb, which is a vessel of water. We could once breathe underwater, right? Let's look at ourselves. What are you going to find in your own water? Can you survive without it? No, not really. Do you think it would benefit you to learn more about your ancestors' connection to it? And how would that knowledge benefit you now in developing a connection to it so that when things start to happen, where there's scarcity, will that inspire you more to fight for it? Would you fight for it as you would for your siblings or other family members? Is that something you could extend to an element that you need? It's not like you don't need it. Have the courage and curiosity to enter the space to explore the differences of relation and connection. Because that's what we are. Really bring in that awareness to how reliant you are on the connections you have to it. It's already there. It's just not in your awareness. Again, look into how people in the past have connected to it. There are people today that see it clearly as an ancestor. Are you willing to open yourself up ... even though it's already a part of you?"

I reflected on how a lot of people struggle with this because so many of us are already fragmented: "Those of us living in this fast-paced, modern-day society are metaphorically cut off at the head. So, then we struggle with this idea that we're related to anything. There's this block of being not related to anything, unless it's a sibling or parent or child. Even ideas that come forth about being related to non-human anything, whether it's land, the animals in their house even, or the house plants that they care for seems outlandish. So many things are just othered. Then with some type of basic established connection, through making attempts, it is interesting to see how that is fostered through dreams. Will dreams that connect us with these elements and bring with it a real, felt experience manifest or show up? Maybe they will, maybe they won't."

Diya said, "Some say, 'Well, I don't remember my dreams,' and that's part of it, but do you want to? Is there a mental block there?

Have you decided to establish that type of connection with yourself? It's not just, 'Oh, I don't remember my dreams, it's not going to work.' It's talking about a deeper relationship to yourself. So how is your relationship to yourself anyway?"

I added, "Right. As humans, we dream every night and we are anywhere between 50 to 75 percent water throughout our lifespan."

Diya exclaimed: "So there you have it! It begins with awareness and understanding that when it comes to relationship there's a connection there and it's reciprocal. It's balance in both ways. There are seven principles that I was taught in my dreams and four of them are especially wonderful. One being relational reciprocity. Reciprocity is relational. It's not even if you do this, I will do this. It's literally our relationship already equates to reciprocity. It's already there, it's already inherited. And then there's the integrity. Are you honoring the integrity of that relational reciprocity? There's the sacredness of spirituality. Spirituality is sacred, right? Life is sacred. Life is spiritual, all of that. It's not one or the other. It's both."

I noted how "when this starts to grow in a person, you're going see it through dreams and hopefully that inspires people to act to care for the Earth."

Diya shared that "by the time that that takes root and it's growing and you're nourishing it, what you are experiencing in here"—she pointed to the heart region—"you're going to project outward into the world. That's the bottom line. With what you're experiencing in your heart, you're going to project onto the world in the ways that you're growing, or in the ways that you're experiencing. Of course, what you're seeing through your experience doesn't necessarily mean that's exactly what's happening. What you assume to be versus what is isn't always going to be the same. It's helpful to keep in mind that you are going through this beautiful experience, and you want to see it in the world around you. But you have to be mindful that even though you want to see that, there are things happening that are not going to be in alignment. You'll see the world as it truly is, and then ask yourself, 'How do I still protect what I'm experiencing that is sacred, while at the same time, seeing that in what's happening in the world the sacred is not being honored?'"

Ecological Dreaming

From the perspective of ecopsychology, humans exist as part of an expansive nexus to include everything in our world—from sea to sky. We, as humans, exist with it all and are much more interdependent than it appears in today's split-off contemporary Western society. What we need to live well is present in the knowledge held within the land. How do we affect nature and what are her effects on us? Sadly, through rampant unconscious industrial processes, we have lost our clear vision of our place on the web of interconnection; relations with ecology on a broad level are fragmented. Bogzaran & Deslauriers (2012) wrote about how "the Indigenous perspective, with its spiritual and participatory orientation to place and all its living inhabitants, has historically been at odds with the overly rational aspects of science" (p. 140), and now science is screaming loud and clear that, when it comes to our environment and the survival of all living creatures (humans included), we are in big trouble. As awareness of our interconnectedness continues to rise, albeit at a snail's pace, we come to face today's ecological crises.

If you look at the Institute of Noetic Sciences (IONS) home page, noetic.org, you will learn that one astronaut's experience led to this group's creation. On the IONS homepage it reads: "Inspired by a profound experience of personal discovery, Apollo 14 astronaut Dr. Edgar Mitchell created IONS in 1973 to explore the interplay between scientific knowledge and inner knowing. Today, we have the world's largest team of multidisciplinary scientists conducting research on frontier topics in consciousness and its impact in our lives." For this reason, I have always had an appreciation for the work conducted through IONS. The IONS 19th international conference was held from May 30 through June 2, 2024. Among the presenters were those whose work centers on environmentalism.

Pachamama Alliance co-founder Lynne Twist and University of California, Davis, professor Philippe Goldin, PhD, co-led a session titled "The Environmental Crisis and Humanity's Evolutionary Leap." They discussed the crisis in our climate as well as our consciousness, considering how these crises might be unfolding to push us toward the next stage of evolution. After all, we must shift, and quickly; otherwise, without acting on solutions for climate justice, we are doomed.

Lynne described a transformative experience, visions over a period of time just prior to the creation of Pachamama Alliance. From her years of work with those indigenous to the Amazon rainforest, Lynne and her community strive toward generating a critical mass of conscious commitment in order to birth a positive future for the next generation. She encourages people to bridge gaps in relationships with the world's people who have been so negatively impacted by industrialized nations' mindless ways. For example, our way of life in the United States negatively impacts the survival of rainforests and jungles. The most pristine ecospheres, such as the Amazon rainforest, house trees that the entire planet needs standing so that we all have clean air to breathe.

Considering how our liberation is bound to the liberation of others, even those quite geographically distant, what action steps need to happen? As we become liberated from the "over-consumption nightmare," so too are Indigenous people liberated in that their home is not being destroyed by outsiders, foreigners, who take their resources and pollute their natural homes, such as by way of deforestation and poisoning natural waterways.

In that session, Philippe Goldin, PhD, spoke about climate anxiety moving through the minds and hearts of people—young people especially. The negative side is that depressive and anxious symptoms have grown. The positive aspect of climate anxiety is that it appears to lead to engagement and activity for positive climate action. Dr. Goldin and colleagues created a course called "Climate Resilience and Activism." Students learn that they are not alone and can connect with other active peers to do the work toward positive change. University professors across the UC system are considering how they can implement a "Climate 101" course for all students to provide literacy on climate science and climate resilience. When I heard this, I felt a surge of excitement and deep appreciation for those members of the older generation who deeply care about environmental stewardship so that the Earth they leave behind will be inhabitable for generations to come.

Lynne shared her thoughts on the concept of "pro-activism," rather than simply activism. She asks, "What do you stand for?" not "What are you scared of?" For her, this means staying centered on the vision for the world and doing the work to "hospice" the unsustainable structures and systems as they die. Consider the fossil fuel industry. She acknowledged the benefit of what we've gotten out of that industry. Instead of being angry at that industry, be grateful for the gifts it gave us while hospicing the natural death of that unsustainable system. Being proactive means we midwife the new way, as opposed to using our activist efforts toward anger and going against. This distinction in consciousness allows love to grow and spread as activists, or rather pro-activists, as we drive the pro-climate agenda forward.

Lynne reflected a very touching level of empathy for the young people now inheriting this planet. She reminded us that since we created the climate crisis, we can reverse it. Hopelessness and apathy do us no good. It's time to stand up, collaborate, speak out, demand change in the name of love for the future.

Philippe brought forth questions and exercises coming out of Indigenous-based realities. What is it like to sit by or between a rock and a tree and listen to them speaking, being, emoting? I thought about how people can also engage with minerals and plants in lucid dreams and out-of-body experiences so to learn about those realities and ways of existing in the world. In the waking state, we can write letters. Philippe suggested writing a letter to the Earth. He also suggested writing to the next generation. Will you take the time to do so? If you did, what did you get out of it? How did it change you?

The film *He Kau Heahea A Hi'iaka: A Call to Restoration* opened my eyes to climate change impacts from the perspective of Native Hawaiians. *He Kau Heahea A Hi'iaka* opens with an origin story of Hawaii, showing how the gods joined together to bring forth life here. At the beginning of the film we are asked, "How did we get here?" in reference to the destruction across the planet, as we see a pregnant woman expressing a look of concern, rightfully for the future of her child-to-be. Included in *He Kau Heahea A Hi'iaka* are alarming statistics: half of the coral in the Great Barrier Reef has died; the Great Pacific Garbage Patch contains more than 1.8 trillion pieces of plastic; coastal cities and towns are threatened by rising water levels—parts of the Marshall Islands may be underwater by 2035.

Then, another voice: "Let me help you remember." This poetic, yet powerful film features goddess *Hi'iaka* returning to plant seeds for change. As the film concludes, we are asked, "Now do you remember?"

Inspired toward action, we are reminded that it takes a community to rise up for change. The pregnant woman is offered guidance: "One single voice is not enough. We must unite, steadfast in the wisdom of our ancestors combined with the science of this era." The future generations are watching....

Today's children are very concerned with what's at stake, as we've seen from ecology-targeted demonstrations and protests led by youth across the globe. When I asked children in my own extended family about whether we faced big problems currently unfolding on planet Earth, they had some things to share. Here was our dialogue:

"What are some of the problems you think we have right now on planet Earth? It can be small things, big things. It can be about interpersonal things like between people; it can be about the land ... anything."

Immediately, the 13-year-old named the issue of "climate change," and the 10-year-old listed problems of accumulating "trash and pollution."

When I asked to hear more about what climate change means and what it does, the 13-year-old spoke up about "melting icebergs" and how the "water levels are rising really quickly." To challenge him, I asked him why this was a problem: "What's so bad about water flooding in on the land?"

He said, "If the water level keeps rising, it will go up and up and run into cities and stuff. It will keep overflowing over time until you can't live there anymore ... flooding houses and stuff. I mean, you can't, like, breathe underwater."

Since the 10-year-old brought up pollution, I asked him, "What does polluting mean to you? Is pollution something that you have a problem with?" He exclaimed, "Well, it makes the world worse! There are these chemicals in the air around the world and if you keep pollution going, well...." His face said the rest.

I looked at them both and asked, "Do you want to live in a world that's polluted?" Together they stated a loud "no," and then the youngest added how he does not want a world with toxicity, particularly "toxic" air. I pushed back, asking why that would be problematic. "It would make it hard to breathe," he explained. "You could die."

I prodded a little more, albeit gently, on the "trash" he named earlier in the conversation. "Littering is a problem, for sure," he claimed, while also sharing with me how he was bothered by watching people litter in his town and not take responsibility for their actions.

When the older child chimed in, he took it a step further to include pollution coming from factories—ones that allow toxic gases to flow into the air he and his friends have no choice but to inhale.

For me, the saddest part was when he linked these current problems on our planet with increased personal stress.

Reflecting empathy as best I could, I asked, "Is there anything you'd like to see done differently then, or done better, when it comes to the Earth?" (After all, they both talked about pollution and climate change, straightaway.) As children, naturally they did not have all the solutions to best protect our planet, and they shouldn't have to. They did agree, however, that world leaders, like "the president," should make decisions that reflect great care for the Earth, as they understood how such decisions would protect them and their lives. Near the end of our conversation, the older child made a final plea directed toward today's world leaders: "Make the Earth in a way so I'm not stressed."

If compassion and care live in our hearts, we must take these pleas seriously and act. I have seen the stress bleed out of my nephews as they live in an area where on some days they must remain indoors due to lack of clean outdoor air. While I've sat on the sidelines as entire communities in my beloved home state of California burned to the ground over just the past handful of years, then relocated to Maui to find the same taking place, many questions have arisen. In response, I conduct searches so I can read more about ecological needs alongside disasters (all caused by human neglect and misappropriation of some kind) across the globe. On the other side of the world from where I was born, destruction of ecology is also rampant. Ngāti Kahungunu tribal member Rhys Jones is a public health physician and associate professor in Māori health. Jones (2023) wrote about the harsh and deadly impact of storms and floods that year with the corresponding social, economic, health and environmental consequences. Settler colonialism exacerbates the impact with examples "in the intersection of market driven livestock farming and exotic plantation land use with severe weather events on the east coast of Te Ika-a-Māui" (Jones, 2023, p. 2202). Jones explains that loss of soil and erosion of land result from irresponsible practices—logging, land clearing for animal agriculture, draining natural wetlands—that increase sediment and debris in coastal environments including lakes and rivers. The risks include the resulting devastation we've seen from flooding (Jones, 2023). We need responsible leadership with decision-making for long-term sustainability. At the same time, everyday people can demand action. If we have not been touched directly, the problem can seem distant. This is misguided, as scientists have told us time and time again how we are at the tipping point.

Jones (2023) proposes addressing the climate crisis directly, through an Indigenous lens, by calling for the rebuilding of environmental relations and the dismantling of systems built on exploitation instead of taking the convenient route, which would still center and support exploitation through the disguised demands of the largest, most powerful corporations across the globe. Jones (2023) calls for the non–Indigenous "to remember their own ancestral 'original instructions' and revitalise their own ancient ways of knowing, being, and relating to Mother Earth and all her inhabitants before patriarchal colonial capitalism took hold" (p. 2202). When looking towards solutions to the crisis we are in, we are unlikely to find them on the surface, for the problem at hand is much too deep. The societal transformation cannot be a shallow one, if it is to be effective (Jones, 2023).

Nalini Chhetri is a clinical professor at Arizona State University's School for the Future of Innovation in Society and School of Sustainability. With regards to climate change, she said, "Anthropogenic climate change and inequalities can harm us, certainly. But we—humanity—created them both, and we have the power and wherewithal to address them and to bring us back from the brink" (Terrill, 2024). She is absolutely correct. We grew this problem, so we can "ungrow" it.

So, how can we live in a more responsible, balanced way? To take these things seriously, direct experience can help. This is where Dreaming comes in. Dreaming for the health of the land and its inhabitants is commonplace among Indigenous peoples. For those of us, like myself, whose familial ancestors migrated to the United States a few generations ago, we can investigate our distant past, our imaginative genealogy to learn how our own ancestors connected with the Earth and how they had a relationship with the dreamtime. A fairly well-known example is rooted in Asklepion Dream temples and practices of ancient Greece. First, dreams can reveal sickness (and healing) of something larger than an individual. Dreams can reflect illness and wellness of community and ecosphere as well. In a conscious dream, we can feel the Earth's presence. We can ask her directly what she needs at any given time. The all-encompassing impact of climate change, or global warming, is shown in dreams. Furthermore, individuals, groups, and communities can participate in a kind of dreaming that identifies larger world issues, re-establishes relationship and affinity with the Earth, and even raises social consciousness. The world and everything in it are experienced as *alive*, and that which sustains us, as well as all life, is no longer a lifeless object for extraction and profit. Additionally, dreamers engage in a holistic process of correcting imbalances and embodying natural rhythms.

Dreaming for and with the Earth is more common than many know. There are groups and publications in existence all focusing on such a task. Jaenke (2020) has written about her own earth dreams and from those experiences has come to understand how "dreams carry the wisdom of the natural mind, capable of restoring humanity's psychic kinship with the earth" (p. 14). She also notes, "Considering the earth-human relationship through the lens of dreams provides an approach to the global ecological crisis rooted in human subjectivity and evolutionary psychology" (Jaenke, 2020, p. 14). We need direct experiences of inter-relationship and connection with our planetary home because it is sadly apparent how basic awareness and education alone do not incite change ... at least not to the level needed to stop what looks like will soon be human extinction. From her own experiences and research, Jaenke (2020) claims that "earth dreams illustrate the process of restoring humans to a participatory relationship with the earth" (p. 14).

One of several groups that exist in order to dream together for environmental and global healing is 350 Dreamers. Tzivia Gover created this group in 2009 as a response to another environmental group's call to action. The group began with just a handful of members and since that time it has grown. Currently there are over a thousand participating in the 350 Dreamers Facebook group for global healing. How does it work? This worldwide network chooses a night for intentional group dreams. On the chosen night, dreamers focus their dream intention on helping the environment to heal. In addition, these group members look to the dream to learn about their role as activists and advocates for planet Earth. Tzivia told me how "one woman in Paris stopped using her car. Others were directed by the dream to heal themselves. Some dreamers learn what might be holding them back from engaging more in the environment. While other dreamers feel into the earth's voice and channel her messages."

In the morning, group members post their dreams and reflections about their dreaming process. The group members are also free to comment on each other's dreams and note the patterns among individual dreams, as well as what the collective dream is reflecting. These dreamers have built a strong community dedicated to expanding their abilities to imagine environmental balance and healing. They recognize that their waking state day-to-day actions matter as well as their dream state activity—dreaming consciousness is connected with waking dreams for a healthy, healed environment and world.

Tzivia's website, Third House Moon, lists the group's values, including a belief in the power of dreams, a belief in the beauty of community and communal action, and a commitment to healing on all levels from personal to planetary. Tzivia didn't know what she believed about the power of group dreaming and what if any impact there might be when she started the group; however, through the process she came to learn how dreaming with a group for global healing helps us to realize how we are not alone and to be able to face something, something too painful to look at, with presence and optimism.

We must tell new stories that reflect the peace and equity we desire. We can dream up these stories. In her book *Dreaming on the Page*, Gover (2023) wrote, "Dreams and storytelling are inherent to all people all over the world, to people of all language groups and all ethnic, racial, and religious groups. They come equally to people no matter what their economic or educational background" (p. 228). Nothing is required for us to dream, except for our presence. Gover (2023) notes how "writing and dreamwork are forms of inner work that help us activate healthier relationships within ourselves, our close circle of family, friends, colleagues, and community. These practices can make us more thoughtful, responsive (instead of reactive) activists as well" (p. 221). We can practice in solitude or in community, without ever having to leave our home (if we don't want to). She said, "I believe that personal growth is essential for our happiness and inner harmony—and that's very important. But the ultimate purpose of healing and becoming whole is to be able to be a more emotionally and consciously skillful member of the whole ... and to serve the greater good. ...these days we're primed to look out for #1, and we don't generally prioritize the big picture or the larger community." We agree that every person, every family, every community makes a difference. How will you share a new story for the world's healing?

With the passing of the harvest moon and the approaching autumnal equinox on my mind, I reflected on the development and direction of, what was at that time, this manuscript. What more could my dreams show me about community and service? How could they continue to guide me as we enter the coming new season? By chance, I happened to check Tzivia's 350 Dreamers page one evening. I saw the current posting that read, "Tonight is our group dream for global healing!" A couple of hours later I got in bed recalling how I would like to participate. Given the group's purpose, I chose to incubate a healing dream for the Earth. I also hoped for strong dream recall the next morning.

In response to that call for global healing, I awoke on Saturday, September 21, 2024, with a memorable dream in the forefront of my mind:

> I'm with an acquaintance, Enrique (a pseudonym), who is a Mexican artist and healer residing in California. We are at someone's house—it's one I do not recognize—but I believe it may belong to one of his friends. The weather is very pleasant and calm—no humidity.. It's sunny and feels like springtime. I'm wearing light layers as the gentle breezes are warm in temperature, rather than cold. We are speaking about someone we know and a change ... a death perhaps, or related topics. Then, I have somewhere I need to go, so I change clothes, but before I leave I bump into two faraway friends I've known for a long time. We are all outside now. These friends are burning some plants in ceremony. This grabs my attention, yet I know I need to get going and depart soon. I follow Enrique around a corner and he tells me to look out because there are a lot of bees buzzing about. I see the bees and lower my head, then sit down on the grass to look at the bees. I want to be with them in a conscious way. In admiration, I lie down to observe the 12 or so bees, as I realize there is nothing to be afraid of. I trust I won't get stung. As I admire the group of bees around me, appreciating the important role they play in human and animal survival, two children appear. They could have been anywhere from six to eight years old. The younger one is male with light brown skin, who I sense is from Asia, Pacific Islands, or possibly Latin America, while the older child is female with fair skin, long blond hair and an accent which I guess is an Australian one. I feel that we are together for the purpose of healing yet realize I do not have my typical child therapy tools and materials. What is it that I am supposed to be doing, I wonder. But quickly I know I can simply lay down with them and cuddle as a form of nurture. I don't need to be in my professional

166

role. After a few moments of that, I place my hands on the boy's chest and back, resting on each side of his heart, breathing love into that space; visualizing love moving through us, and all around us under the warm sun. Love is flowing between us all.

As I feel myself waking up in my bed, I know that that is what I am supposed to be doing. With appreciation for the beauty of this dream—this gift—I recognize the interconnection among all beings and how love is primordial.

There's been a lot discussed so far. Some of the topics might bring up worries or leave us feeling overwhelmed. When we have those days where we feel these things, or maybe even feel lost or disconnected, we can touch our divine nature through dreams, prayer, and silent stillness. An expert in the history and theology of spiritualities, Matthew Fox quotes Hawaiian elder Nana Veary in his 2018 book *Naming the Unnamable*: "Silence means no repetitions, no affirmations, no denials, only a conscious acknowledgement of God's allness. In the silence, one is beyond words and thoughts" (p. 138). This pure stillness by which we can come to know our true essence, what some call God, is at the heart of popular practices today, such as yoga nidra, as well as other forms of meditation, such as mindfulness. When I have prayed or meditated in a dream, I've found myself in an expansive black void—completely silent, completely still. Like an experience of deep love, I know all is well.

Deepak Chopra has said that the purpose of meditation is to know reality, and that God is the deeper reality. We can pay attention to the names and images appearing in our dreams, according to Fox (2018), as a way to know God, Source, the Divine. This *reality* is behind all existence, sustaining all that is. Your life and mine, as well as all creation. When we come to realize, and importantly, directly experience who we truly are and how everything is interconnected, there is no way we can turn our back on the health of this planet and its inhabitants if we are to call ourselves sane. It doesn't matter whether one leans more toward atheism, science and technology, or religious doctrinal beliefs, or even nature-communing direct experiences, or any combination of those, because everyone dreams and it is through dreams by which we enter the source of creation.

Dreaming is one way by which we can support a new vision for a positive climate future, thus benefiting us all. With that inspired vision, we are compelled to take action. If life is one great, never-ending ceremony, how will we show up in it?

7

JOURNEYS INTO
THE DREAM ARTS

Love is the bridge between you and everything.—Rumi

I love to talk to people about *the dream arts*, which in my view encompasses all of the phenomena mentioned in this book. Through those special states of consciousness, we can access the energies of the Earth and ancestral connections, this opening to the memory of our original instructions.

At this time in history, with access to geographical movement much more extensive than our ancestors, many people live in places that their great-great-grandparents likely never even heard of, let alone traveled to. Such modern capabilities, like rapid air travel, place us willingly scattered across the globe. While this is great for a variety of opportunities, the drawbacks are a loss of connection to the traditional place of origin. So many of us have voluntarily exiled ourselves. Of course, historical factors such as fleeing war, dictatorships, famine, and poverty also fill in the back story.

Remembering how dreams and visions come in service of our development and growth, we can work with these and related states so that we may connect to the new territories on which we might be residing. I've lived in a handful of different nations, yet only one of those is connected to my human ancestry of this lifetime. Through the dream arts, I am more able to reorient and reconnect with my inner compass, my soul compass if you will. As people of European ancestry, it can be a challenge to remember our traditional ways, as they were swept away by kings and empires, or buried (literally) by the church. Yet the ancient stones remain underground, the sacred wells still flow underneath chapels built on top of them, and the magic inside burial mounds remains under unkept grasses and overgrown vegetation. The truth remains intact in the Earth herself, and through the dream arts we can discover so very much.

Celtic peoples of the past described locations where the veil between this world (the world of form, ego, density, matter) and the other world (the world of spirit) is thin or porous. These spaces were referred to as *thin places*. Thin places are locations of a mystical quality, sacred spaces that may provide intense encounters with the numinous, the divine, with Creator, God or Great Spirit (among other names). When we consciously alter our state of consciousness (with deep breathing, prayer, meditation, for example) while holding the intention of contacting Spirit, might any location then become a thin place? *Ke Akua* is infused in everything. Everywhere, anywhere is a thin place.

Today, using altered states of consciousness for beneficial purposes of the Earth as well as for self-empowerment is gaining attention and popularity, as noted throughout this book. This is good news because dream, vision, deep meditation, and liminal states of consciousness can direct us, guide us, show us how to live, how to show up in life! Many are looking toward the past, toward their ancestral ways of doing such work to heal the planet, animals, and themselves.

The spiritual journeys we embark upon go by various names, as noted earlier. Regardless of how we label them, we can easily access them, then return to an ordinary state of consciousness with information that can be used for creating more harmony, community or individual assistance, or healing. The dream arts embody much more than altering consciousness through sleep. We can also use our breath, vocal toning, chanting, mantras and song, and even through sonic driving, as well as rhythmic movement (anywhere from swaying to dance). These methods are nothing new. Specific methods come down to specific periods of time—contemporary or ancient times—as well as geographic location, community, and simply what was or is available.

It is important to recognize that many of the experiences

described here, and throughout this entire book, are *normal* within the human condition. They are typical, or normal states of being, from the lens of Indigenous Mind, as I am reminded by Dr. Apela Colorado. Only Western perspectives consider them unusual, or "altered." As a writer trained in Western ways, I use the terminology you see here.

Furthermore, in humans, brain waves (measured in hertz) increase or decrease naturally. Our consciousness shifts and expands throughout the 24-hour cycle. We experience heightened awareness earlier, while later in the day not so much. Lucidity flows along a spectrum as well. We know more nowadays due to scientific instruments and measurements. Just a few decades ago the notion of dream-state metacognitive functioning was dismissed completely. Kahan and LaBerge (1994) have challenged psychology's limited views on human cognitive processes, such as metacognition, due to the field dichotomizing sleeping consciousness abilities and waking consciousness abilities. It's best to think of capacities for awareness along a spectrum or as cyclical. Regarding cognitive science, Kahan and LaBerge (1994) stated, "Evidence of reflective awareness during dreaming raises questions not only about consciousness but also about self-representation and self-awareness over the sleep-wake cycle" (p. 259). They added, "Lucid dreaming reveals high order cognitive skills during sleep—skills previously assumed to be unique to waking cognition" (p. 257). Thus, the terms "altered" state or even "nonordinary" state of consciousness are misnomers.

We are not constrained in our potentials for consciousness. Limitations of the English language do not help. The following terms have been used to describe natural consciousness-based processes through which one can work from within: soul flight, waking dream, waking dream journey, controlled out-of-body-experience, vision, trance, trance-vision, hypnotic trance, hypnotic vision, ecstatic trance, ecstatic journey, imaginal journey, shamanic journey, and of course, the general terms altered or nonordinary state of consciousness. Again, these are all normal within Indigenous models, and with practice, we can consciously guide ourselves into such experiential states. When we apply ourselves, the magic of the natural world that unfolds because of dedication and consistent long-term practice comes down to attention and intention, two ordinary mental skills (Radin, 2018). Getting into this "altered" state of mind, however, comes about via various means. Still, we can access the greater universe ... what lies beyond the dream.

While I prefer to gather all of the terminology listed above and allow them to exist in the same basket, for the sake of ease, many scholars and researchers note specific distinctions. The differences and the details are important when conducting research or when teaching or writing instruction manuals, for example. When it comes to differentiating between hypnotic trance and ecstatic trance, Brink (2022) explains, "These forms of trance are similar in that they bring us to communion with the spirits, but they are different in their energy and rituals for induction" (p. 9). He continues on, noting a distinction given the differences in energies: "The energy of hypnotic trance is slow, quiet and letting go of thoughts. The energy of ecstatic trance is stronger, more directed and intentional" (p. 9). Brink then goes on to explain the different ways to induce these types of trances. He wrote, "The induction of hypnotic trance is through words with a rate of speech to match a person's rate of breathing, while the induction of ecstatic trance is with rapid stimulation to the nervous system, stimulation from the rapid beating of a drum or shaking of a rattle at around 210 beats per minute" (p. 9).

In my own experience, I had come from a background of meditation, beginning in my martial arts training, which then led to a greater interest in nonordinary states. After being turned on to it by a professor in my Master of Counseling program, I began experimenting with hypnosis in 2004 on my way to certification. This unfolded alongside lucid dreamwork and conscious OBE travel, having also spent time being trained into it by a local group of gnostic mystics. It wasn't until over a decade later that I would enter the domains of ecstatic trance and journeying as part of core shamanic practice. While all of the experiences and training have influenced my view of the nature of consciousness in this multiverse, I have found that the most precise information can be obtained through building relationships with the spirits, or otherworldly essences, that come forth to the practitioner of those domains and asking them directly. All we really need is our consciousness. If we want the rewards that come with training and long-term practice, we must apply ourselves, show a commitment, persist and make it a priority.

Practice Safety

While Kremer (2007) wrote, "Dreams and visions, the poetic inspiration of visionary trance states—whether during sleep or induced by chanting, singing, drumming, or entheogens—play a central role in the acquisition and application of indigenous knowledge" (p. 35), for us urban contemporary types, psychoactive substances, such as hallucinogens from parts of the world with which we are unfamiliar, are not only not needed whatsoever, they may actually be harmful, in more ways than one. I advise engaging in this work completely clean, completely sober, where it is one's consciousness through breath, intention and mental focus that controls the shift in one's state of consciousness. For example, consider the current fad among those descended from Europeans of consuming ayahuasca. This kind of tourism is big business, but it is not always safe. Some self-proclaimed shamans are even administering ayahuasca or other entheogenic substances in places like New York City. I hold a couple of opinions that ruffle some feathers from time to time, such as the opinion that medicine is dreamt up by certain peoples for their communities. Partaking in it outside of the place from where it originated may have negative consequences. The plants needed to make ayahuasca do not grow in "The City." I also hold the opinion that those of European origin have their own sacred medicine and therefore it may not be wise to self-elect consuming medicine created for others, regardless of where you consume it.

In February 2024, the *HEAL* podcast hosted by Kelly Noonan Gores featured Sara Eaglewoman, an Indigenous Medicine Woman and Intuitive Healer of Apache Chiricahua descent. The conversation between Sara and Kelly was beautiful.

Sara began by sharing her personal story, speaking of her time with the elders when she was initiated into her medicine. Discipline is at the center of doing healing work. We must be pure ... we must be medicine. Holding integrity and honor in the sacred space comes with the responsibility of the role.

Sara spoke about how the elders and medicine people on the reservations do not administer hallucinogenics, as it is not necessary. The use of hallucinogenics is a form of escapism. Furthermore, the person ingesting a hallucinogen does not know where they will be going ... where they will end up. It could be unsafe. Sara spoke of fragments of the soul getting stuck because of these experiences. Sometimes those parts are stuck in very dark places. "Have the courage to do the work stone cold sober," she says. Stay here, consciously, and learn your lessons from a place of sobriety.

Sara mentioned dreamwalking. In my last book, *Dream Medicine: The Intersection of Wellness and Consciousness*, you will find a chapter on this topic. Dreamwalking is "a process by which a shaman ... enters into a person's dream for benevolent purposes," such as for providing consolation, giving a warning or offering instructions (Mascaro, 2021, p. 52). Furthermore, "not only can dreamwalking allow for teaching and instruction to occur through the dream state, but by entering one's dream, a shaman might administer treatment so that healing can take place" (Mascaro, 2021, p. 54). When Sara dreamwalks, she will meet with her client's, or patient's, aspects of their soul, and work with their blueprint, or what she calls the soul grid. Sara was taught to work with the soul first, and the effects of that will move down into the physical so that shifts will be experienced there.

Kremer (2007) states, "As the descriptions indicate, such shamanic initiations are not mere psychological processes. They are a process always resulting in actions capable of manifesting healing" (p. 36). This is not metaphorical. True shamans can work with Spirit in such a way that changes in matter, in form, manifest.

Sara shares a memory from those who have guided her. Forget what you know, remember what you forgot. Remember the sacred union, where you came from. Once you do that, all will evolve.

Some guidance she shared that was particularly meaningful for me was this:

When you are triggered (in fear, from childhood, etc.), go straight and directly to love—all the love you have received in your life. Treat this like a practice so we can feel safe at home in ourselves. When I hear Truth, I often calmly and softly cry. The Truth throughout this conversation between Kelly and Sara did just that to me today.

Sara then spoke of her own near-death experience and the knowledge imparted to her. You are not judged in the spirit realm, but you are measured, she explained. You are measured by the amount of love you have received, as well as the love you gave. It really is all about Love.

As the interview and conversation neared the end, I was surprised, and pleased, to hear Sara speak about the relationship between martial arts and the healing arts. I have always sensed a strong link between these two arts and have spent a large portion of my life in both worlds. Holding space, presence, silencing the mind, embodiment and maintaining sharp focus come together in these seemingly opposing art forms. But instead of being in opposition, they blend seamlessly and can be of great support when one begins conscious dreamwork.

Prior to engaging in the practices described below, I encourage clients and students to conduct a grounding exercise as well as set up intentional "sacred space." Grounding exercises are among any group of practices that facilitate a psychological coming home into the body through tuning into sensation. An example is running ice water over the hands and even splashing some on the face. Personally, I have found this very effective, especially when I am staying in the High Sierra region around Lake Tahoe during the winter months as the tap water is practically freezing. Nothing focuses my attention like that! Another grounding exercise that I have noticed gaining much attention is Five Senses Grounding. Here, one moves from sense to sense in a 5-4-3-2-1 fashion. First, look at five things around you ... really look. Look at each one at a time. Second, touch four things around you. Really feel the texture, weight, temperature, one at a time. Third, turn your attention now to auditory sensations. Can you hear three different sounds in your environment? One of the sounds might be your own breath. Next, go into the olfactory senses and discover what you smell around you. Take in two different scents and simply notice. There is nothing more to do. Lastly, turning your attention to the mouth, taste one thing ... perhaps the last thing you ate or drank. Using your sense of taste, what can you detect? This practice of Five Senses Grounding supports us to slow down and bring our full conscious faculties back into the body. This practice is especially helpful when we have had a busy day, running around like a chicken with its head cut off, as the saying goes. Five Senses Grounding can be done in rounds—two or even three times in a row. You can do it any time of day or night, literally anywhere; just not while driving, please.

Once we are grounded and ready to move along, setting up an intentions sacred space comes next. This is an important initial component of any ritual, as we want our space-place of eco-spiritual work to be set up with loving attention, and an acknowledgment of the whole purpose of why we engage in these activities in the first place. There are numerous ways by which to go about sacred space dedication. Welcoming and honoring the four directions and elements is a good place to start. We can do this simply with intention; however, some prefer to verbally express a prayer, song, or poem woven into their personalized verbal acknowledgment. Ancient sacred words may be spoken while envisioning a protective circle forming around you. Additionally, some people like to include burning dried plant material to smoke the space, or spritzing the area with salt water, which can be infused with essential oils. However, the powers of the mind via a strong, clear intention are really all that is required. You can set an intention for protection by calling in your protectors, such as a spirit guide from your culture, or one you might already be working with, through the power of imagination and voice. See and feel your guide(s) all around you. Create sacred space with great intention, humility, and respect.

Once the above is established, the conditions might be optimal for turning attention toward a journey into the imaginal realm, the dreamscape, or the worlds beyond by way of altering consciousness. These experiences, what we bring back with us from time in these realms, can carry us forward along the path of psycho-spiritual learning and development—necessary processes for growth and evolution.

Lucid dreaming has been highlighted earlier in this book, but I'll return to that phenomenon here, albeit briefly, in order to share examples of naturally occurring spiritual experiences in that state. Since not everyone easily achieves full consciousness while dreaming, we will explore dream incubation next, as such a practice can impact any type of dream state, lucid or otherwise. In his book *Lucid Dreaming: Dawning of the Clear Light*, G. Scott Sparrow (1988) describes how his lucid dream life gave way to humbling, transformative experiences embodying a state of surrender. He shares several experiences that progress along a spiritual path, concluding with what happens from the lights that begin to approach him from the impact zone (this is where a meteorite has hit the earth in his lucid dream): "They are moving directly towards me in a parallel fashion. I wait until the lights are directly overhead. Then I know it is time to close my eyes and meditate. Immediately a tremendous energy wells up within my body. I try to surrender to it. As I do, light begins to fill my vision. There is a tremendous sense of warmth and love, which continues for a good while" (p. 51). After sharing his dreams of this nature, Sparrow notes how these experiences of light and energy appear to be "universally recognized in literature on meditation and contemplative prayer as actual communion between the individual and the Divine" (p. 51). Through all the experiences brought forth here, we can see how with consistent practice the separation between oneself and the One, the All, a.k.a. Source, begins to diminish, so long as we can surrender to and move through the fear that naturally arises as a result of conscious awakening from such powerful transformational processes at work. Through uncompromising surrender, we experience greater freedom along the path to genuine wholeness (Sparrow, 1988).

Dream Incubation

My last book, titled *Dream Medicine: The Intersection of Wellness and Consciousness*, featured clinicians and practitioners of hypnosis and yoga nidra. Those practices are especially close to my heart because they have helped me during some of the most difficult times of my life (please consider reading *Dream Medicine* for more information, and for connecting with others because the end of the book includes a page filled with resources to various practitioners, just as this one does). Here, I will dive into the practice known as dream incubation, not because I haven't in the past, but because it is a wonderful launching pad for anyone wanting to further engage with their dreams. I encourage everyone to learn all they can about incubating dreams. Again, it is through our dreams that we can have a direct experience (i.e., *gnosis*) of the aliveness of the Earth, and far beyond it. I learned about traditional practices for healing purposes among those of my grandfather's ethnic group. Altering consciousness in order to communicate and commune with saints, ethnic Italian Calabrese combine the use of prayer and dream incubation (*l'incubazio*) in order to facilitate healing (Krippner et al., 2011). The historical ancestral link left me wondering about my own experiences with dream incubation, as it seemed so effective and natural. While not explicitly discussed in my own family, researchers report how "folk magic traditions also seem to have been part of the social fabric for longer than we can trace, despite being in opposition to what the Church deems acceptable for someone who identifies as a Catholic" (Puca, 2019, p. 115). Those who left Italy to settle in the United States, such as members of my family lineage, naturally lost a direct living connection to their history and through the process of acculturation would adopt spiritual and religious practices weighted more toward Catholicism over a previously community-based, place-centered folk practice. Still, it is becoming common knowledge that ancestral memory is passed to the next generations through memory beyond the explicit and declarative memory systems of the brain. We remember through our bodies and through dreams, so we can call them in through incubation.

In December 2022, Ryan Hurd was a guest blogger on my website, ConsciousChimera.com. In that article, Hurd referenced the ancient skill of dream incubation. He explained that the term comes from the Latin *incubare*, which means to lie down upon, or as we say today: just sleep on it. Dream incubation is about calling dreams, asking for guidance or clarity, Hurd claims. I couldn't agree more, for I view the practice of dream incubation as something everyone can do for support and with ease. With consistency comes greater fluency. It's a skill we can build upon.

Hurd contributed further thoughts on this practice known as dream incubation in that blog: "In its weakest form, dream incubation can be represented by a wish for a certain kind of dream while lying down before sleep. ... In stronger variations, common ritual drivers can include affirmations said throughout the day, meditation, prayer, fasting, seclusion, drumming, and the ingestion of a tonic, pill or smoked herbs. Sound familiar to the 'new tactics' posted on lucid dreaming forums? All of these techniques have been used for millennia across the world and in many cultures to ignite altered states of consciousness."

There are so many questions for which we can ask the dream for answers. Dream incubation has been viewed as helpful for wellness-related concerns, as you may have already considered. We can be given guidance, warnings, or receive encouragement in the dream state. Those diagnosed with anxiety disorders appear to experience bad dreams or nightmares at a frequency significantly higher than the general population (Rimsh & Pietrowsky, 2022), yet I wonder about the interplay from anxiety that may bubble up from a new chronic illness diagnosis among those with a deep-rooted solid dream incubation practice. I have seen that the information provided in these incubated dream memories relieves burdensome thoughts and worries for some, especially between scans, such as an MRI, for example.

A dream incubation ritual or intentional dreaming practice can look different for different people (Hurd, 2014). Some of the key components I include are setting a strong intention and holding it clearly in the mind with deep feeling and faith. Even writing the intention down on a slip of paper placed under a pillow can help encourage results. And it goes without saying that you'll want your dream journal next to you as you fall asleep so that as soon as you awaken, you can write your recollections down on paper before memory has a chance to fade.

In the previous chapter, I introduced Tzivia Gover and her community of 350 Dreamers. Here she offers an exercise. Tzivia encourages dreamers to do this "healing meditation for self and Earth" before going to sleep:

> Place your left hand on your heart, and connect to your individual self, your unique passions and desires for the planet.
>
> With your right hand, symbolically and energetically connect with the Earth by placing your palm face down beside you (if you are in bed, place your hand on the mattress; if you're seated on the floor or on a chair place your hand on the floor, rug, or the seat of your chair) as you connect with the Earth, our shared source of all life.
>
> Now breathe slowly and intentionally as you connect with your individual unique self and our common shared source, our mother Earth.
>
> Set an intention to focus your dreaming heart and mind on bringing divine light and healing energy to yourself and to the Earth.
>
> Then, holding onto your intention, place your hands in front of your heart with palms together and feel the two spheres: your individual desires and the Earth's need coming together.
>
> Hold this focus as you enjoy three more breaths, or until the practice feels complete.
>
> Now settle into sleep. And in the morning, notice if your dreams responded with any messages for personal or collective healing.

Try this exercise each night before bed for a week or more. Remember to take note of what you discover. I hope you have a lovely experience with this gentle, compassionate exercise.

In other blog articles in 2022 and 2023, I wrote about sleep hygiene because it is necessary for solid sleep and for cultivating clear dreams. Sleep hygiene and dream incubation go hand in hand. So do not expect dream guidance if you are chronically sleep-deprived or consuming large quantities of alcohol or greasy meals before bedtime.

When I led a retreat at Hollyhock on Cortes Island, Canada, dream-related endeavors were included. After being introduced to the practice of dream incubation, participants practiced together for several nights in a row. A memorable remark was when one woman, after a couple nights of success, exclaimed, "This stuff really works!" While I knew this to be true in my own life, how inspiring it was to introduce someone new to the idea, guide them each night, and witness what they experienced!

Having practiced dream incubation techniques for over a decade myself, I can promise that the practice can become one of your best guides in life—your most trusted inner advisor, if you stick with it. Dreams can show us what we already know deep down but have been afraid to see or acknowledge. Nature is honest—she doesn't lie. We can ask our dreams to reflect to us the living truth inside our bodies. With that said, be sure you truly want to know what you are asking about when doing dream incubation practices. Sometimes the truth is not what we are psychologically ready for. Always *be clear with yourself* before diving into dreamwork of any kind.

Now I'll tell a little more about the foundations of this practice. It's best to practice dream incubation for more than one night—a week's time is best. Every night in any given week, focus on the same question. Avoid a yes/no type of questioning. Often, I like to use "Show me what's happening with _____ (you fill in the blank)," as part of an incubation process. This way you can accumulate information if one dream provides little, or rather you recalled little from the dream. Additionally, practicing with the same intention allows for gathering and accumulating bits of information in an open-ended manner. You can even ask the dream to show you more information about the situation or circumstance.

Expect to receive information from all senses (sight, sound, etc.), even a deep feeling or emotion. Be sure to keep a dream journal because dream fragments, no matter how initially powerful, can fade. Once you have gathered your dream evidence, consider your choices. If you have the opportunity to verify incubated dream recollections, play the role of an investigator. This can build confidence, especially in the initial phases of learning. Furthermore, know that just because you learned of something or have been guided in a particular direction, doesn't mean you must speak or act. Sometimes it's best to observe, and simply sit with the information provided from the incubation process for a couple of days (or longer if appropriate).

Know that one does not have to be lucid in a dream to be shown valuable information. However, a lucid dream experience can allow you to consciously travel to a place, even going beyond current space-time. What's so cool about this practice is that some people can have a powerfully vivid, even lucid, dream on the very first attempt. I've witnessed it happen among those I have coached in dream incubation. And for the record, an option to dream consciously with clear lucidity can be THE intention. Give it a try!

We can practice dream incubation alone or with others in an online community or in our household. Communities of dreamers can be truly powerful. Participation in such a community has the potential to transform one's life (and I'll say more about this in the next section). The Dream Portal is one such community. It was created by Ryan Hurd, author of the book *Lucid Talisman*, whose work I mentioned earlier. The Dream Portal is a unique membership community that includes courses, workshops and other events, as well as discussion rooms, all focusing on the miraculous world of dreaming and the imaginal. By early fall 2024, I completed the Preparing for Lucidity minicourse, which he created. Through it I was reminded of Ryan's background in archaeology. When he spent time on Isla Ometepe (an island emerging out of Lake Nicaragua), he visited megaliths that had been carved with circles and spirals by the ancient people of that place (Hurd, 2011). From earlier in this book, I'm sure it is clear just how much I am drawn to ancient artifacts, but most notably, the spiral. This symbol is found, historically, across the world. Humans from earlier times knew how to access altered states, and it has been proposed that carving circular shapes moves one into an altered state, or rather higher state, of consciousness. While the sound of rock scraping over rock will be absent, we can sit down with a pen and paper and begin to make spirals. As we breathe with attention, we can slow down our rhythms and intentionally make that circular motion with the pen and paper to induce a nonordinary state. This is a wonderful exercise to begin with as part of a dream incubation practice. As we make the spirals—and I suggest doing it with your nondominant hand—set the intention for your dream that night. Then, tuck yourself into bed and hold that intention in your mind as you drift off into sleep. When you wake up the next morning, grab that pen and paper once again and write down the dreams you recall … the dreams initiated by that spiral.

Collective Dreaming

Maybe you've heard of one of my favorite podcasts—it's called *The Dream World*. On her podcast, Amina Mara produces some exciting discussions, with equal credit to her guests. One thread that has come up is how dreaming has the potential for changing the world for the better. The host and producer, Amina Mara, interviewed psychologist and professor Dr. Angel Morgan about collective dreaming on her May 25, 2024, podcast. Dr. Morgan explained a distinction among types of collective dreams and then went on to share stories from both categories. She described two sub-categories of collective dream phenomena. For example, the term *mutual dreaming* involves two or more people who report similar features in their dreams such as recalling an object, person, or place. Next, she moved on to the second sub-category known as shared dreaming.

Now shared dreaming is juicier! In the podcast discussion, Dr. Morgan explained how shared dreaming provides more evidence that people are sharing an actual dreamscape, including imagery, interactions, environment, and more. When we keep a dream journal, or diary, we can track these things. These practices reveal powerful abilities of human beings and can be enhanced when working with a group of other dreams. As you may have noticed, dream groups are on the rise, especially since the spark of COVID. Furthermore, those who engage in planned shared dreaming might make a waking state plan, often with other experienced lucid dreamers, to meet up together in a dream and take a specific action. My favorite is when people use these intentions and dream skills to heal the Earth, our living planet, or project peace and love to the Earth.

A couple of months after Dr. Morgan's podcast episode, Amina

Mara and I spoke at length about how shared dreaming can be beneficial at this time of great conflict and destruction of our planetary home and all of its inhabitants. She is so passionate about shared dreaming that the topic is the focus of her research. Amina's master's thesis was on lucid dreaming for creative inspiration. After her graduation she felt inspired to continue her studies in sleep and dream science. She's currently in a graduate level dream studies program and plans to do future research for a doctoral dissertation focusing on aspects of collective lucid dreaming. Again, we can think of collective dreaming as an umbrella term, and under that umbrella are dream phenomena such as mutual dreaming and shared dreaming. These topics really excite us both!

Amina and I agreed that one does not have to have lucid dreams to experience inspiring and curious results, as far as collective dreaming goes. Amina said, "Even if you're not lucid, you can have mutual dreams of similar dreamscapes and overlapping elements." Of course, dreamers must track their dreams in a journal of some sort and later share them with a dream buddy. It's the only way one can know if mutual dreaming is taking place.

Next, Amina expanded on what shared dreaming entails. "With shared dreaming, two or more dreamers share a storyline." For example, two lucid dreamers might make a plan to meet up in the dream space and do an activity.

With any of these phenomena, dreamers can work together to self-experiment, or test things out in small groups of trusted friends. Neither one's geographical location nor spiritual orientation matter because time and space do not exist in the way we know it in the dream, and the dream is just that ... everybody dreams regardless of background or belief system. We can dig in anytime, anyplace.

Amina added: "Dream groups via a social media platform also report similar patterns amongst people that regularly talk about dreams together. It's really cool. This can help to normalize dream sharing in the community. I love when I tell people about a random dream I had and see how they get excited to start talking about their dreams."

I added how even those who record or track their dreams in

isolation or as a solo practice can join a dream group anytime, likely leading to quicker results than a total newbie, because solo practice is practice. The energy can benefit the group, should one want to dream with community. The additional attention to practicing the dream arts can even spark increased lucidity.

Amina shared a memory: "I have a couple of friends that are experienced lucid dreamers. Together we get lucid on a frequent basis, frequent enough to where we can go in the lucid dream and look for each other or even do specific tasks together. We've been doing these experiments for years—trying to actually meet up in the dream space and exchange a keyword. Now, we don't know each other's word in the waking state. Additionally, we've tried all different variations of shared dream experiments, and it's been cool. We've had some really interesting results!"

Amina reminded me how it's best to engage in shared dreaming experiments for a specific period of time. For example, if you agree to engage in the "keyword" guessing dream game among friends, just as she noted above, consider doing it for a week or even a month. There's too much pressure if the experiment runs just for one night. "A friend and I tried to exchange keywords in the dream state for a good month or two. We didn't have a specific day that we did this— we were in different time zones. Remember, in the dream world, time is not relevant. It's not linear. Anyway, we had some interesting results. This friend had never been to my house, but she had a dream where we met up and she was in my house. She specifically described an orange wall. And I did have an orange wall in my house, but I had recently painted it white. She didn't know that. In the dream, she saw the orange wall, which existed until just days before that dream."

Amina provided additional examples of her and her friend's experimentation with collective dreaming. "Also, over the course of the month, we started to have some interesting dream symbols overlapping. My keyword for her to guess was 'sushi.' So, every time I would dream of her, I would tell her in the dream state, 'My word is sushi.' And every time she would dream of me, she would ask me for my word. There were a couple of failed attempts where she just couldn't get it. But then one day, she reported how she had a dream and couldn't find me in the dreamscape, so she sent me a text message in the dream state, asking for my keyword. She told me how in her dream, I sent her an image."

At this point Amina showed me the image on her cell phone. Truly, it was one of those cake rolls, similar to a jelly roll except it was chocolate with cream—black and white like nori and rice. The next day, Amina's friend asked her if her keyword was cake. While the word was incorrect, the image from her friend's dream was shaped and structured just as sushi is.

In another example, Amina's friend chose the keyword "strawberry." In a lucid dream, Amina tried to identify her friend's keyword. In that dream, Amina saw a symbol. It was a red-colored spade. This is arguably another interesting structural similarity.

Amina asked, "If we cannot be certain about the target, do our brains just translate into whatever we might think the target could be, or how we interpret it?" We agreed that shared dream experiments are almost like the game of broken telephone. These not exact "hits" are common. They are similar enough to get us scratching our heads! Consciousness is mysterious, indeed. We look forward to further research both in and out of the sleep lab in order to inspire the great capacity of human potential.

If we, as dreamers, have the inherent ability to gather a group of friends, make a plan before falling asleep to meet in the dream space and take action, thus exchanging information and energy, what might we be able to accomplish? If we can consciously direct our energy in such a way, might we be able to transmit something beautiful from a place of prayer, for example?

Amina has combined her skills of Reiki and lucid dreaming to offer healing and love to people, animals, and the Earth. "I've had some dreams where I am seeing tragedies and natural disasters—wars and things like that. There's not much that I can really do in the grand scheme of things, but I can use dreams to intentionally send positive energy to those who are hurting or in harm's way. I feel like, energetically, it makes a difference. I think if enough people thought that way, then maybe the world would be a better place. We can do good in our day-to-day lives, and also in our dream states. Dreaming doesn't only reflect reality, it also co-creates it. The dream may have a real and strong impact upon awakening, influencing our thoughts, beliefs and actions. I show up in my lucid dreams how I want to show up in the world, leading with compassion and love. For example, I don't just murder all my dream characters thinking its 'just a dream with no real consequences.' It's reality to me because I am there experiencing it. I treat my dream with love and kindness, even when that's not what I'm receiving from it. If you look around right now in waking life, it's very likely that almost everything you see once originated as a thought in someone's mind. The mind is powerful and creates our experience on Earth."

I nodded and exclaimed, "We can give love to the Earth no matter what state of consciousness we are in, which is nice. Sure, we can make changes in our everyday lives, such as where we spend our money, what we buy, who we support ... all kinds of changes for the highest good. At the same time, it is really cool that anyone can practice dream work or dream consciousness so that they may send out that love and care that they carry in their hearts. I believe that most people do care, but they may not know what to do, or whether their actions will have any lasting impact. I believe no matter where we stand or what we have access to, anyone can project love to our oceans, our trees...."

Amina added more to the conversation: "In a lucid dream, I can manifest things, making things appear out of thin air. It's immediate gratification, usually. Could it be that's why people see this as an unrealistic dream world? Obviously, in the physical world, when you make an action or do things or put effort into things, there's usually a delay period, and with linear time, maybe something has to play it out a certain way, so it's not as instant, or immediate. But it is important to understand how our dreaming self really does have this interplay influence with our waking self—they do influence each other. I think if we have an intention in the dream world, we can do the things in the waking world. I consider it to be a nice balance. There is already research about how visualization helps people perform better and reach goals, and lucid dreaming even helps with improving skills. Lucid dreaming is a form of enhanced visualization, like a fully immersive virtual reality with all the senses functioning."

There's a lot being discussed at this time in theoretical physics, as well as physiological and psychological research. For example, if we have a scary dream, our physiology changes in the dream. You can measure it when we wake up as well. From there, our thoughts, behaviors, and feelings are going to be impacted by that scary dream. Similarly, when we have loving, kind dreams we are also impacted. These effects occur whether we are lucid (aka aware) or not. But when we experience lucidity in a dream, especially for the first time, the experience can literally shift our paradigm. Our long-held beliefs about consciousness are suddenly questioned. While this can be uncomfortable, I believe the shift is worth the initial discomfort. That is because we need to have these types of direct experiences to encourage and motivate positive action for change, especially at times like this when our modern lifestyles are harming the planet and all the natural resources provided for us to live and thrive.

Amina reminded me that we don't have to go it alone: "It's so healing to find a dream community for more than just dialog and process. Such a community holds space for us to grow and evolve on this path. I think it opens space for a ripple effect. There's healing one person, and then more and more people, and then going further to help heal the Earth. This can make such a huge impact. This is evolution."

Amina also shared her dream experiences helping loved ones, such as her grandmother, transition through death. In one of a series of dreams Amina described the following: "I am lucid, and in a town. It is run down and distressed. People are struggling. My grandmother tells me how it is representative of what is taking place in the world. The people in the dream approach me for therapeutic healing. There is this one tree in the dream which I understand to be hundreds of years old. The scene is a beautiful one, really, with a river. And although it is so beautiful, it is such a sad town. The tree is also in distress. I see the inner fibers of the tree, and I understand that the tree is hurting. My grandmother demonstrates how to conduct dream Reiki so I can repair this tree. There are people living in the tree, and they are thankful for the healing. How often am I out in this universe doing this healing work? All I do know, for certain, is that I woke up feeling really good and really happy from that dream. The experience has had a positive impact on my psyche. I show up better in the world. So whatever impact that has, I do think one person can have a ripple effect, and I always try to show up in my life that way, and my dreams have helped me do that, just to show up with love and happiness even when things are hard."

I was touched. I thanked Amina for sharing this tender dream and was reminded how such experiences can really help us see the bigger picture. There's a much bigger story unfolding.

We acknowledged how a lot of agonizing events are taking place in the world right now. Amina recalled how, some years back, a large bridge collapsed, causing death and destruction. She said: "I'm very much empathetic, and I think about all of the ripple effects such a catastrophe can have, like all the people that have been hurt, or the people that are survived by somebody who has died. Additionally, there's impacts to infrastructure, and even those that need such infrastructure to get to and from work. So in that case, I went to sleep with the intention of just thinking about that, and hoping to elevate the universal consciousness or just put out good energy to that place. Why not? I have nothing to lose. Later, a dream showed me the aftermath. I wasn't active in that dream. I was just observing a fast-forwarded time lapse of rebuilding the bridge, and how people were arranging detours and things like that. I was just observing the dream and offering prayers. That was really all I could do."

I thought, *That is something*. Amina continued, "So sometimes I'll do that when some major event happens. I'll invite it into my dream space, then pray to send good energy."

I added how I believe this to be just as effective as sending loving energy from the waking state, through prayer, meditation, or another form on intentionality. I feel sad when I recognize how rivers are being poisoned for various reasons, or how natural waterways have become toxic. I think about how nice that is to offer healing, not only to the people, but also to the ecosystem that has been negatively impacted by catastrophes and disasters. It can be challenging to find a balance.

189

Amina shared a dream with me and as I listened I found it to be so powerful. She said: "In the dream I am doing two types of healing, plant medicine and dream-related healing. It feels important and powerful. There are inter-dimensional schools that teach dreamers how to affect reality and manipulate the dream. I am also going around helping other dreamers become lucid for the first time to increase the loving vibration of the Earth. One of the other teachers tells me that dreams can come true, like premonitions. She tells me that she is also a lucid dreamer whose body is currently sleeping. She tried to tell me where she lives and what her contact information is. I find my way to a tennis court, wondering why it looks so deserted. It feels lonely. I am lucid and I see a man sitting under a tree. He is glowing and I get the sense that he's incredibly intelligent and sentient. I go up to him and ask him the meaning of life. He says one word, 'unity.' He holds my hands, and we start spinning into the abyss."

Amina expressed what has stood out to her through a lot of these different healing dream experiences: "There's this polarity between beauty and destruction, which I think relates to the world we live in. It's like both sides of the spectrum, and my dreams definitely reflect that. For example, even if there is a war-like apocalyptic scene in my dream, I can usually experience it from multiple perspectives and find the smaller beautiful moments. A dream filled with bombs and missile flares may look like beautiful fireworks from a bird's-eye view. I'm thinking, 'wow, this is beautiful—I'm lucky that I'm here experiencing this lucid dream,' yet at the same time it's also sad because the scene is so destructive. It speaks to this duality or polarity, like yin and yang. There's beauty and destruction. There's goodness and there's evil and they're intertwined. I've come to understand that this is how the universe is built."

I chimed in: "There will always be both sides of the coin, I guess. It is inevitable. It is like a never-ending balancing act."

Amina acknowledged how difficult it can be because we, from a Western mentality, exist through a linear framework, making perspective an issue. We see things differently based on where we stand at the time. She said, "Dreams can guide through these challenges and time of confusion. Even when dreams can sometimes be hard or scary, I still feel very trusting that what we're being shown is to help our guidance in some way. Challenge and struggle are transformative."

Collective dreaming sure does have a way of showing us that there's something bigger to this life. Through it, I see something larger than myself, as an individual, or any individual. Just as the term indicates, we are part of a collective, a collective dreaming every single night.

Sure, highly skilled lucid dreamers are the minority. But the vast majority of people are dreamers, and that is all we need to begin. While everyone dreams, some do not recall a whole lot. So, starting with the basics, we can send a signal to the conscious mind reminding it that dream recall is important. Amina reminds us how we don't have to be a lucid dreamer to do these kinds of activities discussed in this section. Still, she claims that it's good to have a dream plan anyways ... just in case you get lucid. Even better, prepare to get lucid!

As I told Amina how I have found that just one lucid dream has the potential to totally shift somebody's life, she offered a few suggestions: "So have an idea of what it is you want to do in your dreams! Anyone can incubate a nonacid dream and influence the content and the storyline. So always have that intention in the back of your mind and think about it as you're going to sleep. Make the intention as specific as possible. So exactly what do you want to do? What do you want to dream about? Also recall that community is really powerful. Start by normalizing dreaming, just as our ancestors did. Start talking about dreams, because a lot of people, while they may not immediately feel comfortable, might actually be dreamers and just don't have anybody to talk about it with. So really start to challenge yourself by telling your friends and family if you dreamt about them. This act can normalize it for them, and they might start telling you about their dreams where you made an appearance! These simple, albeit vulnerable, acts increase your lucidity and your dream recall in general, just because you're talking about it more often and making it like a part of your life. Open up that dialog."

When you've joined a dream community, or simply talk about

dreams at work, share with them your dream plan as well. Who knows, maybe they'll want to join in by committing to the same dream plan. It's really cool, Amina recalls, when a group of friends all dream of the moon and try to meet up at the moon. I can tell she's done this before! She stated, "It's fun. And the more people doing it the more fun it can be. Dedicate a couple of weeks, or even an entire a month to the task. That way it is flexible ... not so rigid."

During our conversation, I thought about all the ways an individual or community can direct healing dream energy to those suffering. For example, how about animals living alone in the cages of an animal shelter, or animals suffering from factory farm confinement, or even the fish swimming in rivers polluted by mining. I personally get so much out of my dreaming with animals, so why not give something back there.

Amina chimed in, "I love dreaming with animals. I've had a couple of funny dreams with that in mind. One of them was with my dog that passed away. Similarly to how I helped my grandma transition, in this dream I was helping my dog transition over. My dog was 17 years old and struggling with multiple health issues. My family had been grappling with the tough decision to put him down or not. I decided to ask him in the dream state, so I incubated a dream by going to sleep asking him what he wanted us to do. I had a dream in which I was walking him for the last time, and a squirrel came by and started talking to me. Although the talking squirrel did not trigger lucidity, it told me that our dog has been ready to die, he was just waiting on me to accept that it is his time, and he gave us permission to let him go."

Amina then shared dreams about plants: "Also, around that same time, I recalled a dream where one of my plants really needed to be repotted. My plant was talking to me in the dream, telling me to re-pot her. So, I woke up and checked the plant, which I haven't looked at in a while, and she was completely rootbound. Needless to say, I repotted this plant just as requested in the dream."

In the backyard of a house she lived in for about 20 years (her mom's house), there have existed several huge trees. Amina stated, "They have literally watched me grow up and have seen so many things happen over the decades ... they are really intelligent beings that have been around for so long watching us, you know. Witnessing the good and the bad. I practically view these trees as my grandparents. In one dream, these trees were guiding me and supporting me, like family members, and kind of like the book *The Giving Tree*. These experiences have opened my mind up to the way that we don't just collectively share the world with each other but also with animals and nature. They are just as conscious as we are, and they even dream. My compassion has grown as a dreamer. Now, I look at the trees a little differently and I talk to them, especially after dreaming with them that day. It's similar to telling your friend, 'Hey, you were in my dream last night.'"

Questions and contemplations regarding sentience arose in my mind. By dreaming in these ways, collective, lucid, intentional, how might we choose differently? How might we behave differently? As someone raised in the Unites States, I have witnessed how our industries have poisoned or destroyed a lot of what we need to stay alive. With dreaming, we have this free, accessible tool that allows us to have a direct experience of the aliveness of the natural world. If we knew that dreaming with the aliveness of our awareness could lead to profound impacts, would we be motivated to do so? After all, change can be scary.

Furthermore, to recall dreams, we can't just pop out of bed, grab our coffee and go about the day on autopilot. Sure, it's easier to objectify things with that kind of lifestyle, but with meaningful dream experiences, would we want to? For dreams feed us a more relational way of walking in the world. Dreams foster resilience and enable healing (Ward, 2024).

Amina gives a few tips for recalling dreams. She says, "Consider slowing down, and in the morning when you wake up really try to bring that dream back into consciousness. Then, take notes, do a sketch, anything to have a record of it. But sometimes dream recall can be low, naturally. Like anything in nature that ebbs and flows ... it's totally normal. This is why some people may not remember dreams for a while."

I like to use the flower as a metaphor for that. Imagine this beautiful flower in your neighborhood, and then you walk by it again a few weeks later, and it's withering. Then a month later it's gone. But then, there's a little sprout next to where it was, on the same vine. Dream recall can come in cycles, just like the cyclical nature of all life. Honoring those cycles and ourselves is important too.

Radically Proactive Hope

Even in the face of power, greed, theft, and tyranny, there is hope. Holding onto hope brings up good feelings but can be passive. If we are going to make positive changes in our societies, we must be active, yet not reactionary. Being proactive requires that we think critically and stay ahead of the curve. Through participation in localized actions in our communities, we demonstrate possibilities for the world. Motivating forces behind local action can become far-reaching and inspire others to do the same. Hope is a radical act.

Some dream experts say that both dreaming and daily waking living are thought-responsive environments—an important thing to consider when it comes to the nature of the universe. It's easy to become frustrated, angry, and even rageful as we witness and live through what is unfolding all around us. Sure, there is an option to mentally project hate and destruction outward onto our perceived enemy. We can even send energetic poison in the dream space or dreamscape itself. Recall that the general wisdom we give we also get. So, just like the healing energy we can send to Mother Earth through conscious dream arts, so too can we send the energies of love and compassion to our environment in everyday affirmative statements and thought patterns. Radically active hope is not spacey, ungrounded wishful thinking; instead, it encompasses a strong inner knowing that this is all we've got. Any other way leads to our own demise.

Remember Greta Thunberg? She's the young Swedish climate justice activist who became famous when she challenged world leaders to do the right thing for the environment. Greta quickly became well known. She inspired others—both youth as well as adults—everywhere across the globe, including myself. Her message was heard around the world and was a source of inspiration locally and globally. When we weave together everything we've covered so far, we can rest assured that we have everything we need inside of us to spark positive change and powerfully envision a just and equitable future for all. We can harness that fierce and inspiring energy to deliver loving action.

Let me tell you about another wonderfully inspiring woman whose actions for the Earth I greatly admire. "Human rights don't make sense to me without the rights of nature," says University of Murcia law professor Teresa Vicente, who is a 2024 Goldman Environmental Prize recipient (*https://www.goldmanprize.org/recipient/teresa-vicente/#recipient-bio*). With great passion and expertise in environmental law, she has dedicated many years to building awareness around what had been responsible for the destruction of the Mar Menor ecosystem. Located in Spain, and considered a national treasure, Mar Menor is Europe's largest saltwater lagoon. Vicente demanded that the endangered lagoon be protected from irresponsible practices related to rapid tourist infrastructure and industrialized agriculture. The big businesses who chose profit above all else poisoned the water, flora and fauna of this marine ecosystem due to toxic run-off. What's more, the water became so deprived of oxygen that the fish literally jumped out of the lagoon and onto the shore in an attempt to survive. Overall, millions died from suffocation whether they remained in the water or not. Due to Vicente's relentless activism and deep love for the environment, she rallied the community to protect Mar Menor, which eventually resulted in the Spanish parliament granting legal personhood to the lagoon. In 2022, and for the first time in European history, legislation was passed acknowledging the lagoon's right to exist with the promise to protect and restore the area.

Given the reciprocal relationships among various diverse species and the natural world in order to ensure the survival of all, humans need to step up to their roles and responsibilities as actors in maintaining the delicate balance. A strictly for-profit reductionist-materialist model kills us all. Gather your community and choose radically active hope—it starts with us.

As this book has only a few pages left before wrapping up to a close, I offer you both a creative exercise and a long-term practice. As a woman who has built shrines and altars for decades as part of her solution for soulful living, I share a bit of guidance below so that you too may feel inspired to create your own sacred space for healing, which can also serve as a place for restoration, contemplation, and reflection. After all, activists need all of the above in order to manage living in an unpredictable world from a place of grounded soulfulness.

If you enjoy crafts or the process of artmaking as I do, consider creating a small shrine or altar for the Earth. The tangible nature of such a sacred space can serve as a reminder to do the inner work for healing on all levels. Such creative workings act to demonstrate commitment and encourage ceremonial life through one's IM.

While you can build outdoors, you might also consider building an Earth-based sacred space in your home, even your bedroom, to remind you to dream with the Earth and for her. Such a dedicated space can also serve to remind those in the household to consider planetary needs over personal ones. There is no right or wrong way to engage in this practice so long as it is done with love, from the heart. Be as simple or as colorful as you like. Include the entire family if that feels right to you.

After such a space is constructed, offer a poem, song, or prayer in commemoration. The best time for this might be when you have an evening with some calm, quiet, and peace. Remember this is a space for healing all sentient life, including planet Earth. So, your dream incubation practice can be ultra-inclusive.

Once you recall a healing dream, you can anchor the experience by showing gratitude with a votive object, or *ex voto*. *Ex voto* (or more fully *ex voto suscepto*) comes from Latin. It means "from a vow" made, or "in pursuance of a vow." *Ex voto* are devotional objects found at sacred sites throughout southern Europe. While the size of such objects varies across the region, the *ex voto* I have seen are typically small, not often much larger than my open hand. They can be made with a variety of materials. The point is to place the *ex voto* offering at the foot of the shrine or altar to show devotion and give thanks. For our purposes here, *ex voto* can be offered to demonstrate a commitment to dream ways or as an expression of gratitude for the healing energy that came through in the dream. Knowing this connection, the *ex voto* you craft should be relevant to your practice. For example, when I was in Sicily, I entered a cave shrine with *ex voto* mirroring the healing that had taken place in a person's body. If the person prayed for healthy or healed feet, then the *ex voto* would show that. Another example I recall from Portugal was wax cast. If a person prayed for a pregnancy, a healthy-looking baby cast out of wax was present. You see, the *ex voto* you construct can embody your hopes and dreams as well. Just be intentional about it and make the offering with grace and/or in gratitude for the gift you received in dreamland.

8

CONCLUSION

We are not here to undo what has happened in the past.
We are here to become conscious enough not to repeat it.
—Caroline Myss

What can our ancestors teach us at this juncture? How can their mythic power, which lives through us at a cellular level, guide us in these turbulent times? While not at the same pace, we all move along the path of a heroine/hero's journey. Each person's experience of separation, initiation and eventual rebirth is unique. For us Western European–American people, what did it take to retrieve the original instructions (those which existed centuries before Christianity) and be in relationship with our Indigenous Mind?

How have the synchronicities and signs living through this collective waking dream provided direction and solace? Maybe the compassion that grows through dedicated spiritual practice has renewed a spirit of activism ... for your children, for those you love, for Mother Earth.

Everything, all creation, comes from the safety and security of pure darkness—as we emerge from the same void, everything is a web of interrelations, and it is all alive (Colorado, 1995). When we cause harm to life outside of ourselves, we are harming ourselves, too. It is obvious that the Earth cannot sustain us if we continue to stay silent about what's harming her.

Every action matters, and so does every thought-form! The vibrational frequency behind those can stimulate life, or wither it, causing further harm. It is our responsibility to improve the fate of humanity, the Earth, and its inhabitants, whether plant or animal.

A woman residing on Cortes Island, Canada, impacted me with

an exquisite tarot reading about a year and a half ago. During that reading, looking me straight in the eye, she recalled the works of renowned poet Rumi. She kindly, yet firmly stated, "Don't go back to sleep." I was curious but unfamiliar with those words coming from Rumi. This woman, however, knew that poem well, sharing with me the entire piece. You might be familiar with it. It begins like this:

> The breeze at dawn has secrets to tell you.
> Don't go back to sleep....

What must we do? What must we practice while living in this industrialized, fast-paced world in order to stay alert and awake? As you've read, we can shift our consciousness through meditation, prayer, and healing rituals and ceremonies to connect with a higher power for wisdom. Again, it is best to alter consciousness naturally without substances that might be linked with hidden motives such as the avoidance of responsibilities, or the seeking of status, thrill or pleasure (Katz, 2017), or even harm to one's body. Either way, we must recognize that community is everything. No one got to where they are by themselves. We all have been supported, and lifted, by those that came before us. I heard someone say, "If you blame them for your trauma, you must also blame them for your resilience." So, how can we use the resilience gifted to us by our ancestors to make this a better place for all? Katz (2017) wrote, "A central condition, indeed requirement, for spiritual transformation is that individuals contribute to the well-being of the community" (p. 183).

When gods and elements are ancestors and relatives who look after you, you also look after them. By caring for the Earth, the land, and all those living here, we participate in a reciprocal relationship. The concept of stewardship supersedes and dismisses the notion of land ownership because how can anyone truly own something so great, something meant to sustain all life? It's time to bury the greed and invite strangers to sit with us at the table so we can learn from each other and care for, or steward, these lands together, in cooperation.

When we consider the tasks laid out before us, which include changing our own perceptions, it can feel daunting. It can feel hopeless. But only at first, as there is hope and it is alive. This is evidenced in, most often, youth-led movements for a sustainable, clean future, where equity, protection of the Earth and all creatures are acknowledged for the integral role each plays in this web of life. Additionally, there is hope in that more and more people are dreaming again and coming to understand how inner experience is highly valued direct knowledge that powerfully informs how to tackle the challenges noted throughout this book with ways we can be supported in a new, loving vision.

When one speaks of illness, Western minds quickly think of physical matters gone wrong. But people can become ill on a spiritual level, too. All illness can be considered an opportunity to heal not just ourselves but, from a spiritual standpoint, our lineage as well. If we see illness as a tool to do things differently, what could that mean for us as a society? Just as a tumor in the body (something we can find and see) might develop as an opportunity to save one's life, screaming for change, so too can catastrophic events erupt in a way in which we simply cannot go back to sleep. By slowing down, we become more conscious, more aware of not only what we say and do, but to what degree we participate in cycles of harm or healing.

Given these wise words, we might wonder what gets in our way here. Today's fast-paced existence has become a barrier to psycho-spiritual awareness. We are cut off, severed at the neck. Our heads are running faster than our bodies, and our bodies simply can't catch up as we live a life of compulsive activity. Such a way of life perpetuates the war inside us, not allowing for our consciousness to confront the real issues—the shadow that surfaces in our nightly dreams, the skeletons in the closet of the mind. This results in a disconnected consciousness, one where we lose contact with ourselves and the radiant life all around us. We cannot *be the light*, not only for ourselves, but for anyone else, if we are not in touch with our heart essence, our soul's home. Breathe, go back into the body, touch the inner pain gently and with great compassion—that is the way home.

Transform your own wounds, so as to not act them out on others or the world at large. Heal self, then heal community and the planet. Sometimes relational injustices in our personal, individual lives can wake us up to the social injustices experienced by the collective throughout the world today. Currently, I think about Maui and the history of injustice here. The social injustices continue.

What needs your attention on the land where you reside? Find your soul community, the group that will take loving action for positive change. Maybe you know them now.

When we are at home in ourselves and in touch with what is around us, we ask good questions. Some of those are about service to humanity. We might ask, "How can I serve?" "How do I serve now?" "What are the most impactful ways in which I can serve, without deleting my own reserves?" Service only requires an open heart and perhaps a little time. There are many things it does not require. Because of the hundreds of options, service does not require money, status, high education, or special skills. There are many, many ways to show up in life through love. Providing free guided meditations each week online to a global community is the way I currently serve and have served for the past few years. Prior to that, it was a couple of decades of nonprofit work with children and families. Both hold space for others and provide nurturing. That's how I serve. And you?

> Do not take lightly small good deeds,
> Believing they can hardly help.
> For drops of water, one by one,
> In time can fill a giant pot.
> —Patrul Rinpoche (1808–1887)

Practice awareness, intentionality, gratitude, responsibility, reciprocity. At times, we might feel down, succumb to the weight of the world, grief-stricken, and falsely believe that actions taken by one individual may not be enough. Take pause. Be still and know. During those times especially set aside our culturally embedded reductionistic programming and recall the wisdom of Rumi—you are not a drop in the ocean, but the entire ocean in a drop. So be like water. Memory and energy are carried in and through water. One person's gift (the energy of giving, actually) radiates through all and everything ... all at once. It matters. You matter.

> *'A'ohe pu'u ki'eki'e ke ho'a'o 'ia e pi'i*
> No cliff is so tall it cannot be climbed.

EPILOGUE:
AS IT STANDS TODAY

As I write this section, the one-year anniversary since the devastating August 8, 2023, fires that destroyed several regions of Maui, including multiple homes in Kula and the entire town of Lahaina, has just recently passed. In addition to the 102 people killed in these fires, there was additional loss of human life. According to a January 8, 2024, ABC News report, the Maui Police Department has confirmed that at least 10 others died by suicide in the few months' aftermath. They can't be certain the suicides were because of the losses due to the fire, but it is an unusually high rate within just a few months' time. The suicide rate is particularly high among Maui's men, according to a May 21, 2024, Hawaii New Report article written by Chelsea Davis in reference to information provided by the Hawaii Department of Health. Davis included how Maui Family Support Services has been offering men's groups across Maui and even in Lahaina in order to offer support to survivors. It's just one of the many efforts made to ease the pain from such tremendous loss.

So many also lost foundational necessities of life, such as their housing and vehicles. Family pets were killed as well. The negative mental health impact can still be seen. Many still suffer from post-traumatic stress, yet there are not enough licensed mental health providers available with the qualifications to treat this kind of trauma.

Then there is the unknown with regard to the long-term physical health impacts. No one can truly know how far and wide toxin exposure has spread within the environment. This not only impacts people and animals on land, but what is it doing to marine health?

After all, it was then, as it is now, "hurricane season." High winds have the potential to spread anything.

Today, a year and a few months post fire, dozens of families are still without permanent housing. Many people are underemployed. Trauma is rampant. The economic burden is incredible. The cost to maintain fire insurance has skyrocketed. The FEMA process continues to be daunting. These are the conversations taking place among Maui's residents—I listen to them almost every day—many of whom are "so stressed out," as they have told me. These concerns are at the forefront of our minds.

Memorial events took place throughout the month of August 2024, such as well-attended Obon ceremonies, community gatherings, and paddle-outs. These remind us that the island of Maui carries an incredibly strong and resilient community. These events also remind us that we must stand up to those prioritizing corporate interests above safety, well-being, and security. Additionally, we must speak out on behalf of the land and all other sentient beings. The way to begin is with each of us and within us. Are we established within our own bodies? Are we in balance, living through the heart? How have we used "The Dreaming" to guide right action? Do we consider the collective? Are we fully aware of the impact of our settler colonial behaviors, and what are we willing to do about that?

As for me and my own inner world, I spent the end of the 2024 summer season reflecting on the two dozen dreams recalled over a period of 14 to 15 months. These dreams did not involve the island's fires, but instead reflected the healing landscape unfolding within me after an interpersonal trauma—the painful fracturing of my relational world and what I had believed was my new home. I'm ready to walk forward with renewed faith, while I carry with me the lessons Spirit has provided. In the words of David Kaonohiokala Bray, "Everyone you meet is a teacher."

Just as I was about to send the final version of this manuscript to my publisher in North Carolina, Hurricane Helene hit, killing hundreds. That same week, I also flew to Seoul, South Korea, to guest lecture about the power of dreams at Yonsei University. During that brief trip, I commented to two decades-long residents on how the high temperatures and humidity "surprised me this time of year." They told me how Seoul was experiencing record-breaking heat— they never expected it to be this warm at this time of year either. It is another reminder of how voices for the Earth are especially critical at this time, as global warming and resulting climate-related disasters are on the rise. When the planet suffers, we suffer.

As I prepare to say goodbye to Maui as my place of residence, I will remain connected to those with whom deep relationships have been formed. I've grappled with the belief of how I should have never moved here in the first place, while simultaneously affirming the multiple synchronistic events that have occurred here, and just prior to my relocation here. I believe that not only everyone, but also every "thing" or rather every experience is a teacher as well. Perhaps Maui as Trickster energy was at play ... and I will respect that. I will continue to tell those I meet about the injustices that have happened here and share all I have been taught about this island's history including the resistance and the resilience of the local people. From back in my own home state, I will send what I consider acts of love and kindness to Maui. As noted on the Acknowledgments page, half of the proceeds from the sale of this book will be directed to Maui-based organizations. So please, spread the word, or even better, spread the love.

~

If you or someone you love is in emotional distress or crisis, call or text 988 now.

Providing free and confidential emotional support, seven days a week, 24 hours a day, the 988 Lifeline is a national network of local crisis centers in the U.S.

GLOSSARY

Alchemy: From a Western standpoint, alchemy is a process of transformation, as it is about turning base metal, like lead, into gold ... a metaphor for transmuting dense frequencies of impulsivity and animalistic desires, even matter, into higher frequencies of creativity, love, wisdom, and spirit.

Aloha 'āina: Love of the land, yet also including an active responsibility (*kuleana*) to its defense and stewardship.

Ancestors: One's literal and imaginative genealogy of human origins to also include the complex of the people, places, and beings that came before this current lifetime.

Dependent Origination: A circular model from the Buddha revealing the process of suffering. Through 12 linked steps (*nidāna*), we see how suffering arises and is perpetuated through cycles of birth and rebirth. We may be born into any kind of body, such as a human, animal or spirit body.

Dream Incubation: A pre-sleep practice or way of cultivating dreams done in order to gain understanding, solve problems, connect with something greater than oneself, and more. Dream incubation can be practiced before daytime naps or as part of one's nightly bedtime routine.

Ecocolonialism: Sometimes called colonial environmentalism, ecocolonialism is used to describe ways colonialism has impacted the environment, particularly the natural environments of Indigenous peoples around the world. Examples include exporting toxins to underdeveloped countries, mineral and other resource extraction, deforestation, introducing invasive plant and animal species, and general alteration of native ecosystems.

Ethnoautobiography: Similar to autobiography in that it is an account of a person's life, yet also expands to include a greater dimension of experience considering a person's tribe, people, ethnicity, indigeneity, or

207

nation. Several elements such as, but not limited to storytelling, place, nature, community, ancestry, gender, history, dreams, creativity, myth, ritual, spirituality, religion and beyond are included in ethnoautobiographical accounts and acknowledge their relational web.

Ex voto: Devotional objects, typically small in size, found at sacred sites throughout southern or Mediterranean Europe. *Ex voto* offerings are placed at the foot of shrines or altars to show devotion and give thanks.

Indigeneity: While not synonymous with the term "indigenous," and more specific than the term "ethnosphere," indigeneity refers to a larger, global collective, sensitive to the needs and aspirations of Indigenous groups, and in consideration of one's fundamental orientation relating to land as ancestor, culture, knowledge, belonging, memory, inclusive of justice and respect for original ways.

Indigenous Mind: A cultural worldview, paradigm, or consciousness of living and being in this world which is holistic and active in maintaining balanced relationship with ancestors (nature, place, history, astronomy, spirit).

Indigenous Science: A science that is multidimensional, holistic, and indigenously minded in not only data collection methods but also in the way in which knowledge is held, shared, and related to.

Initiation: Initiations are entry points into processes of transformation. The old self is discarded, or symbolically dies, so that a new self can be reborn, thus allowing for entry into a new, or next, phase of life.

Kama'āina: Literally translated to "child of the land." A Native Hawaiian person or a person born within the Hawaiian Islands.

Kama'āina Hapa: A person of part Native Hawaiian ancestry, born within the Hawaiian Islands.

Kānaka Maoli: A person of Native Hawaiian origin and ancestry.

Kānaka 'Ōiwi: A person of Native Hawaiian origin and ancestry.

Kuleana: Responsibility.

Kumulipo: Sacred Hawaiian creation chant, poem, myth. An account of the creation of the world according to Hawaiian tradition. *Kumulipo* means Beginning in Darkness, describing how the world and life began according to the *kūpuna*, the ancestors.

Labyrinth: With rich historical roots, modern-day labyrinths have one way in and one way out and are often used as a meditation practice or for purposes of inward reflection.

Lucid Dream: A dream in which the dreamer knows they are dreaming. Lucid dreaming is sometimes referred to as conscious dreaming.

Megalith: A large stone forming a prehistoric monument.

Normative Dissociation: The social norm of disconnection, self-shielding, or splitting off from our origins, place, time, history, nature, and from wholeness, therefore leading to an ever-expanding cultural shadow. See the works of Jurgen Kremer for more on this concept.

Original Instructions: Fundamental advice and principles emerging from a knowing of how all life is an interconnected web or relations. Original instructions inform how a tradition sees the world, including values and responsibilities for how to care for and relate to everything (humans and more-than-human) from the earth, the sky and everything in between. At the heart of original instructions is maintaining balance.

Sacred Activism: An interconnected, transformative way of being, interweaving social justice activism with spiritual practice. While a modern-day term, these ways have existed across time.

Shadow: Individually viewed as hidden, repressed parts of oneself or collectively as hidden, repressed parts of the collective values of the society in which we participate. The shadow is that which we do not see or acknowledge. Neither good nor evil. In mythology, it is the Trickster. See the works of Carl Gustav Jung for more about the shadow.

Synchronicity: The simplest definition is a meaningful coincidence. While this term has been expanded upon in this current age, it was originally coined by Carl Gustav Jung. As quoted in the *Dictionary of Psychology*, synchronicity is "the simultaneous occurrence of events that appear to have a meaningful connection when there is no explicable causal relationship between these events, as in extraordinary coincidences or purported examples of telepathy" (American Psychological Association, n.d.). According to Jung, "some simultaneous occurrences possess significance through their very coincidence in time."

Traditional Ecological Knowledge (TEK): When a people have lived in a place for millennia, through all its adaptations, those people acquire a deep knowledge of that place in a way outsiders or foreigners could never know. This multigenerational experiential knowledge is TEK.

Trickster: Usually male, these spirits or energies live at the boundaries and liminal spaces. They are paradoxical. Tricksters challenge, deconstruct, destabilize, shake and break things, yet are neither good nor bad. By going through the lessons of the Trickster, we are given an opportunity to grow.

Visitation Dream: A category of dreams by which the dreamer reports having received a visitor of some kind. Commonly, a visitation dream includes the perceived presence of a deceased individual or group of deceased people in the dreamer's dreamscape.

Waking Dream: While used loosely among dream enthusiasts, the *APA Dictionary of Psychology* describes a waking dream as "an episode of dreamlike visual imagery experienced when one is not asleep."

Resources

The list below provides names, websites, and contact information of those offering a variety of services and education through their books, podcasts, tours, and workshops.

Alessandra Belloni is an author, musician, theater director, and traditional cultural practitioner. She hosts workshops, such as Rhythm Is the Cure, that connect those of the Italian diaspora to their ancestral and ancient roots: alessandrabelloni.com.

Apela Colorado is an Indigenous scientist, author, and the founder of the Worldwide Indigenous Science Network: WISN.org.

Alaya A. Dannu (a.k.a. Diya Dannu) integrates and embodies the ancient wisdom of the ancestral dream knowledge she was raised on and aims to share this knowledge with the collective to assist with solving real-world problems. She offers immersive workshops, sacred dance-healing circles, classes, and more: houseofamma.org.

Tzivia Gover brings her expertise in creative writing and blends it with an array of unique services, including dreamwork: thirdhousemoon.com. She is also the creator of the group 350 Dreamers.

Ryan Hurd offers a thriving online dream community: The Dream Portal. He is also an author and authority on lucid dream studies and dream-work: dreamstudies.org.

Melissa Johnson created *The Dream Hub Podcast* as well as the sleep and dream supplement, Night Nectar. She also offers a variety of services, including a free e-book about dreaming: dreamhub.au.

Amina Mara has created one of the best lucid dreaming podcasts to date, *The Dream World Podcast*, which also serves as a community resource and support system for dreamers everywhere: thedreamworldpodcast.com.

Angel Morgan is the founder of Dreambridge, which helps adults and children to connect with their dreams and their creativity. Dreambridge also provides educational Dream-Arts opportunities, expands cultural awareness of the link between dreams and creativity, and enriches the community with authentic and meaningful Dream-Arts contributions: thedreambridge.com.

Dominique Pauvert is a traditional practitioner deeply involved in cultural work and scholarship. He helps people who have origins from southwestern France to rediscover their traditional ancestral history and practices. For private or group gatherings, meetings, or tours, he can be reached at dominiquepauvert88@gmail.com.

Bibliography

Alessa, L., Kliskey, A., Gamble, J., Fidel, M., Beaujean, G., & Gosz, J. (2016). The role of indigenous science and local knowledge in integrated observing systems: Moving toward adaptive capacity indices and early warning systems. *Sustainable Science, 11,* 91–102.

American Psychological Association. (n.d.). Ritual. In *APA dictionary of psychology.* Retrieved July 1, 2024, from https://dictionary.apa.org/ritual.

American Psychological Association. (n.d.). Synchronicity. In *APA dictionary of psychology.* Retrieved August 18, 2024, from https://dictionary.apa.org/synchronicity.

American Psychological Association. (n.d.). Waking Dream. In *APA dictionary of psychology.* Retrieved August 18, 2024, from https://dictionary.apa.org/waking-dream.

Bastien, B. (2003). The cultural practice of participatory transpersonal visions: An indigenous perspective. *ReVision, 26*(2), 41–48.

Beckwith, M. (1976). *Hawaiian mythology.* Honolulu: University of Hawaii Press.

Belchik, M. (2004, July 23). Fight for fish to feed a way of life. Scotsman.com. http://www.klamathbasincrisis.org/Poweranddamstoc/powrscotsmanbelchik072304.htm.

Belloni, A. (2019). *Healing journeys with the Black Madonna: Chants, music, and sacred practices of the great goddess.* Rochester, VT: Bear & Company.

Berent, I. (2023). The "Hard Problem of Consciousness" Arises from Human Psychology. *Open Mind, 7,* 564–587.

Berney, C. (1991). David Kaonohiokala Bray: A Hawaiian Kahuna. In R-I. Hinze (Ed.), *Shamans of the 20th Century* (pp. 42–61). New York: Irvington.

Bogzaran, F., & Deslauriers, D. (2012). *Integral dreaming: A holistic approach to dreams.* New York: SUNY.

Brazier, C. (2018). *Ecotherapy in practice: A Buddhist model.* New York: Routledge.

Brink, N.E. (2022). *Listening to the spirits: Surviving the coming apocalypse with ecstatic trance.* Rhinebeck, NY: Red Elixir.

Brown, J.W. (1975). Indigenous Science: Native American Contributions to Science, Engineering, and Medicine. *Science, 189*(4196), 38–40.

Brown, M.A. (2022). *Ka Po'e Mo'o Akua: Hawaiian reptilian water deities.* Honolulu, HI: University of Hawaii Press.

Brown, S.V. (2000). The exceptional human experience process. *International Journal of Parapsychology, 11*(1), 69–111.

Brown, S.V., & White, R.A. (1997). Triggers, concomitants, and aftereffects of EHEs: An exploratory study. *Exceptional Human Experience, 15*(1), 150–156.

Bulkeley, K. (2008). *Dreaming in the world's religions: A comparative history.* New York: New York University Press.

Butzer, B. (2021). Does synchronicity point us towards the fundamental nature of consciousness? An exploration of psychology, ontology, and research prospects. *Journal of Consciousness Studies, 28*(3–4), 29–54.

Bynum, E.B. (2021). The African origin of familial consciousness and the dynamics of dreaming. *Dreaming, 31*(2), 91–99.

Campbell, J., & Moyers, B. (1991). *The power of myth.* New York: Anchor.

Cohen, K.S. (2023). What is indigenous science? *Explore, 19*, 498–499.

Colorado, A. (2021). *Women between the worlds: A call to your ancestral and indigenous wisdom.* Carlsbad, CA: Hay House.

Colorado, A., & Hurd, R. (2018). To re-enact is to remember: Envisioning a shamanic research protocol in archaeology. In D. Gheorghiu, G. Nash, H. Bender & E. Pásztor (Eds.), *Lands of the shamans: Archaeology, cosmology and landscape* (pp. 258–270). Havertown, PA: Oxbow.

Colorado, A., & Hurd, R. (2023). Break in the reef of time: An indigenous science approach to the Olowalu petroglyphs on Maui. In J. Hunter & R. Ironside (Eds.), *Folklore, people and place: International perspectives on tourism and tradition in storied places* (pp. 109–121). New York: Routledge.

Colorado, P. (1995). Remembrance: An intercultural mental health process. *First Reading, 13*(3), 18–21.

Cowen, T. (1993). *Fire in the head: Shamanism and the Celtic spirit.* San Francisco, CA: Harper.

Davis, C. (2024, May 21). Nonprofit underscores suicide's heavy toll with special prevention message in Lahaina. *Hawaii News Now.* https://www.hawaiinewsnow.com/2024/05/22/maui-program-aims-reduce-suicide-rates-men/.

d'Isa, R., & Abramson, C.I. (2023). The origin of the phrase comparative psychology: An historical overview. *Frontiers in Psychology, 14*, 1174115.

Dumont, J. (2002). Indigenous intelligence: Have we lost our indigenous mind? *Native Americas, XIX* (3&4), 15.

Duran, E., & Duran, B. (1995). *Native American postcolonial psychology.* New York: SUNY.

Edgar, I.R. (2011). *The dream in Islam: From Qur'anic tradition to jihadist inspiration.* New York: Berghahn Books.

Eliade, M. (2004). *Shamanism: Archaic techniques of ecstasy* (2nd ed.). Princeton, NJ: Princeton University Press.

Estés, C.P. (1995). *Women who run with the wolves: Myths and stories of the wild woman archetype.* New York: Ballantine.

Ewing, K.P. (1990). The dream of spiritual initiation and the organization of self representations among Pakistani Sufis. *American Ethnologist, 17*(1), 56–74.

Foor, D. (2017). *Ancestral medicine: Rituals for personal and family healing.* Rochester, VT: Bear & Company.

Fox, M. (2018). *Naming the unnamable: 89 wonderful and useful names for God...including the unnamable God.* Pawcatuck, CT: Little Bound Books.

Frank., R.M. (1995). Hunting the European sky bears: When the celestial bear comes down to earth. *Vistas in Astronomy, 39*(4), 723–724.

Frank, R.M. (2015). Bear Ceremonialism in relation to three ritual healers: the Basque salutariyua, the French marcou and the Italian maramao. In E. Comba & D. Ormezzano (Eds.), *Uomini e orsi.* Accademia University Press. https://doi.org/10.4000/books.aaccademia.1363.

Frank, R.M. (2016). Sky bear research: Implications for cultural astronomy. *Mediterranean Archaeology and Archaeometry, 16*(4), 343–350.

Frost, S.B. (2001). *SoulCollage: An intuitive collage process for individuals and groups.* Santa Cruz, CA: Hanford Mead.

Gabriel, H. (1999). *Jewelry of Nepal.* Boston: Weatherhill.

Gabriel, H. (2007). *Ceremonial Jewelry of Nepal.* Beadwork Magazine.

Ghannaee Arani, M., Fakharian, E., & Sarbandi, F. (2012). Ancient legacy of cranial surgery. *Archives of Trauma Research, 1*(2), 72–74. https://doi.org/10.5812/atr.6556.

Gheorghiu, D., Nash, G., Bender, H., & Pásztor E. (2018). Introduction: Towards a landscape for shamans. In D. Gheorghiu, G. Nash, H. Bender & E. Pásztor (Eds.), *Lands of the shamans: Archaeology, cosmology and landscape* (pp. 258–270). Havertown, PA: Oxbow.

Ginzburg, C. (2013). *The night battles: Witchcraft and agrarian cults in the sixteenth and seventeenth centuries.* Baltimore, MD: The Johns Hopkins University Press.

Gmelch, G. (1989). Baseball magic. In A.C. Lehmann & J.E. Myers (Eds.), *Magic, witchcraft, and religion: An anthropological study of the supernatural* (pp. 295–301). Mountain View, CA: Mayfield.

Gores, K.N. (Host). (2024, February 8). Indigenous wisdom and intuitive healing with a modern medicine woman [Audio podcast episode]. In *HEAL with Kelly.* https://www.youtube.com/watch?v=ufZ7wItgoy4.

Gover, T. (2023). *Dreaming on the page: Tap into your midnight mind to supercharge your writing.* Oakland, CA: The Collective Book Studio.

Graves, R. (1960). *The Greek myths.* New York: Penguin.

Griffith, E.M. (1902, March 5). *General description of Hawaiian forests, 1902.* https://dlnr.hawaii.gov/forestry/files/2013/09/Appendix-G-Hawaiian-Forest-Description.pdf.

Gutmanis, J. (2024). *Kāhuna Lā'au Lapa'au: The secrets and practice of Hawaiian herbal medicine* (2nd ed.). Mililani, HI: Island Heritage.

Hallowell, A.I. (1926). Bear ceremonialism in the northern hemisphere. *American Anthropologist, 28*(1), 1–175.

Hamilton, N. (2014). *Awakening through dreams: The journey through the inner landscape.* London, UK: Karnac.

Harden, J.K. (2021). Understanding Native Hawaiian land relations through Kānaka Maoli literature. *Oregon Undergraduate Research Journal, 18*(1), 94–141.

Harrison, P. (1993). More to it than low blood sugar: Kason explores mystical experiences. *Canadian Family Physician, 39*, 2316–2320.

HeartMath Institute. (n.d.). *Expanding our capacity to love.* https://www.heartmath.org/gci/.

Heinze, R.I. (1991). *Shamans of the 20th century.* New York: Irvington Publishers.

Hiraishi, K. (2023). Maui's double-hulled canoe. Hawaii Public Radio. August 16, 2023. https://www.hawaiipublicradio.org/local-news/2023-08-16/hokulea-crew-loses-moolele-oldest-double-hulled-canoe-lahaina-wild fires.

Hoss, R. (2017). The journey of transformation. In R.J. Hoss & R.P. Gongloff (Eds.), *Dreams that change our lives: A publication of the International Association for the Study of Dreams* (pp. 11–31). Asheville, NC: Chiron.

Hurd, R. (2011). Integral archaeology: Process methodologies for exploring prehistoric rock art on Ometepe Island, Nicaragua. *Anthropology of Consciousness, 22*(1), 72–94.

Hurd, R. (2014). Unearthing the paleolithic mind in lucid dreams. In R. Hurd & K. Bulkeley (Eds.), *Lucid dreaming: New perspectives on consciousness in sleep, Volume one* (pp. 277–324).

Hurd, R. (2022). *Lucid talisman: Forgotten lore.* Dream Studies Press.

Hurd, R. (2022b). The ritual practice of lucid dreaming. *Conscious Chimera.* Accessed online at: https://consciouschimera.com/2022/12/08/the-ritual-complex-of-lucid-dreaming/.

Jaenke, K. (2020). Dreaming with the earth. *ReVision, 32*(4)/*33*(1), 14–24. doi:10.4298/REVN.32.4.14–24.

Jenkins, T.A., & Martin, M. (2023). You are what you dream: The dark tetrad and dream content. *Dreaming, 33*(4), 434–445.

Jessen, T.D., Ban, N.C., Claxton, N.X., & Darimont, C.T. (2022). Contributions of indigenous knowledge to ecological and evolutionary understanding. *Frontiers in Ecology and the Environment, 20*(2), 93–101. doi:10.1002/fee.2435.

Jones, R. (2023). To tackle the climate crisis, we need to transform systems according to ancestral original instructions. *British Medical Journal, 383,* 2202.

Kahan, T.L., & LaBerge, S. (1994). Lucid dreaming as metacognition: Implications for cognitive science. *Consciousness and Cognition, 3,* 246–264.

Ka'ili, T.O. (2016, July 15). The demigod Maui: Modern day lessons from ancient tales of Oceania. *HuffPost.* https://www.huffpost.com/entry/the-demigod-maui-modern-day-lessons-from-ancient-tales_b_5788c6e7e4b0cb f01e9f8508.

Kalolo, J.F. (2022). Promoting indigenous science in the realm of modern science in developing countries. *Thinking Skills and Creativity, 45.*

Kalweit, H. (1984). *Dreamtime & inner space: The world of the shaman.* Boston: Shambhala.

Katz, R. (2017). *Indigenous healing psychology: Honoring the wisdom of the First Peoples.* Rochester, VT: Healing Arts Press.

Kellermann, N. (2013). Epigenetic transmission of Holocaust trauma: Can nightmares be inherited? *Israel Journal of Psychiatry and Related Sciences, 50*(1), 33.

Kime, P. (2019). Synchronicity and meaning. *Journal of Analytical Psychology, 64*(5), 780–797.

Kimmerer, R.W. (2013). *Braiding sweetgrass: Indigenous wisdom, scientific knowledge, and the teaching of plants.* Minneapolis: Milkweed.

Kramvig, B. (2015). Gifts of healing: Connecting to Sámi epistemic practice. In

B.H. Miller (Ed.), *Idioms of Sámi health and healing* (pp. 183–208). Edmonton: University of Alberta Press.

Kremer, J.W. (2003). Ethnoautobiography as practice of radical presence: Storying the self in participatory visions. *ReVision, 26*(2), 5–13.

Kremer, J.W. (2007). Dreams and visions in initiation and healing. *ReVision, 29*(1), 34–48.

Kremer, J.W., & Jackson-Paton, R. (2018). *Ethnoautobiography: Stories and practices for unlearning whiteness decolonization uncovering ethnicities* (2nd ed.). Dubuque, IA: Kendall Hunt.

Krippner, S. (2016). Transpersonal dreams as spiritually transformative experiences. In F.J. Kaklauskas, C.J. Clements, D. Hocoy, & L. Hoffman (Eds.), *Shadows & light: Theory, research, and practice in transpersonal psychology* (Vol. 1: Principles and practices) (pp. 151–171). Colorado Springs, CO: University Professors Press.

Krippner, S., Bogzaran, F., & Percia de Carvalho, A. (2002). *Extraordinary dreams and how to work with them.* Albany: State University of New York.

Krippner, S., Budden, A., Gallente, R., & Bova, M. (2011). The Indigenous Healing Tradition in Calabria, Italy. *International Journal of Transpersonal Studies, 30*(1–2), 48–62.

LaPointe, F.H. (1973). The origin and evolution of the term "psychology." *Rivista Critica di Storia della Filosofia, 28*(2), 138–160.

Lavrillier, A., & Gabyshev, S. (2021). An indigenous science of the climate change impacts on landscape topography in Siberia. *Ambio, 50*, 1910–1925.

Leonard, L., & Dawson, D. (2023). Client experiences and understandings of dreams in contemporary Australian psychological practice: An IPA study. *Dreaming, 33*(4), 476–494.

Madden, K. (1999). *Shamanic guide to death and dying.* St. Paul, MN: Llewellyn.

Mallory, J.P. (2016). *In search of the Irish dreamtime: Archaeology and early Irish literature.* London, UK: Thames & Hudson.

Marker, M. (2018). There is no *place of nature*; There is only the *nature of place*: Animate landscapes as methodology for inquiry in the Coast Salish territory. *International Journal of Qualitative Studies in Education, 31*(6), 453–464.

Mascaro, K.R. (2013). *The effects of announcing dreams: An investigation of pregnant women's perceived communication with their unborn* (Doctoral Dissertation). Retrieved from ProQuest Dissertations and Theses Database. (AAT 3602488).

Mascaro, K.R. (2016). Announcing dreams: Perceived communication with baby-to-be. *Journal of Prenatal and Perinatal Psychology and Health, 30*(3), 191–207.

Mascaro, K.R. (2016b). The effects of announcing dreams: An investigation of pregnant women's perceived communication with their unborn. *International Journal of Dream Research, 9*(1), 7–14.

Mascaro, K.R. (2018). *Extraordinary dreams: Visions, announcements and premonitions across time and place.* Jefferson, NC: Toplight.

Mascaro, K.R. (2021). *Dream medicine: The intersection of wellness and consciousness.* Jefferson, NC: Toplight.

McCubbin, L.D., Cristobal, N., & Chin, S. (2021). The case of Kahewai: Indigenous ways of knowing and Kānaka 'Ōiwi well-being. *Asian American Journal of Psychology, 12*(4), 255–264. https://doi.org/10.1037/aap0000244.

Mesaki, S. (2009). Witchcraft and the law in Tanzania. *International Journal of Sociology and Anthropology, 1*(8), 132–138.

Moody, R., & Perry, P. (2010). *Glimpses of eternity: Sharing a loved one's passage from this life to the next.* Paradise Valley, AZ: Sakkara.

Moss, R. (2015). *Sidewalk oracles: Playing with signs, symbols, and synchronicity in everyday life.* Novato, CA: New World Library.

Nelson, M.K. (2008). *Original instructions: Indigenous teachings for a sustainable future.* Rochester, VT: Bear & Company.

Pelusa, D.M. (2004). "That Which I Dream Is True": Dream Narratives in an Amazonian Community. *Dreaming, 14*(2–3), 107–119.

Puca, A. (2019). The tradition of *Segnature*: Underground indigenous practices of Italy. *Journal of the Irish Society for the Academic Study of Religions, 7,* 104–124.

Radin, D. (2018). *Real magic: Ancient wisdom, modern science, and a guide to the secret power of the universe.* New York: Harmony Books.

Raduga, M., Shashkov, A., Gordienko, N., Vanin, A., & Maltsev, E. (2023). Real-time transferring of music from lucid dreams into reality by electromyography sensors. *Dreaming, 33*(4), 495–507.

Reid, J.B., & Taylor, K. (2011). Indigenous mind: A framework for culturally safe indigenous health research and practice. *Aboriginal & Islander Health Worker Journal, 35*(4), 4–6.

Rimsh, A., & Pietrowsky, R. (2022). Characteristics of dream and nightmare in patients with anxiety disorders. *Dreaming, 32*(3), 314–329.

Robbins, J. (2018). Native knowledge: What ecologists are learning from Indigenous people. *Yale Environment 360.* https://e360.yale.edu/features/native-knowledge-what-ecologists-are-learning-from-indigenous-people.

Rowe, G. (2014). Implementing indigenous ways of knowing into research: Insights into the critical role of dreams as catalysts for knowledge development. *Journal of Indigenous Social Development, 3*(2), 1–17.

Sciorra, J. (1989). Yard shrines and sidewalk altars of New York's Italian Americans. *Perspectives in Vernacular Architecture, 3,* 185–198.

Sheridan, J., & Longboat, D. (2014). Walking back into creation: Environmental apartheid and the eternal—Initiating an indigenous mind claim. *Space and Culture, 17*(3), 308–324.

Soholm, H. (2020). When the ancestors call, how do we answer? *ReVision, 33*(3 & 4), 66–71.

Sparrow, G.S. (1988). *Lucid dreaming: Dawning of the clear light* (8th ed.). Virginia Beach, VA: A.R.E. Press.

Stumbrys, T. (2018). Bridging lucid dream research and transpersonal psychology: Towards transpersonal studies of lucid dreams. *The Journal of Transpersonal Psychology, 50*(2), 176–193.

Terrill, M. (2024, January 11). New book makes a case for climate optimism. Arizona State University News. https://news.asu.edu/20240111-creativity-new-book-makes-case-climate-optimism.

United Nations Permanent Forum on Indigenous Issues. (n.d.) Who are indigenous peoples? [Fact sheet]. https://www.un.org/esa/socdev/unpfii/ documents/5session_factsheet1.pdf.

Walsh, R. (2014). *The world of shamanism: New views of an ancient tradition.* Woodbury, MN: Llewellyn.

Ward, J.T. (2024). Indigenous resilience and healing through dreams and spirituality. *Dreaming, 34*(3), 257–273.

Waters, J.W. (2022). American Indian traditions and religious ethics. *Journal of Religious Ethics, 50*(2), 239–272.

Watkins, M. (1998). *Waking dreams* (3rd ed.). Washington, D.C.: Spring Publications.

Weiler, M., Acunzo, D.J., Cozzolino, P.J., & Greyson, B. (2024). Exploring the transformative potential of out-of-body experiences: A pathway to enhanced empathy. *Neuroscience and Biobehavioral Reviews, 163*, 1–7.

Woollacott, M.H., Kason, Y., & Park, R.D. (2021). Investigation of the phenomenology, physiology and impact of spiritually transformative experiences—kundalini awakening. *Explore, 17*(6), 525–534. https://doi.org/10.1016/j. explore.2020.07.005.

INDEX

221

www.ingramcontent.com/pod-product-compliance
Lightning Source LLC
Chambersburg PA
CBHW031428270326
41930CB00007B/621